Ireland and
Anglo-American Relations
1899–1921

Ireland and
Anglo-American Relations
1899–1921

Alan J. Ward

Toronto: University of Toronto Press

First published in Great Britain by
Weidenfeld and Nicolson Ltd.
and the London School of Economics 1969
First published in Canada and the United States by
University of Toronto Press 1969
Reprinted in 2018
ISBN 978-1-4875-7247-1 (paper)
8020 1627 8
Printed in Great Britain by
Ebenezer Baylis and Son Ltd.
The Trinity Press, Worcester, and London

Contents

Abbreviations

AARIR	American Association for the Recognition of the Irish Republic
AIHS	American Irish Historical Society, New York
AOH	Ancient Order of Hibernians
CAB	Cabinet Office Records, Public Record Office, London
FO	Foreign Office Records, Public Record Office, London
Foreign Relations	U.S., Department of State, *Papers Relating to the Foreign Relations of the United States*
FOIF	Friends of Irish Freedom
IRA	Irish Republican Army
IRB	Irish Republican Brotherhood
Parl. Debs.	Great Britain, *Parliamentary Debates*
State Dept.	State Department Records, National Archives, Washington, DC
UIL	United Irish League
von Igel	Papers of Wolf von Igel, State Department Records, National Archives, Washington, DC

Preface

This book was written because of an interest in the relationship between domestic and international affairs which I have had since my undergraduate days at the London School of Economics and Political Science. This relationship is an aspect of the study of international relations which has been largely ignored. Too often international relations is thought of simply as a subject dealing with the relations between personified states which act in an international society as if they were people. At other times, international relations is seen as a subject dealing exclusively with foreign offices and statesmen. 'In this romantic view,' wrote Adolph Berle, 'Foreign Policy has been presented as the creation of Talleyrand or Castlereagh, of Metternich or Bismarck, or Roosevelt, Churchill or Stalin. Execution of Foreign Policy is thus an art practised by men of stupidity or talent, of stubbornness or genius.'[1]

The first of these views, that involving the personification of the state, is a convenience – for we personify all human groups, from schools and trade unions to football teams and social classes, but it is also a necessary legal and diplomatic fiction without which the semi-civilized activity of international relations and international law could not proceed. The second view of the subject is, however, shortsighted. No foreign office exists in a vacuum and no statesman can be understood without reference to his society, the political system in which he operates, his ideology – in fact the environment in which he spends the great bulk of his time. This need to relate statesmen and decisions to the societies from which they emerge has not been very systematically investigated. We know very little, for example, about the relationship between foreign policy and the press, public opinion and interest groups. A great deal of exploration in the form of case studies needs to be done. I chose to work on one case study, the role of the Irish in

1 Feliks Gross, *Foreign Policy Analysis*, New York: Philosophical Library, 1954, Foreword.

Preface

Anglo-American relations and the way in which the problem of
Irish independence, on the face of it, a problem for British
domestic politics alone, influenced Britain's relations with the
United States of America.

I could have chosen many other topics, but I was influenced by
Professor Louis L. Gerson under whom I studied and with whom
I worked at the University of Connecticut. His own book, *The
Hyphenate in Recent American Politics and Diplomacy*,[2] was
published in 1964 and his earlier *Woodrow Wilson and the Rebirth
of Poland*[3] illustrated the role which Polish-Americans and Polish
émigrés played in the formulation of American policy towards
Poland in and immediately after World War I. I chose to work
in a similar field during a similar period. It is enough to say that
the Irish question appealed to me as one which was important and
interesting, but the period chosen requires further explanation.
It is, of course, possible to examine a contemporary problem and
uncover a great deal of valuable information about interest
groups, their organization, their mode of operation, the societies
in which they operate and so on. By polling, interviewing and
sample surveying, the contemporary social scientist can investigate contemporary events. He can assess the truth of claims made
by men who pretend to speak for millions. He can measure public
opinion and the effect of pressure group activities on that public.
All these things he can do, but his weakness is that he can usually
only infer the actual relationship between pressures and policy
decisions. Journalists are as well equipped as university scholars
to do this and many of them do it every day. It is sophisticated
guesswork. The fact that one can chart the probable or possible
flows of opinion, demands and pressures does not necessarily
mean these reach the decision-maker or that he is influenced by
them. We need evidence.

An alternative is to look backwards into the laboratory of
history to a period for which Foreign Office, State Department,
presidential, Cabinet and other documents are available for study.
The methodological problem here is that it is much harder to piece
together a picture of the society as it was, or the interest groups as
they were, or to use modern techniques of the social sciences. As
compensation, however, one very often has no longer to infer

[2] Lawrence, Kansas: University of Kansas Press, 1964.
[3] New Haven: Yale University Press, 1953.

x

relationships between, say, interest group activity and foreign policy decisions. For example, it becomes clear from the documents that in the formulation of certain policies in Britain and America, the Irish and the American-Irish were an important, and sometimes the determining factor. We can assess more accurately the extent to which decision makers were, or thought themselves to be, free agents. This course, or at least the way in which I pursued it, may be less sophisticated but it is a legitimate exercise in the study of political behaviour, and it is the one I chose.

What follows in these pages is less an attempt to dissect the complex international ramifications of the Irish problem than to illustrate just how complex it was. I have tried to weave a web from very diverse events, people, institutions and organizations. The result of my work as I present it here is, of course, incomplete in the sense that one does not easily cover more than twenty years of history in a few hundred pages, and one does not easily travel from continent to continent as the requirements of research for such a subject would ideally dictate. However, I have made an attempt to be not encyclopaedic but reasonably and relevantly comprehensive and what I have written would have been impossible but for the help I received from a variety of sources. These are Professor Louis L. Gerson of the University of Connecticut for his advice and encouragement; the British Association for American Studies for the award of a fellowship from its Rockefeller Foundation grant; the London School of Economics and Political Science which awarded me a Montague Burton Studentship in International Relations with a supplementary grant on two occasions during the doctoral studies which ultimately led to this book; the British Council for its award of a Commonwealth University Interchange travel grant; my former employer, the University of Adelaide, South Australia, which so generously assisted me through its study leave fund; the College of William and Mary, Virginia. I wish to thank the President and Fellows of Harvard College for permission to quote from Elting E. Morison, ed., *The Letters of Theodore Roosevelt*, Cambridge, Mass.: Harvard University Press, copyright 1951, 1952, 1954; Mr Henry Cabot Lodge for permission to use and quote from the papers of his grandfather, Senator Lodge; the Meredith Publishing Company for permission to quote from Thomas A. Bailey, *A Diplomatic History of the American People*, 4th ed., New York:

Preface

Appleton, Century, Crofts, copyright 1950; Mr Joseph P. Tumulty for permission to quote from his correspondence; the Yale University Library for permission to quote from the papers of Edward House and Sir William Wiseman. For the use of their collections and facilities I would particularly like to thank the Library of Congress, Washington, and, in addition, the National Archives, Washington; the Public Record Office, London; the National Register of Archives, London; the National Library of Ireland; the British Museum; the Bodleian Library, Oxford; the New York Public Library; the Yale University Library; the Massachusetts Historical Society, Boston; the American Irish Historical Society, New York; the National Library of Australia, Canberra; the British Library of Political and Economic Science, London. Finally, I must thank my wife, Helene Ward, for her many services to me on this project.

1 The Anglo-American Problem of Ireland

'How is it that the Government of England is blind to the ruin that a people so numerous and powerful in foreign countries, and hating her so intensely, is sure to bring on her in her hour of trouble? It might be politic to try conciliation, instead of coercion, on such a people.'

D.P.CONYNGHAM, 1869

Nineteenth-century American foreign policy was set in the mould of the Founding Fathers, away from the cares and problems of Europe. Or so it was thought. 'Europe,' said George Washington, 'has a set of primary interests which to us have none or a very remote relation.' Europe's frequent controversies were, he believed, not America's concern and his advice to the American people was that they should remain free of the 'ordinary vicissitudes of her politics or the ordinary combinations and collisions of her friendships or enmities'. But this advice could not be accepted by millions of Americans who lived after Washington had passed from the American scene. The United States was an immigrant society, drawn from many lands, and the affairs, loyalties and hatreds of Europe were indelibly printed in the hearts and minds of every refugee from hunger or oppression, and every lonely immigrant who pined for the family and friendships he had left behind.

Washington was, in fact, addressing an early America. 'With slight shades of difference,' he wrote, 'you have the same religion, manners, habits, and political principles. You have in common cause fought and triumphed together.' But the America of the nineteenth and early twentieth centuries was not a united country of predominantly Protestant, British stock, it was a 'menagerie of

1

nationalities'.[1] Vast numbers of Americans identified with the lands of their origin, loving or hating them according to their motives for leaving, and no matter how neutral the United States might be in any legal or diplomatic sense, these immigrants could never share this detachment.

Immigrant groups have always had an important influence on American foreign policy and none more persistently than the Irish. None could exceed their devotion to their mother country, though it was very commonly a land known only through tales imbibed by Irish-Americans growing up in the American ethnic ghettos of their birth. There were vast numbers of such 'Irishmen' for the Irish had begun to flood America during the great Irish famine of the late 1840s and it was with the advent of the great mid-century wave of Irish immigrants, pushed by famine and pulled by the promise of economic opportunity, that the Irish in America became the regular diet of British ministers and consuls. By 1860 there were 1,611,000 Irish-born people in the United States, mostly Catholic, two-thirds of them in Pennsylvania, New York, New Jersey and New England, and almost exclusively dwelling in urban areas.[2]

Perhaps as many as half a million Irish, largely Protestant and of Ulster stock, were in America as early as 1783, but the years before 1840 were only a prelude for the Catholic Irish. From that time on they grew in power and influence. Their press, which had been struggling for survival in earlier years, became powerful and vigorous. They came to control the Democratic Party in the large cities from Chicago eastwards; they supported large numbers of dependants in Ireland; they supported and encouraged both extreme and moderate Irish nationalists in Ireland itself; they contributed in large measure to American anglophobia, and they profoundly influenced the course of Anglo-American relations. As the result of their activities the question of Irish self-government became an American question as surely as it was a British one.

The power of the Irish was firmly based. Most important was their sheer numerical weight. The census of 1910 records that

---

[1] A phrase used by Thomas A.Bailey, *A Diplomatic History of the American People*, New York: Appleton, Century, Crofts, 4th ed., 1950, p. 610.
[2] Maldyn A.Jones, *American Immigration*, Chicago: University of Chicago Press, 1960, p. 118.

Irish-Americans, those born in Ireland or with at least one Irish-born parent, numbered 4,504,360 and this made no count of the millions whose grandparents and great-grandparents were Irish and who still strongly identified themselves with Ireland. Irish-American propagandists in the twentieth century not uncommonly claimed twenty million Irish-American supporters and they may have been justified for Irish-American nationalism, as it has been called, was an extremely resilient commodity. Three million Irish arrived in the United States between 1845 and 1891. They were poor and having left the potato culture of Ireland, they settled not on the land, for which they were ill-equipped both financially and by training, but in the cities where they provided unskilled labour for the rapidly developing industrial society. There they lived in almost exclusively Irish districts. It was a poor life and the memory of hardships in the Old World was compounded by the urban misery of the new. Responsibility for it all was easily assigned to England.

The rural, green Ireland of Irishmen's dreams was very different from the ugliness of their adopted cities. They were homesick and they were also despised. On the lowest rung of the socio-economic ladder in the 1850s and 1860s, they were subjected to anti-Irish and anti-Catholic abuse. They could hardly be unaware of their Irishness as the nativism of the 'Know-Nothings' reached its peak in the 1850s. They looked inwards to their own community and became fiercely and belligerently Irish, but in their defence, from the earliest times, they enlisted Americanism. The principles of American democracy, they argued, were the principles for which Ireland was fighting. Ireland's struggle for freedom from English tyranny was therefore America's struggle too and the enemy was a shared one. 'It will be not alone Ireland and America versus England,' wrote an Irish-American in 1864, 'but Democracy versus Aristocracy, the rights of man versus the rights of Kings.'[3] During their own war of independence the American colonists had looked to Ireland as a natural ally in a common cause, and now the roles were reversed as Ireland looked to America. Particularly in the last decade of the century Irish-Americans fiercely replied to nativist attacks that the foreign-born were a threat to the United States by championing an aggressive anti-British

[3] Brig. Gen. J.L.Kiernan, *Ireland and America versus England*, Detroit: George W.Pattison, 1864, p. 15.

brand of Americanism. The task of the American-Irish Historical Society, founded in 1898, was to examine and publicize, and often to romanticize and glorify, the role of the Irish in American history, to attack the so-called 'Anglo-Saxon' ascendency in American life and to promote a 'true' Americanism based upon the diverse origins of the American people.

The isolation and persecution of Irish-Americans by other Americans perpetuated an Irish sub-culture in the United States which in turn made them constantly aware of Ireland. As Thomas N.Brown argues, Irish-Americans, even those who had risen above poverty and the ghetto, saw the cause of the difficulties in their path – the social ostracism by a dominant class in which families of British Protestant stock predominated, the nativist antipathy, and further barriers which others had not to cross – in the very humiliation of Ireland. They were persecuted in America because they had arrived as 'slaves'. They could hold their heads high only when Ireland was free. In this sense, Irish-American nationalism was very much an American phenomenon. 'The springs of Irish-American nationalism . . . are to be found in the realities of loneliness and alienation, and of poverty and prejudice,' Brown wrote.[4] It was one way for Irish-Americans to come to terms with America, but it also perpetuated a genuine and deep-seated hatred of England. Millions of Irish-Americans knew England, either from direct experience or from the tales of their elders, as the persecutor and tormentor of Ireland. Their homeland was a hell of absentee landlords and rack rents, of poverty and famine. They could not forget this and even their grand-children could not forget it.

In America the Irish were never able, and perhaps from force of habit never chose, to live their lives without reference to their membership in the Irish-American community. A huge number of Irish fraternal, religious, sporting, political and benevolent societies bore witness to their acceptance of this fact and, as a distinct community within the broader American culture, they were cultivated by three groups of fellow Irish-Americans who had an interest in maintaining the distinct character of the Irish, the easier to manipulate them. In this way their assimilation was hampered, but at the same time these three groups performed the

---

[4] Thomas N.Brown, *Irish-American Nationalism, 1870–90*, Philadelphia: Lippincott, 1966, p. 23.

role for the lonely immigrant of mediating between the old Ireland and the new America. He was not thrust into an alien environment unclad but was first sheltered by his own kind. The first group was the Catholic Church. The Irish arrived in a largely Protestant country and the Catholic Church in America became very much an Irish-Catholic Church. The second group comprised Irish-American political 'bosses' whose power in the Democratic Party was based on their ability to deliver the Irish vote. They cultivated this by welcoming the immigrant and providing a 'welfare state' for him within the urban chaos. They found jobs, homes, offered relief and often bribed. They were closely associated with the predominantly Irish saloon keepers, and they had allies among the many Irish-Americans who took the Irish gift with words into journalism. The 'bosses' were primarily interested in immigrants for the political power they represented, but the Irish community they and the Church nurtured provided an audience for the third group, the Irish nationalists. Some of these were *émigrés*, like O'Donovan Rossa and John Devoy, who were active in Ireland in the 1860s but survived and were still fighting for Ireland from America in the twentieth century. Some, like Daniel Cohalan, were actually born and lived their whole lives in America. Others, like John Redmond and Eamon de Valera, came from Ireland to lead and to agitate for comparatively short periods before returning home. Irish-Americans in the Democratic Party and the Catholic Church were involved in the struggle for Irish independence but they were not its prime movers and Irish independence was not their central concern. From time to time in this study they will appear as participants but the American agitation for Irish independence was organized by Irish and Irish-American nationalists. Irish nationalism was important for the maintenance of the Irish identity in America but it was not the central characteristic of the role of Irish-American politician or Irish-American churchman.[5]

It is the Irish and Irish-American nationalists, encouraged by a number of different philosophies of action and revolution, who form the backbone of this study. But for them there would have

[5] For an interesting and convincing study of Irish-American politicians see Edward M. Levine, *The Irish and Irish Politicians*, Notre Dame: University of Notre Dame Press, 1966.

been no Anglo-American problem of Ireland; but for them successive American governments would have been free from determined attempts to influence American policy towards Britain, Ireland's persecutor; but for them Britain would have been free to handle her own problem of Ireland without constantly having to pay heed to a greater Ireland overseas.

As early as 1866 one observer had written:

> How is it that the Government of England is so blind to the ruin that a people so numerous and powerful in foreign countries, and hating her so intensely, is sure to bring on her in her hour of troubles? It might be politic to try conciliation, instead of coercion, on such a people.[6]

If only it had been as simple as this! Even when the British understood its implications for their foreign policy, the Irish question was still a problem in their domestic politics, the focus of important interests and rigid attitudes which prevented a settlement. In effect, because the British would, or could do so little to settle Ireland's claims, they had to tolerate gross interference in their relations not only with the United States of America, but with other countries, particularly the British Dominions, as well.

The following pages can illustrate only a part of this very complex story, but a most important part, the Irish question as a factor in Anglo-American relations from the Boer War to the Anglo-Irish treaty of 1921.

[6] Capt. David P. Conyngham, *The Irish Brigade and its Campaigns*, Boston: P. Donahue, 1869, p. 81.

2 The Organization of Revolutionary and Constitutional Nationalism, 1899–1912

'*The result of the abortive insurrection of 1848 was to change the base of Irish revolution from Ireland to America.*'

PHILIP H.BAGNAL, 1882[1]

'*When England realizes what the support of this nation means on behalf of Ireland we shall begin to realize our independence.*'

JOHN REDMOND, NEW YORK.
The Times (London), 6 OCTOBER 1904

The year 1848 was one of violent revolutions in Europe and the outer ripples reached as far west as Ireland. In May of that year John Mitchel, a Dublin publisher, was sentenced to fourteen years of exile in Australia for inciting rebellion. Five years later he and his family were dramatically rescued by an Irish-American expedition and in November 1853 they reached New York. There Mitchel made an amazing statement which has been echoed by generations of political refugees in America. He greeted the press:

I am a professed revolutionary now, an adventurer, a seditious propagandist. I mean to make use of the freedom guaranteed to me as a citizen or inchoate citizen of America to help and stimulate the movement of European Democracy and especially of Irish independence. I mean to claim for the revolutionary refugees here, not only the hospitality and comity of America, but also her sympathy and active friendship; nay, I claim for them that America shall be to them

[1] Philip H.Bagnal, *The American Irish and Their Influence on Irish Politics*, London: Kegan Paul, Trench & Co., 1882, p. 111.

7

the very stamping ground prayed for by Archimedes whereon they may plant a lever that shall move the world.[2]

In fact Mitchel moved to Richmond, Virginia, away from the centres of Irish-American activity, and his support of the southern cause in the Civil War cost him any influence he retained, but he set the scene and many were to live by the principles he declared in 1853.

Two organizations carried the burden of Irish-American revolutionary activities before 1900, the Fenian Brotherhood and the Clan na Gael. The Fenian Brotherhood dated from the mid-1850s and in the years immediately following the Civil War it was responsible for military raids into Canada. A minority faction of Fenians preferred direct aid to Ireland and in 1867 a ship, the *Erin's Hope*, sailed from New York with arms and volunteers, only to arrive long after the Irish rising of 1867 had failed. The Clan na Gael was formed in 1867 and it was the Clan, not the Fenian Brotherhood, which survived to renew the fight for Irish freedom in 1900, although, of course, they shared many of the same members. The Fenians were never able to command popular Irish-American support and suffered from outright condemnation by the Roman Catholic Church. Such popular and political support as they were able to muster in the six or seven years following the Civil War was due to the prevailing anti-British sentiment, a product of the war, and to politicians' fears of the growing power of urban Irish-American voters. With the settlement of the most outstanding Anglo-American disputes in the Treaty of Washington, 1871, the Fenian Brotherhood collapsed. It was no longer needed to taunt the British Empire.

For thirty years revolutionary Irish nationalism in both Ireland and America lacked strong direction or real success. In America, the Clan na Gael split in the 1880s over a number of issues, including dynamite sabotage in England, Parnell's leadership and the Irish Land League. In Ireland, the Land League agitation and Parliamentary pressure for home rule subdued plans for outright revolution. In 1900, however, revolutionary Irish nationalism was reborn in the United States. A convention at Atlantic City, New Jersey, in July 1900 marked the reconciliation

[2] Florence Gibson, *The Attitudes of the New York Irish towards State and National Affairs, 1848–92*, New York: Columbia Univ. Press, 1951, p. 65.

of the factionalized Clan na Gael under the direction of Daniel
Cohalan and John Devoy. Their aims were circularized in this
way:

> The object of the Clan is the complete independence of the Irish
> people and the establishment of an Irish Republic, and to unite all
> men of our race in all lands who believe in the principles of Wolfe Tone
> and Emmet. We pledge ourselves to the principle that physical force
> is the only engine a revolutionary organisation can consistently and
> successfully use to realise the hopes of lovers of freedom in lands
> subject to the bonds of oppression.... Our duty is to nerve and
> strengthen ourselves to wrest by the sword our political rights from
> England.[3]

Though American citizens, they could still feel that they had
political rights in Ireland.

Cohalan was born in Middletown, New York, in 1867, the son
of Irish-born parents. He was admitted to the New York bar and
began to practise in New York City where, by 1900, he was well
established in the Democratic Party. He regularly attended
Democratic state conventions from 1900 and was a delegate to
the national conventions in 1904 and 1908. He was, furthermore,
Grand Sachem, the senior officer, of the Tammany Society from
1908 to 1911 and in 1912 he followed the route of many Tammany
members onto the Supreme Court of New York State. He had
always been interested in Ireland and first became prominent in
the Irish nationalist movement during the Boer War. Ireland and
its relationship to American foreign policy came to be his primary
political interest after 1912. In that year he opposed Wilson's bid
for the Democratic presidential nomination and this, together
with Wilson's hostility to Tammany and political bosses,
facilitated Cohalan's drift away from the Democratic Party at
the national level. He opposed Wilson and his administration and
the implications of his opposition will become clear later in this
study.

In the year of Cohalan's birth John Devoy, already twenty-five
years old, was in a British prison, having been convicted for Irish
revolutionary activities. He was released in 1871 and went straight
to New York where he worked as a journalist and began a career

[3] Circular to Clan members, 10 October 1900, in Charles C. Tansill, *America and the Fight for Irish Freedom, 1866–1922*, New York: Devin-Adair, 1957, p. 121.

in Irish-American organizations which was to span almost sixty years until his death in 1928. Unlike Cohalan, Devoy supported the Republican Party for most of his life in America but they combined very effectively in the Irish nationalist movement. Led by Cohalan and Devoy, the Clan na Gael quickly became an object of public attention, with considerable coverage in the daily press. The acting British Consul in New York refused to believe press reports of a Clan resurgence on the assumption that if this was true the Clan would have maintained a conspiratorial silence.[4] He was wrong, although the secrecy surrounding this revolutionary organization has meant that we can know very little of its workings. There is, for example, no data on the strength of the Clan, its membership, finance, or its overall plan of action. Its membership was widespread, but could never have been large, perhaps less than forty thousand.[5] Leadership was, in the main, exerted from New York, the home of the prime movers, but when necessary the Irish of Boston, Chicago, Philadelphia, Baltimore, Buffalo, Cleveland, San Francisco and other cities could be mobilized for mass support. The Boer War presented the Clan with ready-made mass audiences as the Irish rose to protest at British policy and it also enabled it to share a common platform with moderate men, such as W.Bourke Cockran, a New York lawyer and US Congressman, who were opposed to its revolutionary methods. Members of the Clan, however, had no doubt that Ireland needed to be prepared for revolution. This was certainly John Devoy's view and had been for many years. In 1881, for example, he had written:

> If Ireland wins her freedom, she must wade to it through blood and suffering and sacrifice.... The people at home must be prepared – they must be armed.... We in America must do more than make speeches and subscribe money to keep the agitator alive! An agitation that must be fed and fostered and subsidized from abroad has nothing in it. Let us devote some of our spare cash to preparing Ireland for the final ordeal.[6]

[4] Cited by British Chargé Lowther to Foreign Secretary, 7 August 1900, *FO* 5/2428.
[5] Devoy's published and unpublished papers tell very little of the period 1899–1912. Tansill, *op. cit.*, had access to the papers of Daniel Cohalan, but very little is contained in his book on this period.
[6] Bagnal, *op. cit.*, p. 223.

10

Support for this view came in 1901 when John Daly, Mayor of Limerick and until 1896 a prisoner of the British, visited the United States for a series of mass meetings on Africa and Ireland. Daly's message to the Americans was clear, although it was one which found remarkably little support in his native Ireland:

Stop your bickering and hypocrisy and settle down to work for independence. Any man in Ireland who is worth his salt today will spit upon the words constitutional agitation. The war clouds hang over China, France is uneasy, no man knows what Germany may do, and in it all the opportunity for Ireland to strike will surely come. See that you are prepared for the emergency and well prepared, for it is going to be a death struggle.[7]

Daly's attack on the constitutional agitation was timely for the previous year had seen a reorganization of the Irish Parliamentary Party. The party's discipline and unity had collapsed in 1890 over the divorce scandal involving its undisputed leader, Charles Stewart Parnell, and Mrs O'Shea. Parnell died in 1891, but for ten years John Redmond led the so-called 'Parnellites' against the majority of the party, led by John Dillon, whom Redmond attacked for sacrificing Parnell for the sake of the Irish Party's alliance with the Liberal Party. Redmond, who was born in Ireland in 1851, was still a comparatively young man at the time and as both a Catholic and an aspiring politician his refusal to desert Parnell was a courageous act. The easier course would have been to appease the Church and the Liberals. He was rewarded when he became Ireland's spokesman in the British Isles and America from 1900 and so nearly achieved home rule for Ireland. Though courageous, he pursued objectives for Ireland which were essentially moderate but which ultimately failed to satisfy the great bulk of his followers in Ireland and America

The problem of intra-Irish strife in Ireland and at Westminster in the 1890s was compounded by a new policy to alleviate major Irish grievances. Introduced by the Conservative Government which came to office in 1895 it was a far cry from past Tory policies of coercion. Improvements in the conditions of Irish tenancies followed the 1896 Land Act; a Local Government Act of 1898 set up elected county, rural district and urban district councils; and a Department of Agriculture and Technical

[7] *Chicago Sunday Times Herald*, 3 March 1901.

Instruction was created in 1899 under the direction of Horace Plunkett. It was clear that reforms of this kind designed to improve the lives of ordinary Irishmen could undermine the movement for Irish political autonomy if the nationalist movement remained so disastrously divided.

The reunion of the two major factions of the Parliamentary Party in January and February of 1900 involved the acceptance of Redmond's terms, that is, an independent Irish party, tied to no other, dedicated to securing both home rule and the redress of social and economic grievances from any British government prepared to grant them. Redmond became leader and Tim Healy and his few supporters, who had further factionalized the party by attacking the centralized authority of the Parliamentary Party from 1895, were purged through the agency of the United Irish League (hereafter the UIL). This was a new popular organization founded by William O'Brien in 1898, which challenged Healy's support in the constituencies. By the end of 1900 it was accepted as the popular arm of the Parliamentary Party and Healy had been expelled for running his own candidates against its nominees. A strong Irish Parliamentary Party, supported by the new UIL, was now set to recoup the disastrous loss of support and income which had resulted from the divisions of the 1890s.

The United States and the Dominions were essential to the Irish Parliamentary Party as sources for the replenishment of its treasury. Redmond had returned from an American visit in 1899 convinced that Irish unity was essential if more support was to be forthcoming from the United States.[8] The 1890s had proved as financially barren abroad for the party as they were politically barren at Westminster. Like the Labour Party, the Irish Party paid subsidies to enable its members to sit in Parliament. Over thirty nationalists received aid in 1895 and the shortage of money from 1895 to 1900 caused them considerable hardship. This was, then, by no means the slightest of the reasons for reunification and an improvement in the subsidies paid to members dated from the reunion in 1900. F.S.Lyons estimated that more than fifty per cent of the eighty or so Irish nationalist members were receiving substantial sums in aid between 1900 and 1910. The party also had elections to fight and supported various social schemes, such

[8] Tim Healy, *Letters and Leaders of My Day*, London: Thornton Butterworth, 1928, v. 1, p. 443.

as the Evicted Tenants' Fund, and a great deal of the necessary money came from the USA and the Dominions.[9]

The scale of these contributions from overseas was huge. In 1880, Parnell toured the United States and Canada raising funds and regular visits were made by John Dillon, Tim Healy, John Redmond and his brother William, and a number of other Members of Parliament. T.P.O'Connor, for example, made six fund-raising tours to North America in all. In the early 1880s the Irish Land League received hundreds of thousands of dollars, largely collected by Patrick Ford and his Irish-American newspaper, the *Irish World*.[10] Messrs O'Brien, Dillon, Harrington, O'Connor and Sullivan, all Members of the Irish Parliamentary Party, were in the United States on a fund-raising mission at the time of the Parnell-O'Shea divorce scandal, and their absence certainly contributed to the general chaos which followed. One of the major problems of the succession to Parnell was the question of the control of American funds held in Paris for the Irish Parliamentary Party which were not released until 1894.[11]

John and William Redmond began their long series of foreign tours in 1883 with a visit to Australia where, despite adverse publicity from the Phoenix Park murders, they raised $15,000 for the Irish National League. *En route* home they raised another $15,000 in the United States. John Redmond made further trips to the USA in 1886, 1895, and 1899, and the poor returns from this last trip impressed on him the need for Irish unity.[12] The London *Times* of 31 January 1900 echoed this view more cynically: 'The so-called reunion of the Irish party means little beyond the fact that nothing more is to be squeezed out of the Radical party and that the coffers of Ireland in America are empty.'

In the years following the reunification of the Irish Parliamentary Party a successful effort was made to re-enlist American

[9] For an account of the financing of the Irish Party, 1890–1910, see F.S.Lyons, *The Irish Parliamentary Party, 1890–1910*, London: Faber and Faber, 1951, Ch. 6, 'The Payment of Members'. His estimate of £70,000 ($350,000) from foreign sources in the period 1900–10 is probably too low. See also D.C.Lyne, 'Irish-Canadian contributions to the home-rule movement in the 1890s', *Studia Hibernica*, No. 7, 1967, pp. 182–206.

[10] Carl Wittke, *The Irish in America*, Baton Rouge: Louisiana State University Press, 1956, pp. 165–6; Brown, *op. cit.*, p. 121.

[11] T.P.O'Connor, *Memoirs of an Old Parliamentarian*, London: Ernest Benn, 1929, v. 2, p. 187; Lyons, *op. cit.*, pp. 19, 23.

[12] Denis Gwynn, *The Life of John Redmond*, London: Harrap, 1932, pp. 51–3, 56, 85, 93–4.

support. The problem in the United States was complicated, however, by the re-emergence of the revolutionary Clan na Gael and by the independence of the important Ancient Order of Hibernians (AOH), primarily a Catholic social organization. Redmond's first move, therefore, was to create a new Irish-American organization which would accept a subordinate role to that of the Irish Parliamentary Party and the new UIL at home. He wanted nationalist policy to be determined at Westminster and not in the USA. He began to sound out his American friends very soon after the breach was healed,[13] but it was not until 31 October 1901 that he and two of his Parliamentary colleagues, Patrick McHugh and Thomas O'Donnell, arrived in New York to organize the United Irish League in the United States. They were greeted by a former advocate of violence, Patrick Ford, a fact which shocked the London *Times*' Dublin correspondent and to which he often alluded, but Ford was eager to back the UIL with his newspaper, the *Irish World*, and had publicly rejected the Clan na Gael for its advocacy of a revolution doomed to failure. In fact Redmond was greeted by representatives of seventy or so Irish organizations in the USA, including the AOH and the revolutionary Clan. At a meeting attended by prominent Irish-Americans in New York, he clarified his position:

When I came here years ago and asked your sympathy, you told us, and quite rightly, go back and become united among ourselves before appealing to the Irish in foreign lands. I took your advice.[14]

The three Irishmen addressed mass meetings in New York, Chicago, Baltimore, and Washington, DC, where they were received by the President, and in a brief visit to Canada they were received by the Prime Minister, Sir Wilfred Laurier,[15] but the real business of the trip was to organize an American UIL. Following a caucus between Redmond and a handful of the New York Irish in November, a larger meeting of 150 representatives met at the Hoffman House, New York, on 4 December to establish the organization. There was a conspicuous absence of Clan leaders, although many of those present were Clan members. In

[13] For example, Redmond to W.Bourke Cockran, 31 March 1900, *Cockran MSS.*, Box 18.

[14] *New York Times*, 16 November 1901.

[15] *Ottawa Evening Journal*, 22 November 1901.

his address to the meeting Redmond made two important points. The first was that the Irish movement should be controlled from Ireland. He declared:

When Ireland is united she is entitled to decide for herself what is best for her interests. No Irishman in America living 3,000 miles away from the homeland ought to think he has a right to dictate to Ireland. No man who thinks he has that right can justifiably become a member of this new league. This new movement, in fact, should be an auxiliary only of the organization at home.

Such it did, in fact, remain, but Redmond also had to cater for the fact that the rank and file Irish-American was not worried by fine shades of distinction between constitutional and revolutionary activities. Redmond wanted to keep the movement in America out of the hands of Irish-Americans who were known to hold revolutionary views, and to do this he had to appear at least not to oppose revolutionary policies himself. Secondly, therefore, he played to the gallery:

Our movement is not antagonistic to any other movement. We have no quarrel and want no quarrel with any man or anybody who wants to strike a blow at the English Government. In fact, we hope that any man or any such body, if they can strike a blow, will strike quickly and strike hard. But other policies should not prevent our efforts to advance the movement we have instituted for the Irish cause. It is advancing and its effects are bound to be felt.[16]

This was ammunition for his Unionist opponents in later years.

The provisional executive committee of the UIL of America elected by the December meeting was dominated by New York men but it included representatives who ranged from Boston to Savannah, Georgia, and from Washington, DC to Chicago. When Redmond and his party left the United States on 11 December they were able to announce that their mission had been successful, the new organization had been launched with John F. Finerty, editor of the Irish-American *Chicago Citizen* and, like Patrick Ford, a former revolutionary, as National President. William Redmond and Joseph Devlin staged a well publicized tour for the UIL from February to June 1902 in which they too met President

16 *New York Times*, 5 December 1901. Sponsorship by moderate Irish-Americans is clear from the circular invitation to the meeting, dated 27 November 1901. When the provisional executive published a statement later in December it said that physical force was not renounced, but was not immediately practicable.

Roosevelt and by the time they left approximately two hundred branches had been established.[17].

John Redmond was not entirely happy, however. In January 1902 he wrote to Bourke Cockran that the amount of money raised by his trip had disappointed him. In March another letter to Cockran indicated that he was far from confident that the organization in the United States was progressing,[18] but his return to the United States in October that year indicated that the UIL was thriving. The occasion was the first biennial National Convention of the UIL in Boston.[19] Following the convention, at which large sums of money were pledged for the Irish cause, Redmond, with Edward Blake, MP, John Dillon, MP, and Michael Davitt, toured the major north-east cities and collected more money. Redmond could feel very pleased as he returned to Ireland for the Irish Land Conference in December.

The Secretary of the December conference of Irish landlords was Captain Shawe-Taylor whose letter to the Irish press in September 1902 had first sparked interest in a negotiated settlement of the Irish land problem. He returned from a brief visit to the United States in March 1903 just prior to the introduction of the Government's land bill, which provided bounties to landlords and long-term finance for Irish tenants to encourage land sales to those who actually worked the land, and he gave his judgement on one important aspect of the problem in this way:

A final settlement of the land question, by removing the barrier at present existing between Ireland and England, will greatly improve the relations between America and England, and will also link in closer friendship the Dominion of Canada and the British Empire.[20]

In America the passage of the 1903 Irish Land Act was welcomed by the constitutionalist UIL as a first step towards an Irish political settlement, but was opposed by the revolutionary Clan na Gael as a poor substitute for independence. These rival organizations were now at each other's throats and their dispute came

[17] London *Times*, 8 March 1902; United Irish League of America, 'Proceedings of the First National Convention, Boston, Oct. 20–21, 1902', *AIHS*.

[18] Redmond to Cockran, 20 January 1902, on receipt of $3,000 as a first instalment from the American UIL, and 19 March 1902, *Cockran MSS.*, Box 18.

[19] *New York Times*, 21, 22 October 1902; United Irish League of America, *op. cit.*; Lyons, *op. cit.*, pp. 99–103.

[20] London *Times*, 2 March 1903.

into the open on the issue of their rival sponsorship of Robert Emmet memorial meetings in September 1903.[21]

That same month the Clan's own newspaper, the *Gaelic American*, edited by John Devoy, an experienced journalist, published its first issue. Its establishment was a challenge to the *Irish World* which supported the increasingly successful agitation of the UIL. The new paper's policy had been laid down by John Mitchel many years before – complete independence for Ireland and the promotion of the revolutionary nationalist movement in Ireland and the USA. It immediately launched into a sustained attack on Redmond and the constitutional movement.

Redmond's next visit to the United States was for the 1904 National Convention of the UIL in New York. The national treasurer reported that since October 1902, every state of the union had contributed to a total income of $61,665 and even the previously sceptical London *Times* reported that the tour was a success.[22] In 1905 William Redmond toured the USA from coast to coast on his return from a similar mission to Australia and T.P.O'Connor was sent to Philadelphia for the third National Convention of the UIL in 1906. He confessed to Bourke Cockran that, as a result of the January General Election, he had left Britain with the Irish 'war chest' empty, but that the Philadelphia Convention had remedied that. He added, 'I had a most satisfactory interview with the President and he is doing all he can to help.' O'Connor was concerned at the lack of attention shown him by the Clan-dominated Irish leaders of New York, but he still managed to raise between fifteen and twenty thousand dollars there. He also visited Canada with Edward Blake, and when he departed from America two fellow Members of Parliament, Hazleton and Kettle, remained to campaign on.[23]

Redmond and Joseph Devlin attended the 1908 UIL convention

[21] The dispute can be followed in the papers of John Mitchel, a grandson of the Irish revolutionary with the same name, who became Mayor of New York on the 'Fusion (reform) Ticket' in 1909. He was UIL Secretary in New York City in 1903. *Mitchel MSS.*, Box 1.

[22] United Irish League of America, 'Proceedings of the Second National Convention, New York, Aug. 30, 31, 1904', *AIHS;* London *Times*, 1, 2 September, 6 October 1904.

[23] O'Connor to Cockran, 11 October 1906, *Cockran MSS.*, Box 18. Consul General Sanderson, New York, to Ambassador Durand, 19, 29 October 1906, reported on O'Connor's tour in which $60,000 was pledged in Philadelphia, $20,000 in New York and $10,000 in Boston. *FO* 371/160.

17

in Boston and O'Connor was next in the United States in October 1909 seeking financial support for the critical period of the battle over Lloyd George's budget and the attack on the power of the House of Lords. Setting himself a target of $50,000 he exceeded this very comfortably.[24] Then, in 1910, John Redmond and Alderman O'Boyle visited America for the UIL National Convention in Buffalo while O'Connor toured in Canada. Together they raised an estimated $200,000.[25]

By no means all the money raised on these and other tours by members of the Irish Party went into the Parliamentary or General Election funds because Ireland and the UIL had other interests too, but the party was well provided for. One Irish writer in the *North American Review* questioned whether this aid was necessary at all. He estimated that if one million nationalists each contributed twenty-five cents a year the yield for Irish political purposes would be a more than adequate $250,000.[26] But Ireland could not raise these sums and but for aid from the Irish overseas nothing would have been achieved. Redmond clearly indicated this dependence on American support in 1910. For a while in the summer of that year he hoped for an immediate General Election on the issue of the power of the House of Lords, but he confessed that an autumn election would seriously have damaged the finances of his party because his fund-raising trip to America for the UIL convention would have been cancelled.[27] He did manage to go and by the time the election came in December there was more than enough cash in hand.

Missions abroad by John Redmond and other Parliamentary leaders had been consistently successful since 1900 with large audiences and excellent publicity. The UIL was widely dispersed in the United States and accepted, without dispute, leadership from the Irish Party at Westminster. Its actual membership is unknown and is in any case less important than the mass audiences it was frequently able to command. The UIL was certainly

[24] *New York American*, 23 October, *New York Sun*, 23 October, 8 November 1909. O'Connor had already raised $55,000 without tapping New York.

[25] *Annual Register for 1910*, London: Longmans, Green & Co., 1911, p. 226. $153,000 was pledged at Buffalo.

[26] 'Party Supported by Sympathizers in the United States', *North American Review*, October 1908, v. 188, pp. 624–6. The writer argued that the Irish spent $70 million on drink and $17 million on tobacco each year.

[27] Redmond to Elibank, 1 June, 24 July, Redmond to O'Connor, 5 June 1910, *Elibank MSS.*, Box 17.

faring infinitely better than the revolutionary Clan na Gael in this period but its success had been gained at the expense of a certain calculated ambiguity which played into the hands of opponents of home rule. What did Redmond and his followers want, they asked. In Canada in 1901, Redmond claimed that Ireland wanted what Canada already had. 'It was only by the concession of home rule,' he said, 'that the rebellious Canadians were turned into loyal, prosperous and contented citizens.'[28] But Canada was a Dominion, independent in almost every respect and a far cry from the limited autonomy of home rule, and the constitution of the American UIL made clear that its objective was 'full national self-government for Ireland'. In October 1910 John Redmond told the New York Press Club, 'By home rule we mean something like you have here, where Federal affairs are governed by the Federal Government and State affairs by the State Government,' but that same month, discussing the progress of the home rule movement in an address to the UIL national convention at Buffalo, he declared, 'These concessions are only valuable because they strengthen the great goal of national independence.'[29] At Westminster, the Irish Party claimed that by home rule it meant the delegation of purely Irish business to a subordinate Irish parliament in Dublin and the reservation of national, international and imperial matters to the parliament at Westminster. However, in the light of Redmond's contradictory statements, which were echoed by his Irish colleagues, Unionists justifiably asked if the Irish Party could be trusted.

The confusion the Irish created was the result of attempts to find meaningful parallels to the Irish experience for very different audiences around the world and of the less creditable desire to capitalize on local sentiment and local cash by oversimplifying the issues. This quotation from Philip G. Cambray's anti-Nationalist book, *Irish Affairs and the Home Rule Question*, published in 1911, illustrates the problem rather well:

Well meaning persons suggest the granting of Home Rule ... entirely ignoring the fact that the Americans who pay for representation at Westminster do so for motives of which the desire of assisting

28 *Montreal Daily Star*, 21 November 1901.
29 Cited in Ian Malcolm, 'Home Rule All Round', *Nineteenth Century*, November 1910, v. 68, pp. 791–9, and *Parl. Debs.*, Commons, 15 February 1911, 5th Series, v. xxi, 1076.

Ireland to obtain Home Rule is only one. Moreover, the American contributors' idea of Home Rule as wholly satisfying the Irish demand is not a subordinate Parliament, but independence. Enthusiasm which extracts dollars from Irish-American pockets is not engendered by declarations for a petty Parliament and of loyalty to the Empire. For their money they require something full-blooded, and the Irish Nationalist leaders visiting them take great pains to see that they get it. So long as Irish Nationalists are a powerful Party, with great influence in British politics, so long can they look across the Atlantic for the financial assistance without which their agitation would sink to insignificant proportions. It is not too much to say that the contributions are made not more with the intention of assisting Ireland than with the desire of injuring the British Empire. English supporters of Home Rule would have it believed that the dollars are subscribed for the better government of Ireland; but no one who has any acquaintance with the speeches and the literature of the Irish-Americans can fail to be struck by their anti-British spirit.[30]

In the United States, the Ancient Order of Hibernians was able to endorse the Parliamentary Party while maintaining that complete independence, and nothing less, was the Irish goal and at the same time Redmond could say in Parliament, 'I deny I am a separatist'.[31] It was very easy to distrust him.

A similar problem, also connected with the need to campaign abroad, concerned the question of the use of armed force in Ireland. As we observed earlier, Redmond appeared to endorse physical force in 1901 but at all their later meetings in America he and his colleagues counselled caution and attributed recent advances in Ireland to peaceful agitation. Nevertheless, their American associates, particularly Patrick Ford, provided ammunition for Unionist attacks. Ford had renounced force as impracticable by this time and had thrown his weight behind the UIL, but in the 1880s he was a known advocate of violence and dynamite. His *Irish World* was a powerful voice for the UIL but it was also addicted to attacking any suggestion of an Anglo-American alliance. It backed Russia against Britain's ally Japan in the Russo-Japanese war and was generally to be found in the ranks of England's enemies. Joseph Devlin once delivered a speech to an American UIL meeting counselling moderation and

[30] Philip G. Cambray, *Irish Affairs and the Home Rule Question*, London: John Murray, 1911, 2nd ed., p. 133. Cambray was a member of the Union Defence League.

[31] *Parl. Debs.*, Commons, 15 February 1911, 5th Series, v. xxi, 1105.

sat down to hear the Rev. Dr Brann announce from the same platform, 'In America we give hundreds of dollars to Irish Leagues, but we would give thousands if it meant the winning of Irish independence on the battle field. We are hoping for that war too.'[32] There were many similar incidents. However, Redmond's British critics ignored the fact that the physical force faction of the Irish in the United States, the Clan na Gael, openly attacked both the UIL and the Parliamentary Party and it was quite improper for Cambray and others to suggest that it lay behind the whole Irish movement in the USA. Not until the outbreak of World War I did this become true. Not until then did John Redmond lose his hold on the Irish abroad.

Redmond had a great deal to show for his methods. Ireland was beginning to look prosperous and content, as Halévy observed when he visited it in the summer of 1903,[33] and the Land Act was to make it more so. Despite improved living standards, however, the Catholic Irish persisted in sending to Westminster Members of Parliament who supported a measure of Irish self-government. These had traditionally been aligned with the Liberal Party, and as the Conservative administration lived out its last months in 1905 negotiations with the then Liberal leader, Campbell-Bannerman, resulted in his commitment to a measure of self-government which was somewhat ambiguously repeated in the King's speech in 1906. However, the January 1906 General Election gave the Liberal Party an absolute majority in Parliament and it was not dependent on Irish support.[34] The measures offered the Irish in 1906 by the Chief Secretary James Bryce, and in 1907 by his successor Augustine Birrell, were quite inadequate and were rejected by Redmond and the UIL.[35]

It had been clear for decades that the absolute veto of the

[32] *New York Times*, 19 February 1903.

[33] Elie Halévy, *History of the English People in the Nineteenth Century*, London: Ernest Benn, 1961, v. 5, pp, 394–5.

[34] Lyons, *op. cit.*, pp. 113–14. Liberals 400, Unionists 157, Irish Nationalists 83, Labour 30. David Butler and Jennie Freeman, *British Political Facts, 1900–60*, London: Macmillan & Co., 1963, p. 122.

[35] In October 1906, Bryce offered an unrepresentative Irish authority which was required to petition the Imperial Parliament for permission to legislate on any item, and in 1907 Birrell offered an Irish Council of eighty to ninety members, three-quarters of whom were to be elected and the remainder nominated, with powers over primary and secondary education and various technical boards. Its budget was to be granted from the Imperial Exchequer. D.Gwynn, *Redmond*, pp. 135, 142–9.

predominantly Conservative House of Lords was the ultimate obstacle to the passage of home rule legislation and Redmond was reminded of this in November 1906 when he was asked for, and gave, Irish support for the Liberals' Education Bill. In a test of strength the Lords rejected this bill and moved towards the showdown with the government which came with Lloyd George's budget in 1909. The Lords rejected the budget that November and Redmond was able to use the General Election in the following January, which was very largely fought on the issue of the power of the Lords, to secure a much firmer commitment to home rule from the Cabinet. In the Albert Hall, London, on 10 December 1909, the Prime Minister, Asquith, declared, 'The solution of the [Irish] problem can be found only in one way, by a policy which, while explicitly safeguarding the supremacy and indefectible authority of the Imperial Parliament, will set up in Ireland a system of full self-government in regard to purely Irish affairs'.

Asquith went to the country by dissolving Parliament on 10 January 1910, and Irish hopes were raised by the election result which this time placed the fate of the Liberal Government very much in their hands. The Liberals returned 275 members, the Conservative-Unionists 273, Labour 40 and the Irish Nationalists 82. Seventy of the Irish were pledged to the Irish Party, the remainder supported William O'Brien and Tim Healy in opposing the budget. Redmond stood firm. His price for supporting the Government was the abolition of the Lords' power of veto. Asquith agreed and, both to secure passage of the government's legislation and to maintain Irish support, he announced in April the intention to legislate the reform of the House of Lords. On 6 May, however, the question was deferred by the death of King Edward VII and for the next seven months or so the power of the Lords was the subject of constant negotiations and conferences. The Irish had little power in these discussions and at any time could have been undermined by a Liberal-Conservative settlement, but when the still unresolved question was thrown to the country in the December 1910 General Election the Irish retained their power in the House of Commons when the Liberal Party again only marginally held power.[36] The Government

---

[36] For the elections see Butler and Freeman, *op. cit.*, p. 122, and D. Gwynn, *Redmond*, pp. 167–75. The figures in December 1910 were Liberal 272, Conservative-Unionist 272, Labour 42, Irish Nationalist 84.

managed to force reform on the reluctant House of Lords in August 1911 after threatening to create a majority of Liberal peers, and the stage was set for the repayment of the debt to the Irish and for the implementation of the outstanding Liberal commitment to home rule. The upper house could now only delay an item of legislation for two sessions and a home rule victory was therefore virtually assured by 1914. But then came the shock of Ulster's determination to resist by force. For the moment, however, Redmond's policy of patience appeared to have paid off. For ten years it had required very careful management not only of the Irish at home but of the Irish in the Dominions and the United States.

This success had been disastrous for the cause of revolutionary nationalism. Despite rumours of arms shipments and threats of arson and sabotage, actual violence and physical force were not an important part of the revolutionary movement in the years from 1899 to 1914. The *Gaelic American* regularly carried an advertisement offering a Mauser rifle to anyone securing fifty annual subscriptions, arguing that Ireland could only be freed by physical force and that every Irishman needed a rifle to emulate the Boers, and both the Clan na Gael and the AOH had small sections for military drilling, but these very minor activities did not feature prominently during the period. Rather than engage in petty terrorism the Clan was dreaming with John Devoy of a full-scale military rising in Ireland, and but for the rebellious policy of Ulster and the coming of the world war this would have remained a dream. In Ireland the Irish Republican Brotherhood, founded in the 1850s as the companion to the Fenian Brotherhood, had been undermined by the parliamentary agitation, by reforms in land ownership, education and local government, and it barely managed to survive. A member of its Supreme Council confessed that its total membership could be assembled in one concert hall.[37] It was organized in the larger cities of Ireland, Scotland and England, but its numbers were very small. Redmond was very much in control and as the chosen leader of Ireland he was welcomed by the great majority of Irish-Americans whenever he chose to campaign for funds in the USA.

[37] The member was P.S.O'Hegarty. See his *History of Ireland under the Union, 1801–1922*, London: Methuen, 1952, pp. 633–4; *The Victory of Sinn Fein*, Dublin: Talbot Press, 1924, pp. 12–15.

Devoy's own assessment of the revolutionary movement in Ireland was that, 'From 1871 to 1916 it was maintained almost entirely by moral and material support from the Clan na Gael. Envoys from the IRB attended every Convention of the Clan na Gael and went back to carry on the work.'[38] Desmond Ryan recalled the surprise with which Patrick Pearse, who was later to be executed for leading the Easter Rebellion, greeted Devoy and 'other grey-haired Fenians' when he visited America in 1914. 'There were no such men in Ireland,' he said, and this of course was a major reason for the lack of revolutionary activity there.[39] The British had effectively exiled a whole generation of Irish revolutionary leaders, without regard for the repercussions on Britain's relations with the countries of refuge.

The revival of the IRB stemmed from America and it owed much to Thomas Clarke, who suffered fifteen years in British prisons only to die, like Pearse, before a firing squad in 1916. Born in 1858, Clarke was raised in an Ireland of misery and evictions. On his first visit to America in 1881 he joined the Clan na Gael and his arrest in England in 1883 followed his return to England on an abortive attempt at a dynamite sabotage mission. He was released in 1898 and left for America where he became Assistant Editor of the *Gaelic American* and a leading organizer of anti-British agitations. In 1905 he took US citizenship, but by 1907 he was on the way back to Ireland to reorganize the IRB from the cover of a tobacconist shop in Dublin. The IRB had been relatively dormant under the leadership of John O'Leary until his death in 1907, but from that point on Clan money and instructions were channelled via Clarke, a reliable agent for the American-Irish.[40] The precise relationship between the Clan and the IRB is obscure because it was conspiratorial but they had worked closely since at least 1877.[41] They offered reciprocal membership and there are many indications that money in sums of hundreds (and perhaps thousands) of dollars was sent to Ireland. Short of volunteers, equipment and opportunities, the IRB's expenses were slight but even so it needed aid and Clarke

[38] John Devoy, *Recollections of a Rebel*, New York: Charles Young, 1929, p. 392.

[39] Desmond Ryan, *The Phoenix Flame*, London: Arthur Baker, 1937, p. 293.

[40] Louis N. Le Roux, *Tom Clarke and the Irish Freedom Movement*, Dublin: Talbot Press, 1936.

[41] Brown, *op. cit.*, p. 67.

became treasurer to ensure safe delivery of Clan money after $300 was misappropriated.[42]

Progress in Ireland was slow and publicity poor with the New York *Gaelic American* as the only regular weekly revolutionary journal to combat the power of various organs associated with the constitutionalists, notably *Freeman's Journal* and the *Irish Independent*. Clan aid failed to revitalize an Irish journal, *The Peasant* in 1908, but in 1910 Clarke and the IRB managed to start a monthly, *Irish Freedom*, and they augmented printed news with the new cinema medium, bringing nationalist newsreels to packed halls in 1913.[43]

Although the IRB bore the tradition of revolutionary nationalism it became associated in the public mind with the Sinn Fein movement so that to most people Sinn Fein came to cover the whole range of nationalist agitation in its later years. This was unfortunate because Sinn Fein was an original conception for Ireland, unrelated to the tradition of armed rising and dynamite which characterized the IRB and the Clan. The founder of the movement was Arthur Griffith whose policy was built upon the Hungarian example from which the Dual Austro-Hungarian monarchy stemmed. Its platform came from his twenty-seven articles on Hungary's example to Ireland published in his journal the *United Irishman* in 1904. Griffith's starting point was that the Act of Union of 1801 was illegal and that Ireland should assume that the constitution of 1782 and the Renunciation Act of the following year were still in force. His plan called for the establishment of a council of three hundred to determine national policy which would be voluntarily carried out by county councils and local bodies, whilst Irishmen would refuse to sit in the Imperial Parliament. In 1908 a number of separatist groups combined to form the Sinn Fein League and although Griffith himself appeared to allow for the possibility of a Dual Monarchy, the majority of his supporters were Republicans and the phrase 'National Independence' united them all.[44]

The first electoral appearance of Griffith's policy was in

[42] William O'Brien and Desmond Ryan, eds, *Devoy's Post-Bag, 1871-1928*, Dublin: C.J.Fallon, 1948, 1953, v. 2, pp. 382, 401, appendix p. 570.

[43] *Ibid.*, pp. 365–6, 396–7, 410–11; Le Roux, *op. cit.*, p. 90.

[44] Dorothy Macardle, *The Irish Republic*, London: Victor Gollancz, 1938, pp. 64–6; Arthur Griffith, *The Resurrection of Hungary, A Parallel for Ireland*, Dublin: Whelan & Son, 3rd ed., 1918.

February 1907 when Charles J. Dolan, MP, resigned his seat as a member of the Irish Party to fight as a Sinn Fein candidate, and lost. Membership of the League grew slowly and was insufficient to sustain the *Sinn Fein Daily*, a newspaper which failed in January 1910 after a few months' operation.[45] Like the IRB, Sinn Fein seemed to be making little progress as the decade ended.

With the IRB both slow to develop and basically a secret organization, the Sinn Fein League, as a publicly avowed separatist organization, received support from the Clan na Gael and the IRB. Members of the latter were allowed to join it in 1907 and Clan aid to the *United Irishman* saved the paper in 1902.[46] In the spring of 1907 Bulmer Hobson toured the USA for the movement and later in the year the *Gaelic American* began a campaign to boost Sinn Fein. 'Parliamentary Party in the Last Ditch' declared its headline on 31 August. The Irish Party, it claimed, was seeking a quick election before Sinn Fein had election funds to challenge it. On 7 August 1907 a Sinn Fein League was formed in New York under the Presidency of Daniel Cohalan with John Devoy as a member of its executive committee, and a year later the Sinn Fein League of America was founded in Buffalo.[47] Its aim was to raise contributions for the Sinn Fein election fund, but it made no progress.

Although not a real alternative as yet to Redmond's party, the revolutionary Irish in America found Griffith's Sinn Fein League more acceptable. Similarly, the *Gaelic American* was very kind to William O'Brien's 'All for Ireland League', founded in 1910. The League was an attempt to unite all classes and regions in Ireland in a scheme of home rule. In fact, O'Brien's organization was inimical to everything the Clan stood for except the principle of Irish unity itself. It was a party of conciliation and compromise, not of outright independence. Backed by a small number of Conservatives as a device for breaking the Liberal-Irish Nationalist alliance it was occasionally supported with funds by wealthy Americans who had been led to believe that Lloyd George was a dangerous socialist. It was a tool in the British party political battle, despite O'Brien's sincerity and his many genuine supporters, and Devoy and many Anglo-Irish Tories accepted the

45 O'Hegarty, *History of Ireland*, pp. 655–6.
46 O'Brien and Ryan, *op. cit.*, v. 2, pp. 347, 349–50.
47 *Gaelic American*, 10 August 1907 and 15 August 1908.

League for the same reason, because it might weaken the Irish Parliamentary Party.[48]

In 1910 and 1911, however, the Clan na Gael was itself dangerously weak. In New York the Clan leaders faced a challenge from one Mathew Cummings, who was using the United Irish Societies, an organization which had co-ordinated the activities of one hundred or so Irish-American groups since 1899, to try, without success, to unseat them. John Keating, a Clan leader, wrote despondently that the end of the movement was near, and that internal conflict was the cause.[49]

Cummings had already featured in a battle for the control of the Ancient Order of Hibernians, an organization about which we know rather more than we do of the Clan or the UIL.[50] It was, and indeed still is, an Irish Catholic organization, claiming an obscure ancestry to pre-Christian times, which was introduced into the USA in 1836. It gained adherents steadily, particularly during the 'Know-Nothing' nativist crisis, but it, too, suffered from internal dissension and in 1897 it was reunited after twenty years of conflict. By 1910 its membership was 180,000, of whom just under a third were members of its Ladies' Auxiliary. It had a small military wing to attract young adults with an interest in drilling, which complemented the New York State 69th, or 'Irish', Regiment and the 'Irish Volunteers' associated with the Clan na Gael. The income of the order was huge, but most of it was in the form of insurance contributions, for a great many of the divisions were benefit societies. Organization was by counties, and by divisions within these, whilst co-ordination, the organization of the biennial national conventions, and the publication of the *National Hibernian* journal were in the hands of an elected national executive. Involvement in politics was forbidden by its constitution, but foreign affairs escaped this provision and British policy was systematically opposed at all its meetings. Its

---

[48] *Ibid.*, 23 April 1910. See Alan J.Ward, 'Frewen's Anglo-American Campaign for Federalism, 1910–1921', *Irish Historical Studies*, Vol. xv, no. 59 (March 1967), pp. 256–75.

[49] Keating to Devoy, 22 January 1910, 11 August, 16 November 1911, *Devoy MSS.*, 10, 610.

[50] Unless otherwise stated, the Ancient Order of Hibernians material is from John O'Dea, *A History of the Ancient Order of Hibernians and Ladies' Auxiliary*, Philadelphia: Published by the Order, 1923, 4 vols., a detailed, if uncritical study of its history.

non-political interests, however, were wide. The Order established a chair in Gaelic at the Catholic University of America, and it had some success in lobbying for Irish studies in public and church schools. It handsomely endowed the Gaelic League of Ireland and attacked not only the 'stage Irishman' of American vaudeville but the drama of Yeats, Synge, Lady Gregory, *et al.*, for their 'vilification' of the Irish race in their 'Dublin, or pagan, school of art'.

The American Hibernians were not closely associated with Hibernians in Ireland who were, in fact, divided between a small militant faction of about 4,000, who used the name Ancient Order of Hibernians after registering it as a benefit society, and the majority, 60,000 or so in nearly 700 divisions, who added Board of Erin to the title to distinguish themselves. These were led by Joseph Devlin, MP, who was also Secretary of the UIL, and they supported Redmond. The logical association of the AOH Board of Erin with the Americans was prevented by the stubborn insistence of the native Irish organization that it was the parent body to which Hibernians in America and elsewhere should affiliate. As the most powerful Hibernian group in the world, however, the Americans demanded a relationship based on partnership and equality and consequently there was very little co-operation between them.

The American AOH endorsed the Irish Parliamentary Party for most of the period, but it always declared quite frankly its support for complete Irish independence and it did turn against Redmond's party for four years when Mathew Cummings became President in 1906. During his militant reign he concluded an agreement with the National German-American Alliance, in 1907, and declared that in any Anglo-German war the Irish would fight with the Germans. In 1909 he visited Ireland where he sought to destroy the authority of the Board of Erin by appearing at meetings organized by the rival AOH. His attempt to force the American AOH into militant separatism did not go undetected or unresented, and he was narrowly defeated for the Presidency in 1910 by a moderate, James J. Regan. Once again the Parliamentary Party was endorsed, though the Board of Erin continued to reject an alliance.

Redmond and the Irish Parliamentary Party were, then, still riding high in Ireland and America. Their constitutional agitation for home rule was an international movement but the weaker, revolutionary nationalist opposition was also international. In fact the Irish could not have maintained their struggle for self-government in both of these guises, had it not been for the support of the international-Irish and particularly the American-Irish. This fact had an important bearing not only on the organization of the campaign for an Irish settlement but also on the whole course of Anglo-American relations.

3 Anglo-American Relations, 1899–1912

*'Were the Irish capable of adopting hostility to
Great Britain instead of the independence of Ireland
and to pursue objects which would appeal rather to
American interests than to American sympathies, their
influence in this country would become far more
dangerous.'*

SIR FREDERICK BRUCE, BRITISH MINISTER
TO THE UNITED STATES, 19 MARCH 1867[1]

*'Are we not Anglo-Saxons ? The more than seventy
percent of us, who are Germans, Irish, Austrian Slavs,
and persecuted Jews from Russia, must not interfere
with Anglo-Saxon unity, y'know.'*

SHAEMUS O'SHEEL, NEW YORK, 1915[2]

Anglo-American relations at the turn of the century were cordial
and a widespread assumption existed that the United States and
Britain could have no serious differences of opinion. The settlement of the Venezuelan boundary dispute by arbitration in 1899,
the Hay-Pauncefote Canal Treaty of 1901, and the settlement in
1903 of the long drawn-out Alaskan boundary dispute between
Canada and the USA, reinforced the prevailing British view that
conflict between the USA and Great Britain was unthinkable.
Oblivious to the multi-racial composition of American society,
the British press commonly asserted that there existed an Anglo-
American bond through a shared 'Anglo-Saxon' race to justify
British diplomatic concessions to the United States, but in fact

[1] William D'Arcy, *The Fenian Movement in the United States, 1858–1886*,
Washington, DC: Catholic University Press, 1947, p. 238.
[2] Shaemus O'Sheel, *The Catechism of Balaam Junior*, New York: Hugh G.
Masterson, 1915, 6th ed., p. 14.

30

Britain had good cause to court American friendship. She could not compete against the USA in the Americas and retreated. In her Far Eastern policies co-operation with the United States was desirable to check the expansion of European powers, particularly Russia and Germany. In Europe, France was particularly hostile and in 1898 Germany began her mammoth naval construction programme. Britain consequently looked for good relations in her 'rear' across the Atlantic.

In America it was widely accepted that Britain's benevolent neutrality during the Spanish-American War of 1898 had been crucial in preventing a European alliance behind Spain. This popular view exaggerated Britain's role but the American government was able to justify its own benevolent neutrality during the Boer War, which began in October 1899, at least in part by reference to this episode. Henry Cabot Lodge, who has often been accused of anglophobia, summed up his feelings in this letter of 2 February 1900:

> I think we shall manage to keep our neutrality, and that the government will be kept from doing anything in the way of meddling in the Transvaal War. There is a very general and solid sense of the fact that however much we sympathize with the Boers the downfall of the British Empire is something which no rational American could regard as anything but a misfortune to the United States.[3]

In positions of political power, particularly in the Republican Party and among leading academics and journalists in the USA, were many who valued Anglo-American friendship as something unique in international relations. Nevertheless, there was still a considerable amount of anglophobia in the United States which buttressed the traditional American policy of non-involvement in foreign affairs. During the Chinese Boxer Rebellion in 1900, for example, neither the United States nor Britain was prepared unilaterally to undertake strong action to protect their shared interests against China or the European powers involved there, but joint action was equally impossible. John Hay, the Secretary of State, well understood this and to his Assistant Secretary of State he wrote:

[3] Henry Cabot Lodge, ed., *Selections from the Correspondence of Theodore Roosevelt and Henry Cabot Lodge, 1884–1918*, New York: Charles Scribner's Sons, 1924, v. 1, pp. 444–6.

If it were not for our domestic politics, we could and should join with England, whose interests are identical with ours, and make our ideas prevail. But in the present morbid state of the public mind towards England, that is not to be thought of – and we must look idly on, and see her making terms with Germany instead of with us.[4]

Largely responsible for the 'morbid state of the public mind' was Britain's 'suppression' of the Boer republics.

The Boer War does not occupy a prominent chapter in the history of Anglo-American relations but when one searches for a critical event, a historical watershed to mark the beginning of this study, it takes on a special significance. During the war the two major strands of Irish and Irish-American activity which were to create the Anglo-American problem of Ireland during the next two decades were dramatically reorganized. In Ireland a reunited Irish Parliamentary Party spoke out on South Africa as its first act and in the United States the Clan na Gael re-emerged from many years of decline under the leadership of an old Fenian, John Devoy, and an Irish-American lawyer, Daniel F. Cohalan. Revolutionary Irishmen had prayed since the Napoleonic Wars that England's weakness would be their opportunity and the Boer War reminded them of this self-imposed responsibility. To both Irish factions, the 'Constitutionalists' and the 'Physical Force Party', the war marked the beginning of the final march to Irish nationhood, and in America it was also their rehearsal for the attack on the British Empire which began in 1914.

In both the United States and Great Britain there were highly vocal minorities opposed to British imperial policies in South Africa, and their most significant shared characteristic was the presence in them of leading men of Irish birth or extraction. In the House of Commons in February 1900 John Redmond claimed to speak for Irishmen throughout the world when he declared, in supporting the Boer claim to independence:

It is true that whenever the Empire is involved in a difficulty or complication which diminishes its great strength, a feeling of hope and satisfaction runs through the veins of the Irish race at home and abroad.[5]

In the United States prominent Irish-Americans contracted an

---

[4] Hay to Alvey A. Adee, 14 September 1900, *McKinley MSS.*, v. 63.
[5] *Parl. Debs.*, Commons, 4th Series, 7 February 1900, v. 78, 831–2.

immediate alliance with American anti-imperialists, largely Democrats, with anglophobes, and with German-Americans who feared any Anglo-American accord which might disadvantage Germany. Any enemy of Great Britain was, *ipso facto*, a friend of Irish-Americans, and when the Boers turned to the United States for aid they were greeted by Irish patrons who were well established in politics and the press. The United Irish League was yet to be organized in America, but there were hundreds of Irish-American fraternal, religious and political organizations ready to protest at Britain's conduct of the war. In major cities throughout the country United Irish Societies had been formed to co-ordinate the activities of the many Irish groups. The Ancient Order of Hibernians actively opposed the war as did the still factionalized Clan na Gael. Irish-American newspapers like the *Boston Pilot*, the *Chicago Citizen* and the *Irish World* added their strident denunciations of the British to those of the anti-imperialist Democratic press.

As belligerents the Boers wanted men and supplies, but they also wanted to deny these vital items to the enemy. Since Britain monopolized the American trade in arms and war supplies the Boers wanted trade with both sides to be banned in the interests of 'true neutrality', a policy which would have resulted in a net gain for them.[6] This was precisely the case repeated by Irish-Americans and other pro-Germans to weaken Britain in 1914. Another important Boer objective was diplomatic support from the United States government. No one expected military assistance, but American diplomatic intervention by way of mediation or pressures brought to bear through one of a number of negotiations then under way with the British, was at least conceivable.[7]

Rumours of Boer purchases and recruitment in America appear

[6] A few days after the war began in October 1899, the South African Republic appealed to the US Government to ban the export of mules and horses to British troops in South Africa. 191,402 'remounts, mules and donkeys' were shipped during the war, the most important category of war supplies. American trade with Britain grew by $112 million (approximately 20%) during the war. See John H. Ferguson, *American Diplomacy and the Boer War*, Philadelphia: University of Pennsylvania Press, 1939, pp. 45, 50. A useful, though dated, book.

[7] These negotiations included the Alaskan Boundary, the Clayton-Bulwer Treaty revision, American navigation laws and reciprocal trade relations, Bering Sea seals, and Newfoundland fishing rights. See Charles S. Campbell, *Anglo-American Understanding, 1898–1903*, Baltimore: Johns Hopkins Press, 1957.

to have strayed into the British Embassy by design for, in the absence of more positive kinds of harassment, warfare by rumour was a standard item in the Irish-American armoury against the British Empire. With the co-operation of the American government and Pinkerton detectives, the British investigated tales of arms purchases and recruitment, concentrating on Irish-American organizations, but they discovered very little. Boer sympathizers were raising money to send recruits to South Africa, covertly and via Europe, but very few men were sent and in fact the US Treasury Department probably indicated the truth in February 1900. It had been searching for violations of American neutrality by the Boers and concluded that rumours of large enlistments were deliberately planted to influence public opinion.[8]

The most successful act of Boer recruitment was wholly Irish-American and quite public. An 'Ambulance Corps' of about sixty men was equipped and sent to South Africa by the United Irish Societies of Chicago in February 1900. It was ostensibly a non-fighting unit accredited by the American Red Cross and before leaving each man made a declaration that he intended solely to provide medical aid. Despite the open secret that the unit was intended for combat, this subterfuge effectively prevented American or British interference and almost all of them took up arms immediately on arriving in South Africa.[9]

For their part, the British government issued instructions that all American applicants for service with the British forces should be told, verbally and with nothing in writing, that they could not be recruited on United States territory. Consuls were steeled to the task by a memorandum setting out the fate of the British minister and three consuls who were expelled during the Crimean War as the result of 'the work of the enemies of this country of the

[8] Report in Ambassador Pauncefote to Foreign Secretary, 23 February 1900, *FO* 2/319. One elaborate plan by a 'prominent and thoroughly trustworthy Irishman' to send 5,000 men is described in Ferguson, *op. cit.*, p. 66. Reports of rumours and their investigations are liberally distributed in the diplomatic records of the Boer War.

[9] *New York Times*, 26 November 1900; Ferguson, *op. cit.*, pp. 66–7. The Ancient Order of Hibernians contributed $2,700 of its 'Boer War Fund' to sending the 'Ambulance Corps', and $5,000 to bringing them back. See O'Dea, *op. cit.*, v. 3, pp. 1224–5, 1267–8. There was also a so-called 'Irish Brigade' organized as a regular unit in the Boer Army by Col. J.E.Blake, a West Point graduate, from 300 Irishmen and Irish-Americans. See *New York Times*, 16 November 1900, and Edgar Holt, *The Boer War*, London: Putnam, 1958, p. 88.

nature of a conspiracy to create embarrassment and, if possible, a rupture with the United States'. Consuls were also, no doubt, aware of the fate of Sackville-West, the British Minister sacrificed by President Cleveland for the Irish-American vote in 1888.[10]

A small number of Americans, including Irish-Americans, made their way to South Africa to fight with the Boers, but there is no evidence that even this slight contribution in men was matched by weapons or supplies. The British on the other hand acquired large numbers of horses and mules from the United States. Most of these were shipped from New Orleans and it was there that the British were subjected to legal and physical harassment. It is difficult to assess Irish-American complicity in this, although the British took it as axiomatic. For more than a year the very nervous British Consul in New Orleans, Arthur Vansittart, warned of impending disaster at the hands of Irish 'physical force' advocates, and in March 1902 Ambassador Pauncefote finally asked the American Secretary of State, John Hay, to warn the Governor of Louisiana that the 'Irish Physical Force Party' planned to destroy the next shipment of mules and horses. Within a few days he passed on Vansittart's fears that the Consulate was in danger but nothing came of the threats and it is doubtful whether agitators intended anything more than that the British should be put to the maximum of discomfort.[11]

Legal harassment in 1901 and 1902, through recourse to the courts, to the Governor of Louisiana, and even to the President, on the question of supply shipments was largely in the hands of a South African, Samuel Pearson. Pinkerton agents followed him to Washington and New York, where he was seen to associate with Irish-Americans, but they concluded that rather than actually conspiring with them to sabotage the British, his task was to secure publicity for the Boers.[12] Pearson did not hamper

10 Memorandum signed A.Oakes, 7 October and Foreign Office memo. 18 October 1899, *FO* 2/213. Allan Nevins, *Grover Cleveland,* New York: Dodd, Mead & Co., 1933, pp. 428–31.

11 Pauncefote to Hay, 24 March 1902, *Hay MSS.,* v. 21. Pauncefote to Hay, 29 March 1902, Great Britain, Notes to Department of State, v. 136, *State Department.* A minute signed 'T.H.S.' on Vansittart to Foreign Secretary, 18 January 1902, said, 'This sounds very exaggerated and sensational. I daresay the New Orleans people think it would be rather a good thing if Vansittart were diffused in fragments over the universe but I don't believe they would allow the consulate to be blown up'. *FO* 2/622.

12 See *FO* 2/483, 622, 686, and Ferguson, *op. cit.,* pp. 52–60.

British supplies, but his activities contributed to anti-British feeling and suspicion. He found willing allies among Irish-Americans and among Democratic politicians whose target was less the British than the Republican administration in Washington.

Pearson's task was to impress public opinion and politicians by somewhat indirect means, but not so three Boer envoys, Fischer, Wessels and Wolmarans. Their intention was made clear on their arrival in May 1900:

> We should like to have the government arbitrate with England, and undoubtedly we shall go to Washington and try to have an audience with President McKinley. If we cannot induce the government to do what we like we shall try to arouse the people so that they will compel the government to recognise us in that way.

McKinley and Hay undermined their efforts by seeing them within a week of their arrival but for a month they toured the country, from the east coast to Nebraska in the west, addressing audiences which were predominently Irish-American. They left in June to continue their agitation in Europe.[13]

Anti-British forces in America had gone to the country in a series of mass meetings immediately war was declared in October 1899, and the outstanding orator of the largely Irish-American and Democratic campaign was W.Bourke Cockran, a former US Congressman and a New York lawyer who was born in County Sligo, Ireland. The general tone of the campaign was anti-British, anti-imperialist, and anti-administration as the Boers were freely equated with fellow sufferers from imperialism, the Filipinos and Irish. The great boom period for these meetings was the first five months of 1900, but although their frequency decreased, they did continue throughout the period of the war and even later, particularly when there were visitors from South Africa or Ireland to hear. John Redmond and other Irish MPs addressed many of them.

Important sections of the press, including, for example, the *New York Times, New York Sun, New York Herald* and *Washington Evening Star*, whilst increasingly critical of British policies as the war dragged on, nevertheless objected to America interfering in foreign affairs. The *New York Tribune*, though 'neutral', attacked the tactics of the pro-Boers. 'The Irish and German

13 *New York Evening Post*, 15 May 1900; Ferguson, *op. cit.*, pp. 146, 149–51, 155.

voters in the United States', it declared on 18 May 1900, 'are to unite in a sort of political blackmail performance, threatening ruin to any man or any party that declines to do their bidding.' In each major city there were, however, newspapers which opposed the Republican administration and supported the Boers, the *New York World* and the *Chicago Tribune* for example.

The British received a reasonably fair, if not always favourable, press, but they had no reply to the mass meetings being organized by their opponents.[14] In a letter to Henry White in March 1900, John Hay observed:

The Irish and the Germans, for the first time in my knowledge, seem to have joined their several lunacies in one common attack against England and incidentally against the Administration for being too friendly to England. I do not imagine this coalition can survive many months, but for the moment it lifts all our lightweight politicians off their feet.

Hay confessed that as a result of this pressure, and from fear of consequent Congressional expressions of sympathy for the Boers, McKinley had agreed to respond to a Boer request that month and had asked the British government to accept American 'good offices' in settling the war. Since it was known that the British would refuse, the offer was clearly a gesture to Congress and to the pro-Boers.[15]

In fact the pro-Boer agitation and propaganda came to nothing in Congress, although large numbers, perhaps even a majority, of Senators and Congressmen sympathized with the Boers. Resolutions of sympathy were all pigeon-holed or defeated by the Republican majority. President McKinley's private views were rarely recorded, but his administration insisted on the right of US citizens to trade freely. His Secretary of State, John Hay, had written in September 1899 that friendship with Britain was the one indispensable feature of American foreign policy[16] and McKinley's successor, Theodore Roosevelt, wanted the British to win despite his considerable admiration for the Boers' military

14 Note that, as in World War I, the British controlled press wire services between the USA and the war zone. See Ferguson, *op. cit.*, p. 177.

15 Allan Nevins, *Henry White: Thirty Years of American Diplomacy*, New York: Harper Bros, 1930, pp. 151–2.

16 Hay to Henry White, 24 September 1899, Tyler Dennett, *John Hay: From Poetry to Politics*, Port Washington, New York: Kennikat Press, 1963, p. 221.

skill. The British presence in Africa was, he felt, essential to the progress of civilization.[17] When Governor of New York in January 1900, he wrote to his friend Cecil Spring Rice:

The other day some belated Fenians came up to sound me as to what my attitude would be if they attempted an invasion of Canada. I explained to them that in the first place they would not try it, and in the next place that, if they did, I should promptly call out the militia and clap them all in jail. Of course being in a high official position I have been very careful to take no stand publicly beyond notifying the members of the legislature that I would permit no anti-English resolution to pass if it needed my signature.

In March he wrote to a Boer:

By the way, much of the pro-Boer feeling here is really anti-English, and as I have a very warm remembrance of England's attitude to us two years ago [during the Spanish-American war] I have of course no sympathy with such manifestations.[18]

There was so much public interest in the Boer War, however, that both major parties were forced to carry planks on the subject in their platforms for the 1900 elections. The Republicans referred to McKinley's offer of good offices, but pledged themselves to non-involvement pending an 'honourable' settlement. The Democrats went much further by expressing sympathy for the Boers and attacking McKinley's 'ill concealed Republican alliance with England, which must mean discrimination against other friendly nations'. This reference to an 'alliance' was, as we shall see, quite unfounded and was a device to please Irish and German-American voters. When it actually came to the campaign German-Americans occupied the attention of both parties. They were thought to be the 'swinging voters' of the election for, since the Civil War, they had been predominantly Republican. In 1900 their leaders and press appeared to resent American expansion in the Pacific, which encroached upon the imperial pretensions of their homeland, and they also shared with Irish-Americans a fear of an Anglo-American alliance, talk of which had been growing for several years. Germany was clearly the most important of the

[17] See for example, Roosevelt to Henry White, 20 March 1896, Elting E. Morison, ed., *The Letters of Theodore Roosevelt*, Cambridge, Massachusetts: Harvard University Press, 1951, v. 1, p. 523.

[18] Roosevelt to Spring Rice, 27 January 1900, and to F.C. Selous, 19 March 1900, *ibid.*, v. 2, pp. 1146–7, 1233.

'other friendly nations' referred to in the Democratic platform. On the other hand, the Irish were of relatively minor concern in the election. Most of them were traditionally Democratic and there was little fear of their defection. Some, notably John Devoy, Patrick Ford and Patrick Egan, believing that the machine-oriented Democratic Party was interested only in votes and not in Ireland, and distrusting in their own rebellious way the power structure of the party itself, had looked in the past to the Republican Party as the more promising vehicle for Ireland.[19] In 1900, however, they formed a new, non-party organization, the Irish-American Union and campaigned for the Democrat, W.J.Bryan. There was, therefore, a solid anti-imperialist Irish front.[20]

Republican fears were unfounded for McKinley's margin of victory was almost 850,000 votes and in both the popular vote and the electoral college he increased his 1896 majority over the Democrat, Bryan. Some Republicans defected over the issues of the Boer War and imperialism, notably the German-American elder statesman, Carl Schurz, Oswald Ottendorfer, owner of the *New York Staats Zeitung*, and Bourke Cockran who, in fact, returned to the Democratic Party which he had left because of the silver issue in 1896. But they were only marginal. On its monetary policy, on American imperialism, and on the general conduct of foreign affairs, the Republican administration was endorsed by the electorate. This by no means implies that the British were also endorsed. The Boer War had demonstrated that they were the most hated nation in the world and by July 1901 the conservative *New York Times* was prepared to concede that the majority of Americans probably sympathized with the Boers. But the Republican Party was in power for reasons quite unconnected with the distant events in South Africa and the United States was on the crest of a Republican wave. The administration and powerful men like Henry Cabot Lodge in the Senate were sympathetic to the idea of a strong British Empire as an instrument of America's own security and were grateful for Britain's strict neutrality in the Spanish-American War. The combined result was a surprising moderation in American attitudes towards the war in South Africa.

19 Brown, *op. cit.*, pp. 134–5. Patrick Egan, a revolutionary Irish nationalist in the 1870s, left Ireland in 1883 and by 1889 was US Minister to Chile.
20 *New York Times*, 21, 24, 31 August 1900.

Theodore Roosevelt, who became President following McKinley's assassination in September 1901, was certainly pro-British in the war. In August 1899, he attributed the main force of the movement opposing Anglo-American friendship to the 'professional German and professional Irish vote which is at present so hostile to the Republican party because of the party's record of sincere good feeling for England'.[21] Nevertheless he had a belief, little based in fact though he frequently stated it, that a new American character was emerging from the mixture of races and in his view the term 'Anglo-Saxon' had no meaning.[22] He was also over-optimistic in other respects, as this comment he made in 1908 illustrates:

There is just one redeeming feature about all these nationalities, and that is that the entrance of all those new nationalities has diminished what used to be the one feeling of hostility, that against England. The Irish always want to embroil us with England, and therefore feel friendly to Russia. The Jews always want to embroil us with Russia, and therefore feel friendly with England. They also feel friendly with Turkey; but the Greeks feel very hostile to Turkey, as do the Armenians. The Germans would like to see us hostile to both France and England; but the Poles, Danes, and Norwegians wish us to be hostile to Germany, and the Swedes, to Russia. The Italians have a hostile feeling to both the Germans and French, and like the English, as do also the Danes and the Scandinavians generally. The result of this mixture of ethnic prejudice is that in a measurable degree each acts as an antiscorbutic to the others.[23]

He was forced to rediscover the 'hyphenated-American' and the dangers of conflicting national loyalties in World War I.

Roosevelt sympathized with the Boers yet supported the British and in the same way his respect for Britain did not conflict with his personal regard for Ireland and the Irish. One of his closest friends was the Irish-American writer Finlay Peter Dunne (Mr Dooley), and from its foundation in 1897 to his resignation in 1908 he was a member of the American-Irish Historical Society. While President he published articles on early Irish sagas and

[21] Roosevelt to Cecil Spring Rice, 11 August 1899, Morison, *op. cit.*, v. 2, pp. 1049–50.
[22] Roosevelt to Robert J. Thompson, 30 April 1900, and T. St. John Gaffney, 10 May 1901, *ibid.*, v. 2, pp. 1273–5, v. 3, p. 76.
[23] Roosevelt to Elihu Root, 2 July 1908, *ibid.*, v. 6, p. 1104.

communicated with Lady Gregory on the same subject.[24] He was friendly with Sir Horace Plunkett and encouraged him to submit reports on his Irish experience to assist US agriculture,[25] and he addressed the Friendly Sons of St Patrick in New York in March 1905. He first met with Parnellite MPs in 1887, and as President he entertained visiting Irish parliamentary leaders. He also knew Michael Davitt quite well.[26] These facts lend weight to his own claim, made in 1899, that he was a 'Home Ruler':

> I became a Homeruler in consequence of reading Lecky, and have continued so partly because I have thought it would be a good thing for Ireland, and partly because I should like to see the removal of the one great obstacle among the people who speak English all over the world. As you know the Canadians and the Australians have always taken exactly the attitude towards Home Rule that the Americans have.

He used almost identical prose in 1911 when writing to T.P.Gill, a former Parnellite MP who was at that time Secretary of the Department of Agriculture and Technical Instruction in Ireland.[27]

Roosevelt's sympathy was not unappreciated in America and his own hearty Americanism deflected much Irish opposition to his more identifiably anglophile Secretaries of State, John Hay and Elihu Root. In the 1904 election, Patrick Ford's *Irish World* came out in his support and thereby returned to the Republican Party. The influential *Boston Pilot*, edited by the Irish-American James Jeffrey Roche, also backed him, as did the old Irish revolutionary, O'Donovan Rossa. In some ways this was embarrassing, as Roosevelt wryly pointed out to John Hay:

> Oh, John, John, I demand your sympathy! Patrick Ford, James Jeffrey Roche and O'Donovan Rossa have come out for me. Answer me frankly – have you tampered with them in any way! If so, I hope you have not promised any personal violence to the British Ambas-

[24] Theodore Roosevelt, 'Ancient Erse Sagas', *Century*, January 1907, v. 73, pp. 327–37. Roosevelt to Lady Gregory, 8 June 1903, 25 September 1906, 24 October 1907, *Roosevelt MSS.*, Boxes 145, 154, 157.

[25] Roosevelt expressed his thanks to Plunkett through Bryce, 2 March 1909, *Roosevelt MSS.*, Box 162, and warmly commended Plunkett to President-Elect Taft, 21 December 1908, Morison, *op. cit.*, v. 6, pp. 1433–4.

[26] Roosevelt, in London, to Lodge, 7 March 1887, Lodge, *op. cit.*, v. 1, pp. 52–3, and Roosevelt to Davitt, 17 February 1904, *Roosevelt MSS.*, Box 147.

[27] Roosevelt to William Archer, 31 August 1899, and to Gill, 17 January 1911, Morison, *op. cit.*, v. 2, p. 1064, v. 7, pp. 209–10.

sador. At least, have no open rupture until after the dinner to the Archbishop of Canterbury.[28]

However, the *Gaelic American*, first published in 1903, violently opposed the President and there is no evidence that the bulk of Irish-American voters changed their political allegiance as the result of the urgings of a few. Their commitment to the Democratic Party was far too deep.

Though sympathetic to Irish home rule, and on friendly terms with numerous Irishmen and Irish-Americans, Roosevelt was unhappy at their attempts to influence American foreign policy. This was an important period for American foreign policy, as the United States looked outwards under a President with an astute grasp of foreign relations and of America's destiny as a twentieth-century great power. But the formulation of foreign policy in pluralistic America was more complicated than in Britain, where the Foreign Office and Cabinet reigned supreme. In the USA domestic politics impinged far more directly on foreign affairs than in Britain. US foreign policy was democratic, with all the benefits and handicaps which that entailed. Roosevelt's Secretary of State, John Hay, for example, was engaged in a running battle with a very independent Senate which resulted in 'open war', for although the Executive had power to negotiate treaties, it required a two-thirds majority of the Senate to ratify them. The Senate was, and is, however, a body with wide interests, subject to a wide variety of pressures from groups such as the Irish, and refused to be managed by the Executive.

In June 1900 an article in *Harper's Weekly* suggested that the Senate was seeking to usurp treaty-*making* powers. It claimed, perhaps extravagantly, that treaties negotiated by the Executive were dealt with as rough drafts, and that no treaty of importance had passed the Senate in thirty years. The reasons for this, it found, were fourfold: party politics, sectional interests, the ambition of individual Senators and, most importantly for us, a tendency to cultivate foreign-born voters for election purposes. Hay believed that the Hay-Pauncefote Canal Treaty of 1900 with Britain had received such treatment when the Senate drastically amended it. This demonstrated, he believed, that it was a constitutional mistake to give just one-third of the Senate an absolute

---

[28] Roosevelt to Hay, 20 August 1904, *ibid.*, v. 4, p. 914.

veto. 'I long ago made up my mind,' he wrote in April 1900, 'that no treaty, of which discussion was possible, no treaty that gave room for a difference of opinion, could ever pass the Senate.'[29] A few months later he wrote that many opposition Senators were 'craven time servers who think it is always good politics to attack England'. The rest were anti-Roosevelt, anti-Hay, or were honest but narrow-minded patriots.[30] The treaty, signed in February 1900, provided that the United States could build and maintain a central American isthmian canal without British co-operation, thereby abrogating the 1850 Clayton-Bulwer Treaty, but could not fortify it. The Senate used its constitutional power to amend this last provision. The second Hay-Pauncefote Treaty, signed in November 1901, after Roosevelt had succeeded McKinley, tacitly conceded the right to fortify so that the United States could protect its vital investment in the strategically important canal. The British, notwithstanding Hay's fulminations, accepted it.[31]

There were a number of reasons for the Senate's behaviour on this occasion. There was still a considerable traditional distrust of Britain in the Senate. Senator Hale, Republican of Maine, for example, was one who, in John Hay's words, 'declaimed at war – but excepted from his strictures war with England which he longs for. He informed me . . . that God intended to punish England for the Boer War – a statement which impressed me considerably, as of course he would not have made it without authority.'[32] The year 1900 was also a presidential election one and the defeat of the Canal Treaty was certainly an element in the campaign. The Boer War contributed to the anti-British feeling and members of the Democratic Party in Congress were prepared to add their voices to the considerable clamour from Irish and German-Americans, and from anglophobes of all kinds, in opposing any agreement which involved concessions to Great Britain or a watering down of American 'rights' in the Americas. In their campaign platform the Democrats condemned the 'ill-concealed alliance with England', and attacked the 1900 Canal Treaty as a

[29] Hay to J.McCook, 22 April 1900, *Hay MSS.*, Box 23. See also Dennett, *op. cit.*, Ch. 34, 'The Senate and the McKinley Tradition'.
[30] Encl. in Henry White to Arthur Balfour, 12 January 1901, *Balfour MSS.*, 49742.
[31] There was actually some ambiguity about the right to fortify which is discussed in C.S.Campbell, *op. cit.*, p. 216.
[32] Hay to Roosevelt, 14 December 1902, *Roosevelt MSS.*, Box 51.

surrender of American rights.[33] The hard core of the Republican opposition to the Hay-Pauncefote Treaty, however, including Henry Cabot Lodge, fought the treaty on the twin grounds of the Senate's right to amend, and an interpretation of the Monroe Doctrine which gave absolute freedom to the United States in its Latin American policies. The Senate was, in fact, primarily asserting its legitimate authority in foreign affairs and its most enthusiastic supporters in the country at large, for the quite different reason of anglophobia, were Irish-Americans. A similar combination of forces emerged when the administration negotiated arbitration treaties with a number of countries in 1904. Irish-Americans attacked the proposed arbitration treaty with Britain as if identical agreements with other countries had not been made. The British treaty, they argued, was a *de facto* alliance. However, this use of the term 'alliance' by Irish-Americans and some of their anti-British activities should be discussed in more detail at this point before we return to the treaties themselves.

The concept of an Anglo-American alliance persistently embarrassed the US government. Irish-American interest in this concept is explained quite simply. Time had not erased the memory of famines and coercion in Ireland's past and the peculiar immigrant experience of the Irish in America had strengthened rather than weakened their Irish-American nationalism and its concomitant anglophobia. Any friendship between Great Britain and their adopted home was therefore resisted on emotional grounds. Secondly, they argued that Irish freedom should be positively encouraged by the USA and that Anglo-American friendship would necessarily eliminate American sponsorship of Irish independence. Any friendly arrangement between the two, distasteful though this would be, should, many believed, be bought by Britain and the asking price was Irish freedom. As John Redmond argued when addressing the 1904 United Irish League of America convention, 'It is . . . understood that, if there is ever to be an Anglo-Saxon alliance it will be absolutely necessary to grant Home Rule to Ireland first'.[34] The Clan na Gael was opposed to an alliance even on these terms. By publicizing an alleged Anglo-American alliance, Irish-Americans were able to strike to the very heart of traditional American foreign policy –

[33] C.S. Campbell, *op. cit.*, pp. 204–8.
[34] London *Times*, 2 September 1904.

non-involvement in the affairs of Europe and a refusal to engage in entangling alliances.

Irish-Americans preferred tension in Anglo-American relations for reasons both of revolutionary strategy and sheer cussedness. They cultivated an alliance of anglophobes, those who hated England as the enemy of 1776, 1812 and the Civil War, isolationists, German-Americans who dreaded an Anglo-American combination against Germany, and Democrats anxious to discredit the Republican administration.[35] The Boer War set the pattern and throughout the period 1899 to 1912 we find the theme recurring. On 31 December 1899, a New York Democratic Congressman of German origin, William Sulzer, addressed a New York meeting of the United Irish-American Societies in a style which was to become familiar in the next few years:

There is no doubt that there is a secret agreement between the White House and Downing Street. I make this charge publicly and as a representative of the people.[36]

The nature of the campaign and its intention were never hidden. John Daly, the visiting Mayor of Limerick, made it quite clear at a meeting in New York in March 1900:

It's plain what England is after. Her longed for alliance with this country can never be realised as long as the Irish at home and in this country are hostile. McKinley's or any other Administration would not dare to form such an alliance against the wish of the great Irish electorate of this country.[37]

A fierce debate raged in 1898 and 1899 over the appointment of a known friend of England, Joseph Hodges Choate, as US Ambassador to Britain in succession to John Hay who served in 1897 and 1898. At a Union League dinner in February 1899 Choate was praised by Elihu Root as the 'ablest and best we had to represent the American branch of the great Anglo-Saxon race', and even the moderate Irish-American, W. Bourke Cockran, to his probable horror later that year when the Boer War began, praised Anglo-Saxon liberty and justice and spoke of an Anglo-Saxon alliance representing 'God's kingdom on earth by the

[35] *New York Times*, 28 March, and editorial, 'The Chicago German-Americans', 29 March 1899.
[36] *Ibid.*, 1 January 1900.
[37] *Ibid.*, 26 March 1900.

diffusion of justice among both peoples'.[38] But, 'Mr Choate hates the Irish race with a hatred that he never endeavours to conceal,' declared the *Boston Republican*, while the *New York Daily News* prepared its readers for a new 'outbreak of Anglo-Saxon alliance and fellowship talks'. This was but part of a venomous attack launched on Choate, who had made the error of using his biting wit upon the Irish in 1893 when addressing a dinner of the Friendly Sons of St Patrick in New York. He had alluded to the Irish habit of ruling other 'down-trodden nationalities', for example, the Americans. 'For what offices, great or small, have the Irishmen not taken?' he asked. 'What spoils have they not carried away? I propose that you should all, with your wives and children, and your children's children, with the spoils you have taken from America in your hands, set your faces homeward, land there and strike the blow.' The press greeted this with good humour in 1893, although the London *Globe* took the view, amusingly in the light of later developments, that the speech was an incitement to revolution. In 1898, however, Choate's words were put to anti-British, anti-Republican and anti-alliance use.[39]

The Irish and Democratic attack misfired. Choate received widespread support and many asked if the Irish had lost their power. One of the answers must surely be that the Republican Party never counted the mass of the Irish among its supporters and Choate's appointment was a *party* political act. This was also an issue of personalities and not a canal agreement, an arbitration treaty or an alliance, where the Irish would be part of a larger opposition. Here they were virtually alone and, whenever that happened, they failed in their anti-British objectives.

The arguments concerning the supposed alliance during the debates on Choate's appointment, the Canal Treaty and the Boer War were put forcefully enough to be noticed. The *New York Times*, whilst denying the existence of an alliance, held that the natural tendency to act together required no alliance. In October 1899, as the Boer War began, it declared:

[38] *New York Tribune*, 18 February 1899. Choate was a Republican lawyer who had made a fortune in corporation and trust work. He was defeated by Platt for the Republican nomination for US Senator from New York. For British tributes to him see London *Daily Mail*, 28 April and London *Times*, 6 May 1905.

[39] Edward Sandford Martin, *The Life of Joseph Hodges Choate*, New York: Charles Scribner's Sons, 1920, v.i, pp. 440–2. Press reactions are collected in *Choate MSS.*, Scrapbooks 3 and 4.

We cannot afford, either as a matter of decency or as a matter of interest, to allow professional or hereditary Anglophobists to endanger the understanding between England and America which is the best guarantee now 'in sight' for the peace and progress of the world.[40]

On 18 October Hay pointed out to the British Chargé d'Affaires the political capital the Democrats were endeavouring to make out of the supposed alliance and he expressed his view that the Irish-American vote could always be counted on to antagonize Britain, even when this course harmed American interests.[41] A few months later Hay was forced to state publicly, 'There is no truth in the charge that a secret alliance exists between the Republic of the United States and the Empire of Great Britain'.[42] Despite these protestations, the Democratic Party National Convention in the summer of 1900 adopted a plank condemning the 'ill concealed alliance with England' and the alleged alliance was attacked at every opportunity by the anti-British forces at Boer War protest meetings, such as those addressed by Sulzer and Daly, at Democratic campaign rallies, at meetings of the reborn Clan na Gael, at St Patrick's Day meetings throughout the country, and at meetings to celebrate the birth and death of every Irish nationalist martyr.

Pressure for a formal alliance came largely from Britain. The more the British talked, the more alarmed became sections of the Irish-American press. In July 1898 an Anglo-American League was founded in London with a very eminent membership under the Chairmanship of James Bryce. John Hay, then US Ambassador in London, was the willing recipient of its aristocratic attentions[43] and he was pursued for the remainder of his public career by the taunt of 'Anglo-mania'. Joseph Chamberlain, the Colonial Secretary, provided fodder for Irish-American cannons with his outspoken advocacy of Anglo-American union during the great surge of pro-American feeling in Britain which accompanied the Spanish-American War of 1898. 'Terrible as war may be', he said, 'even war itself would be cheaply purchased if in a great and noble cause the Stars and Stripes and the Union

40 *New York Times* editorials, 18 February and 15 October 1899.

41 British Chargé d'Affaires, Reginald Tower, to Foreign Secretary, 18 October 1899, *FO* 2/239.

42 This was in reply to allegations of a secret alliance made by US Consul Macrum of Pretoria on his return from Africa which were used by opponents of the administration. Ferguson, *op. cit.*, pp. 96–103, 122–3.

43 London *Times*, 9 September 1898.

Jack should wave together over an Anglo-Saxon Alliance.'[44]

As A.E.Campbell has suggested, the terribly imprecise notion of a common 'Anglo-Saxon race' played a prominent part in British, and to a lesser extent, American thinking,[45] but it was quite obviously not something to appeal to the many other ethnic groups in the American population. Arthur Balfour, the Leader of the House of Commons and from 1902 Prime Minister, wrote to Admiral Mahan in December 1899 that he would like to see a naval agreement 'between the two great branches of our race'. A year later, in a letter to the American diplomat Henry White, he recorded his belief that Britain and the United States shared essentially the same law, language, literature, and religion and that this produced a fundamental harmony 'compared to which all merely political alliances with other States should prove to be the evanescent result of temporary diplomatic convenience'. However, he did recognize the Irish problem in America for he prefaced his remarks with the words, 'But of course I recognize that large numbers of the most loyal citizens of America are either not of British descent, or, if of British descent, come from that part of Ireland which has never loved England.'[46] This only appeared to modify his thesis, not negate it, for in 1904 he wanted an Anglo-American alliance to enforce the 'Open Door' against anticipated Russian expansion in Manchuria, and even with the Russians well on the way to defeat at the hands of the Japanese in 1905 he wanted an alliance with America in the Far East.[47]

[44] Chamberlain's 'Birmingham Speech' 13 May 1898, C.S.Campbell, *op. cit.* p. 47.

[45] A.E.Campbell, *Great Britain and the United States, 1895–1903*, London: Longmans, Green, 1960, *passim.*

[46] Balfour to Mahan, 20 December 1899, *Balfour MSS.*, 49742, and to White, 12 December 1900, *ibid.*, 49739.

[47] Balfour to Lansdowne, 11 February 1904, *ibid.*, 49728, and draft letter Balfour to Cecil Spring Rice, sent to Lansdowne, 17 January 1905. Lansdowne approved it 18 January, *ibid.*, 49729. Theodore Roosevelt had asked his friend Cecil Spring Rice, to visit America to discuss foreign affairs because of his inability to talk frankly with Ambassador Sir Mortimer Durand. Balfour's letter to Spring Rice contained his 'unofficial' instructions on the 'unofficial' mission. George Monger, *The End of Isolation: British Foreign Policy, 1900–1907*, London: Thomas Nelson and Sons, 1963, p. 181, argues that the letter was probably never sent. Lansdowne in particular was very uneasy at not using regular channels, but the general sense of Balfour's thinking was certainly communicated to Roosevelt. See also Balfour to Percy, 15 January 1905, 'Much ... as I desire a treaty with America, the difficulties – not on our side, but on theirs – are obviously immense'. *Balfour MSS.*, 49747.

President Roosevelt believed that British and American interests were identical in that region but he insisted in 1905, 'there should be no open evident agreement so as to avoid exciting alarm and criticism'.[48] Such 'alarm and criticism' were likely to come from the Senate and from particular interest groups, notably the Irish and German-Americans, which were prepared to support both traditional foreign policies of non-involvement and the Senate's conception of its constitutional power in foreign relations. Hay may have exaggerated the power of immigrant minorities at the expense of other factors in American politics when he wrote the following to Roosevelt in 1903, but his concern for their influence must have had a considerable foundation in fact.

I take it for granted that Russia knows as well as we do that we will not fight over Manchuria, for the simple reason that we cannot. It is a singular ethnological and political paradox that the prime motive of every British [Irish] subject in America is hostility to Great Britain, and the prime motive of every German-American is hostility to every country in the world, including America, which is not friendly to Germany. If our rights and our interests in opposition to Russia in the Far East were as clear as noonday, we could never get a treaty through the Senate the object of which was to check Russian aggression.

Hay added: 'The Irish of New York are thirsting for my gore. Give it to them, if you think they need it.'[49]

Balfour's overtures to the USA fell on barren ground and public talk of a secret alliance was folly. However, the pacific settlement of outstanding Anglo-American disputes concerning a Central American canal and the Alaskan boundary, Britain's neutrality in the Spanish-American War, British sympathy for the American annexation of the Philippines which pre-empted German expansion and brought America into the Far East, US neutrality during the Boer War, and the active propaganda of prominent men on both sides of the ocean, contributed to a novel harmony in Anglo-American relations. Addressing a Pilgrims' Club banquet in New York in 1906, Elihu Root, then Secretary of State, testified to it when he said, 'With a sincere and genuine contract of purpose, if

[48] Monger, *op. cit.*, p. 182.
[49] Hay to Roosevelt, 28 April 1903, *Hay MSS.*, Box 26. A.E.Campbell, *op. cit.*, p. 184, uses parts of the same quotation but omits the reference to ethnic Americans.

not of paper, our relations are sealed as effectively as they might be by a formal agreement.'[50]

The British Government recognized the domestic problems faced by the US administration and never forced the issue of an alliance. As C.S.Campbell reminds us, no miraculous transformation of deep-rooted American traditions and predilections had occurred.[51] The influence of George Washington's farewell address was still strong, and anglophobia, though less rampant than forty years before, was very real. Balfour wrote to Choate on this theme as the Ambassador prepared to leave at the end of his term in Britain in June 1905. He had always been careful to make his words on the common mission of the two countries less strong than his convictions, Balfour wrote, for fear of exciting not sympathy, but suspicion or ridicule in the United States.[52] Public sentiment was a force to be reckoned with in the USA and, as the British well knew, the catalyst was often Irish-American disaffection. No opening could be given it. In 1904, for example, the British Ambassador, Durand, prevented a Rhode Island military drilling association from using the title 'King Edward VII Commandery,' and in 1905 he likewise averted a conference of patriotic British societies which was arranged to organize the purchase of a journal to place pro-British views before the public in reply to many anti-British journals and newspapers. 'I should run considerable risk of stirring up Irish opposition if nothing more', Durand wrote. 'The Americans in general are sensitive about organized action of this kind.' In 1906 he was able to report with pleasure, 'The position of British subjects in America is good enough. They merge easily into the population and do not give offence as the Germans and Irish do by remaining "hyphenated Americans".'[53]

Irish-Americans of all persuasions fought hard against the tacit Anglo-American accord. They not only attacked the 'alliance', but also took more positive action. As each international crisis developed, meetings of the Irish urged on the enemies of Britain

[50] Reported in Sanderson, New York, to Durand, 2 April 1906, *FO* 371/158.

[51] C.S.Campbell, *op. cit.*, p. 162.

[52] Balfour to Choate, 1 June 1905, *Balfour MSS.*, 49742, and *Choate MSS.*, 'A-Carter'.

[53] Durand to Foreign Secretary, 27 July 1904, *FO* 5/2550; 6 April 1905, *FO* 5/2579, and Durand's annual report on the USA for 1906, 2 December 1906. *FO* 371/357. Did he really believe that the Irish were no longer 'British subjects'?

as they had during the Boer War. The United Irish League virtually monopolized Irish-American fund-raising activities in the years before World War I, because Redmond and his colleagues were recognized by the majority of the Irish in Ireland and America as the legitimate leaders of the home rule movement, but when there were opportunities to frustrate British policies around the world and to affect adversely the course of Anglo-American relations, the revolutionary Irish in America, though never wealthy or numerous, asserted themselves in the leadership of virtually the same mass movement which had been nurtured by the United Irish League for other purposes. Although the United Irish League's American leaders and the *Irish World* were often engaged in anti-British activities, the UIL as an organization was not in the forefront of these agitations. However, the more positive attitude of the Clan na Gael was expressed in this resolution read by Daniel Cohalan and approved by a meeting in July 1903:

Ireland's true interests will ... be best served by a steady, resolute, and progressive policy of organization among her own people the world over and the cultivation of alliances with England's enemies with a view to the eventual reconstruction and re-establishment of an Irish nation – the founding of an Irish Republic – on the ruins of the British Empire. To that policy we pledge our hearty and continued support and as citizens of the United States we will oppose by every means in our power any and all forms of alliance or understanding between this country and England and every use of the power and influence of the American Government in support of British policy or British interests in any part of the world.

In an address to this meeting John Keating, a veteran Irish-American nationalist, forecast that France and Russia would soon be united against England and then, he promised, 'The British Empire will be destroyed and Ireland will be free'.[54]

France and Spain had directly aided Ireland in the past but Irish-American collusion with the enemies of England dated from the Crimean War when John Mitchel unsuccessfully negotiated with the Russian Minister in the United States. In 1877, when the British favoured Turkey in the Russo-Turkish War, John Devoy and a committee of the Clan na Gael visited the Russian minister

54 *New York Times*, 31 July 1903.

to discuss Irish independence, but to no avail. The Russians believed that Irishmen wanted only educational and land reforms. In 1900, with Britain under attack from all sides in the Boer War, Judge O'Neill Ryan, chairman of the reunited Clan, interviewed both the Russian Ambassador, Count Cassini, and the French Ambassador, Jules Cambon, without success.[55]

Irish-Americans moved closer to Russia, however, with the signing of the Anglo-Japanese Alliance in 1902, an agreement which was clearly directed at containing Russia in the Far East. In June 1903 the British Ambassador reported that Irish and Russian societies were co-ordinating their activities and that Count Cassini, and more particularly Baron Schlippenbach, the Russian Consul in Chicago, were in collusion with Irish leaders. This lasted for several years, for in 1904 the Baron and his staff attended an Irish picnic which was addressed by the Boer general Cronje, and in New York in 1905 the Russian Consul General, Lodygensky, attended a meeting addressed by William Redmond, MP.[56] Both the constitutional and physical force parties received Russian attention. Letters written by Lodygensky and alluding to Russo-Irish co-operation came into British hands so easily in some way that the British Consul-General in New York, Sanderson, reported, 'I am not at all sure that he is not writing some of these things with the view of their being brought to my notice'.[57] In fact Russian behaviour presaged no real intervention on Ireland's behalf. The Achilles heel of Ireland was simply used, through the Irish-Americans, to prick the British into a little extra worry, and although it was claimed that the Russian Ambassador had asked the Irish to hold pro-Russian meetings, it is far more probable that the Irish needed no encouragement.

During the Russo-Japanese war in 1904 and 1905 the Irish in America again used the familiar technique of mass meetings, with Russian flags replacing those of the Boers. The Irish-American press tried very hard to discredit the Japanese and long articles by Michael Davitt, a former Irish Member of Parliament, were published in the *Irish World*, accusing Japan of 'playing England's game' in the Far East. 'Our Friend in Need', ran a headline on

[55] Gibson, *op. cit.*, p. 67; Devoy, *op. cit.*, pp. 399–400.
[56] Sir Michael Hergert to Foreign Secretary, 19 June 1903, *FO* 5/2523; *Chicago Record Herald*, 15 August 1904; *New York Times*, 25 September 1905.
[57] Sanderson to Foreign Secretary, 28 February 1905, *FO* 5/2587.

16 April 1904, when it 'discovered' that by befriending the USA in 1863 Russia had averted British intervention against the North in the American Civil War. An editorial on 19 March 1904 was headed, 'That Russian Despotism Myth', and from St Petersburg Davitt himself assured his readers that the Russian government had nothing to fear from the labouring classes. Stories of massacres, he had been informed, were exaggerated, and were maliciously spread by the British press.[58] The rival *Gaelic American* attributed Japanese success in the war to 'treacherous violation' of the rules of civilized warfare, and although Japan resoundingly won the war the paper awarded moral victory to Russia at the Treaty of Portsmouth.[59]

This love of the Irish for Russia was in reality hatred of England. Irish-Americans tended to see England as the driving force behind the Japanese, although the Anglo-Japanese alliance was in fact defensive. It was in the British interest that Japan should not be destroyed by a European power in the Far East, but to suspicious eyes English treachery was at work and its fulfilment was the Russo-Japanese War. The record indicates that the British government had grave doubts about the wisdom of the war and on the basis of very bad naval and military intelligence believed Japan would lose. 'We should, I take it, not allow Japan to be invaded', wrote Lansdowne, the Foreign Secretary, who advocated mediation or, at the very least, friendly counsel to Japan so that Great Britain would not have to appear in the role of Japan's deliverer.[60] British doubts were soon removed, of course, by Japanese victories but the renewal of the Anglo-Japanese Alliance, which Britain's enemies claimed was evidence of her complicity in the war, was seen by President Roosevelt, who as mediator certainly knew more than they, as a contributing factor in inclining the Japanese to be more moderate in their demands at the peace conference.[61]

These were the facts and they varied greatly from the versions of the Irish-American press and the leaders of Irish-American opinion. It must be said, however, that with few facts at their

[58] *Irish World*, 4 February 1905.

[59] *Gaelic American*, 13 February 1904, 2 September 1905.

[60] See *Balfour MSS.*, 49728 including Lansdowne to Balfour, 22 December 1903.

[61] Roosevelt to Ambassador Durand and to Whitelaw Reid, 8 September 1905, *Roosevelt MSS.*, Box 151.

c

disposal they may have had no alternative. Emotionally and ideologically, most of them believed that Britain selfishly controlled her allies as she controlled Ireland and her Empire. Many slipped easily into the attack from sheer force of habit though others more deliberately cultivated American anglophobia. It really is impossible to disentangle reasons and motives and assess their weight, but the combined effect was a relatively united Irish-American attack on British policy in the Far East and on any attempted Anglo-American co-operation in that area. The Irish backed the wrong side, however, for the shocking treatment of Russia's Jewish population, particularly the Kishineff pogrom of 1903, caused a great revulsion in America. At the outbreak of the Russo-Japanese War, Roosevelt had observed that the Jews were as violently opposed to Russia as the Irish were in support, but in fact the Jews were more powerful and more than fifty thousand of them marched in protest against Russian anti-semitism through a cold New York in December 1905.[62]

To return now to the arbitration treaty of 1904, many Irish-Americans saw this as the prelude to a further entente or alliance with the British. In November and December 1904 and January 1905, after protracted negotiations, the United States signed treaties with Britain, Germany, other European powers and Japan to arbitrate with the Permanent Court of Arbitration at the Hague any matter affecting the interpretation of any treaty but *not* involving the vital interests, honour, or independence of the contracting parties.[63] In January 1904, Ambassador Durand reported enthusiastic pro-arbitration treaty meetings all over the United States, but in February Consul General Sanderson in New York reported that the Irish 'Physical Force Party', that is, the Clan na Gael and the United Irish Societies, was working up opposition in New York and was attempting to convey to Congressmen an exaggerated idea of the extent of popular feeling against a treaty. Since 1904 was an election year, he noted, it would be difficult to counter the Irish without appearing to meddle in American affairs and thereby supplying a convenient

[62] Roosevelt to Spring Rice, 19 March 1904, Morison, *op. cit.*, v. 4, pp. 759–61.
[63] For details of these and later arbitration treaties see Denna F.Fleming, *The Treaty Veto of the American Senate*, New York: Putnam, 1930, Ch. 5, 'The Action of the Senate on Arbitration Treaties'.

anti-British election issue.[64] Michael Davitt, then writing for the *Irish World*, was deeply involved in this agitation and was lobbying Senators as he had in 1897 when an earlier Anglo-American arbitration treaty was defeated. Several years later Sanderson recalled, 'There is no doubt in my mind that the Irish, helped on by Michael Davitt's presence, exerted a strong influence on Congress at the time that the . . . negotiations for an arbitration treaty were under way.'[65] The Irish were already engaged in the campaign against the 'British War' with Russia in the Far East, and now, in meetings throughout the country and in the Irish-American and Democratic press, the arbitration treaty with Britain was denounced as an alliance.

Hay certainly felt terribly oppressed by Irish pressure. 'They are evidently after me', he wrote in his diary in November. One story put out by the Clan na Gael to arouse southern opposition to the treaty was that Confederate bonds, issued by the South in the Civil War and never redeemed, would be a subject for arbitration. One Senator was anxious about attacks on the British treaty by the Clan na Gael and by the story of the Confederate bonds. He mentioned this to Hay in December 1904. Hay was sceptical and refused to take the opposition seriously. 'They can talk [the treaties] to death,' he wrote, 'but there hardly seems sufficient motive.' His diary entry of 12 February 1905, however, showed a dramatic change, for there he attributed the Senate amendments in large part to the work of the Clan, and he repeated his thoughts in a letter to a friend on 16 February 1905:

I cannot tell you how deeply we are all grieved and disappointed at the failure of the arbitration treaties. I had never heard from any quarter of any possible objection to them, but a drive was made at them, as soon as they were sent to the Senate, from two quarters, one from the Clan na Gael in New York and Philadelphia, who objected to nothing but the English treaty, and the other from certain interests

[64] Durand to Foreign Secretary, 14 January 1904, *FO* 5/2549; Sanderson to Foreign Secretary, 25 February 1904. On 4 March 1904, Sanderson reported that Cohalan was meeting the Russian Consul General Lodygensky to discuss the Arbitration Treaty and the Russo-Japanese War. *FO* 5/2551.

[65] Sanderson to Bryce, 23 February 1907, in Bryce to Hardinge, 7 March 1907, *FO* 371/359. Davitt left in November 1904 after working for many months to defeat the treaty by organizing petitions to Senators. Sanderson to Durand, 2 December 1904, *FO* 5/2551. See also Nelson H. Blake, 'The Olney-Pauncefote Treaty of 1897', *American Historical Review*, v. 50, 1945, p.238.

in the South, who feared – utterly without cause – that the question of their repudiated debts might be brought into arbitration. Ignoble as these attacks were we soon found, to our deep amazement, that they were extremely effective and many Senators who had expressed themselves in the strongest language in favor of the treaties began to take an active part against them.

Hay also agreed, however, that the arbitration treaties involved the question of Senatorial rights and he attacked the Senate directly for its love of power.[66]

On 11 February 1905 the Senate had voted by fifty to nine to so amend all the arbitration treaties that the President refused to accept them. The *Gaelic American* claimed credit for this defeat on behalf of the Clan na Gael for, it claimed, as in the case of the proposed arbitration treaty of 1897, the Clan had exposed every argument used by the government. The *Irish World* also congratulated the Senate on its decision.[67] The Irish must have had a hand in the defeat as Hay himself insisted, but more important, certainly to Republicans, was the question of the Senate's prerogatives. These arbitration treaties had specified that before any dispute was submitted to the Permanent Court of Justice at the Hague, a 'special agreement' was to be signed by the parties concerned defining the exact dispute and the procedure to be followed. In the Senate it was argued that these agreements would be in fact 'special treaties' and that the administration was trying to evade the Senate's right and responsibility to ratify treaties. Senators substituted the word 'treaty' for 'agreement' thereby ensuring that they would constitutionally share in the procedure, and Roosevelt, rather than renegotiate the treaties, dropped them. The parallel with Wilson and the League of Nations is clear, for the issue in each case was international action for peace and each involved attacks on the Senate's role in United States foreign relations. The United States was committing itself to proscribed courses of action regarding unknown future problems, the

[66] Hay's Diary, 1 November, 12 December 1904, 12 February 1905, *Hay MSS.*, Box 27; Hay to Edwin D. Mead, 16 February 1905, *Hay MSS.*, Box 26. The South may have had some cause for concern. Bryce wrote to Grey, 4 March 1911, concerning pecuniary claims against the USA: 'As respects the old claims against the Southern States which disturb the rest of Southern Senators I have kept them so far, in reserve, in order to meet and counter any attempt on the part of the United States to press on us claims we deem inadmissable.' *FO* 371/1266.

[67] *Gaelic American*, 18, 25 February and *Irish World*, 18 February 1905.

nature and details of which could hardly be known in advance. The Senate wanted to judge each problem on its merits as it arose and to act accordingly. What is especially important for this study is that in both cases Irish-Americans joined the opposition for reasons of their own and this combination overwhelmed the agreements. Roosevelt wrote to Hay, 'I am getting to take your view of the Senate under stress of seeing the way they are handling the arbitration treaties.'[68]

Roosevelt refused to compromise until 1908 when he submitted new arbitration treaties in a form acceptable to the Senate, that is they conformed to the amended 1904 treaties. Once again the British treaty was only one of many, but again the Irish, with the notable exception this time of the *Irish World* which had supported the President's re-election in 1904, moved in to attack the 'alliance'. The new Secretary of State, Elihu Root, himself a friend and former legal counsel to some of the more conservative Irish-Americans, came under attack. Lord Bryce, the British Ambassador, telegraphed to London that Root was being bombarded by Irish petitions and was anxious to avoid any delay which might be attributed to their influence.[69] In a letter to Whitelaw Reid, the US Ambassador in London, Root wrote that the Senate Foreign Relations Committee had unanimously agreed to the arbitration treaty with Britain, 'notwithstanding an enormous number of petitions against the treaty from the Clann na Gael [*sic*] and other Irish societies'.[70] The Senate approved the treaty on 22 April 1908, but not before some last-minute Irish activity. Bryce reported, for atmosphere rather than merit, a fairly typical example, a statement from Mr O'Connell, a Boston member of the House of Representatives, in which he urged the building of four new battleships. 'As the sun emerges from the waters of Massachusetts Bay,' he orated, 'and sends its beams over the glistening waves, we are mindful that those same waters may tomorrow or at another time bring forth our ancient enemy of three great wars.'[71]

[68] Roosevelt to Hay, 28 January 1905, *Roosevelt MSS.*, Box 149.

[69] Bryce to Foreign Secretary, telegram, 10 March 1908, *FO* 371/563. Root was a neighbour of Judge Morgan O'Brien and Counsel to Thomas F.Ryan, *Root MSS.*, Box 300.

[70] Root to Reid, 8 April 1908, *Root MSS.*, Box 304, *Reid MSS.*, Box 75.

[71] *Congressional Record* 11 April 1908, p. 4803, in Bryce to Foreign Secretary, 15 April 1908. *FO* 371/563.

Bryce summed up the Irish agitation in a dispatch dated 22 May 1908 which is quoted here in full:

There was at one time, shortly before the approval by the United States Senate of the Arbitration Treaty between Great Britain and the United States, a certain fear that the efforts of the extreme Irish faction, still active and noisy in this country, might wreck the Treaty in the Senate, and even the Secretary of State showed some anxiety lest any delay that might occur in getting it through the Senate should be attributed to the influence of the Irish. An immense number of petitions and remonstrances were received from branches of the Clan na Gael, lodges of the ancient order of Hibernians [*sic*] and other Irish Associations throughout the country, protesting against the Treaty, which they persisted in describing as a Treaty of Alliance, having earnestly declared during the last eighteen months that the aim of British policy was to secure such an alliance and that I had come here for that purpose. A few days before it passed a large deputation came to Washington from Boston, one of the most powerful Irish centres in the country, to interview President Roosevelt and members of the Senate, and thus endeavour to prevent the treaty going through. They heralded their arrival with a flourish of trumpets and announced in the press that a majority of the Senate Committee on Foreign Affairs [*sic*] was on their side. They seem, however, from what the President and certain Senators have told me about their interviews, to have received very little satisfaction – an encouraging sign of the change that has come over American politics, in which the violent Irish faction now counts for much less than it did twenty years ago.

The President gave me a gleeful account of the way in which he had 'scored off' the deputation. After listening to what the Irish 'delegation' had to say, he sent for a copy of Washington's farewell address to Congress delivered at the end of his term of office, and read them the passage dissuading the nation from allowing its policy to be affected by feelings of bitterness towards any Power and from cherishing resentments of any kind. As the authority of Washington is second only to that of the Holy Scripture, the deputation had nothing to answer, and retired crestfallen.

Senators Crane and Lodge of Massachusetts both pointed out that Treaties practically similar with other nations had already been approved by the Senate and that there was no question of a Treaty of Alliance with England. The Irish professed to be surprised at this. They had repeated the fable so often that they had apparently come to believe it. On being asked whether they wished that England alone should be debarred from concluding such a Treaty with America they did not venture to argue further.[72]

Senator Lodge and the Irish had been on the same side in earlier arbitration battles, though for very different reasons, but the 1908 arbitration treaty with Britain demonstrated that though powerful, the Irish were not able to determine American policy alone and certainly not with a Republican administration unsympathetic to their anglophobia and their anti-imperialism.

Despite this setback the Irish in America were still important for their nuisance value in Anglo-American relations. For example, they cultivated other immigrant groups. Until the possibility of an Anglo-German clash appeared Britain's enemies were more obviously Russia or France and for a number of years the revolutionary Irish hoped for a growth of the Anglo-French tension which followed the 1898 Fashoda crisis. However, the French government did not encourage them and there was no significant French-American population with which to combine. The Anglo-French Entente of 1904 destroyed their hopes. The Irish and German-Americans, on the other hand, had pooled their strength in the 1890s and during the Boer War, less in anticipation of an Anglo-German war than in recognition of the facts of the European balance of power and with the determination to prevent an Anglo-American combination developing against Germany and German interests around the world. By 1907 and 1908, however, the likelihood of an Anglo-German war was widely realized and the relationship was cemented more firmly. In July 1908 the Irish-American *Chicago Citizen* declared:

There is not an Irishman in America today, in whose veins good red blood is flowing, who would not rejoice to hear that a German army was marching in triumph across England from Yarmouth to Milford Haven.[73]

In January 1907 an agreement was signed between the German-American National Alliance and the Ancient Order of Hibernians,

[72] Bryce to Foreign Secretary, 22 May 1908, *FO* 371/563. The Roosevelt story is confirmed in Roosevelt to Reid, 18 April 1908, Morison, *op. cit.*, v. 6, p. 1011. The delegation was led by Mathew Cummings, militant National President of the AOH. See *Gaelic American*, 25 April 1908.
[73] *Chicago Citizen*, 11 July 1908.

then under militant control, by which both agreed to oppose American alliances with *any* foreign power, to oppose legislation which might restrict immigration, and to investigate the contribution of all races to the development of America. The Germans represented 6,000 organizations and 1,250,000 members while the AOH membership in July 1907 was 140,173, with an additional 55,000 in a Ladies' Auxiliary.[74] These are sizeable figures but there is no evidence that this arrangement materially altered anything. It would have existed *de facto* in any case in view of the developing tensions in Europe and Ambassador Bryce rightly observed that the Irish called the tune in this partnership.[75] The pattern of Irish control of anti-British movements was now well established in America and German-Americans had no record of great mass meetings of their own until the European war began in 1914. The AOH endorsed this 1907 arrangement at each national convention, even when moderates resumed control in 1910, and when the war came they openly supported Germany.

Another, though less important, alliance contracted by Irish-Americans during this period was with Indian nationalists of the British imperial, not 'Red', variety. Indian nationalism was developing very rapidly and despite the vast distance involved, an embryonic relationship was established between the Clan na Gael and Indian nationalists which was to prove very embarrassing to the British Government. The Irish found American ignorance of India something of an advantage and, although Britain had little to fear of actual revolt from these intrigues, there was the problem of their effect on the British imperial image in America. A campaign was engineered by the *Gaelic American* and the Clan na Gael from 1905 as a result of which exaggerated suggestions of Irish and Indian intrigues and rumours of arms shipments to India gained currency in America. For years British diplomats were set the task of investigating the really very minor conspiracy, and they naturally discovered very little.[76] However, the real victory of the *Gaelic American*, with the considerable aid of the *New York World*, was the growth of interest

---

[74] O'Dea, *op. cit.*, v. 3, pp. 1387–8.

[75] Bryce to Foreign Secretary, 9 August 1910, *FO* 371/1023.

[76] See in particular, Consul General Bennett, New York, and Bryce in *FO* 371/563, 783, in 1908–1909. The British government had Scotland Yard and Pinkerton agents working on the problem and maintained close liaison between the Foreign, Indian, and Irish offices.

in Indian nationalism by the US press. In 1908 the *New York Times*, *New York Tribune*, *Boston Transcript* and other journals and papers carried a considerable quantity of news and comment on India which was not always unfavourable to Britain, but any mention of this largely unknown sub-continent was an advantage to its national cause.

In July 1908 the India Office, alarmed at the spread of what it deemed to be misinformation in America, decided to supply its own information to American editors and journalists, but Bryce counselled caution. American public opinion, he insisted, had not been influenced by the agitation and no Irish-Indian conspiracy had been established. An official British press campaign, he argued, would encourage the agitation and might well antagonize editors. Consul General Bennett in New York added that official backing for such a campaign might rebound against the British in the November American election campaigns and he suggested careful approaches to US correspondents in London.[77] The final method of disseminating information, delayed until 1910, was a safe, official one. Memoranda, copies of acts, and a covering letter were sent to libraries and universities across the country for the information of 'students of imperial administrative systems'.[78] In addition, to the surprise of the Foreign Office, Lord Morley, the Secretary of State for India, asked President Roosevelt to speak on India. With the aid of Bryce, Roosevelt prepared a speech for a scheduled address on missionary work in which he praised the British Empire above Rome. It was a deliberate attempt to dispose of the view that the United States sympathized with India, though his effort would have been unnecessary but for the campaign begun by Irish-Americans to embarrass the British Government.[79]

Roosevelt's term of office ended early in 1909 when William Howard Taft succeeded to the Presidency. The Irish vote had not loomed large as an issue in the election the previous November

[77] India Office memo. prepared for Lord Morley, 18 July, and Bryce minute 3 August; Bennett to Foreign Secretary, 5 October 1908, *FO* 371/563.
[78] Draft by Bryce 14 January approved by India Office 16 February 1910, *FO* 371/1021.
[79] Bryce to Foreign Secretary, 24 December 1908 and FO minute *FO* 371/783; Roosevelt to Sydney Brooks, 28 December 1908, Morison, *op. cit.*, v. 6, pp. 1443–6; to Bryce, 21 January 1909, *ibid.*, p. 1478; to Col. Arthur Lee, 7 February 1909, *ibid.*, pp. 1507–9; *New York Tribune*, 19 January 1909.

and in a dispatch Bryce had commented, 'It is a new feature and a good feature of American politics that men are less and less governed in the discharge of their civic duty by their racial sentiments. One cannot talk of a German vote and the Irish vote now as people talked twenty or even ten years ago'. This was a premature judgement.[80]

Despite an ostensible desire not to court the favour of immigrant groups by doing their bidding, Taft's administration found itself embroiled in immigrant politics several times. Like Roosevelt, Taft was the object of great Jewish-American pressures regarding Russian anti-semitic atrocities. Demands were made by American Jews and their friends for the abrogation of an 1832 commercial treaty with Russia and in 1911, to forestall Congressional action, Taft was forced to declare that he would not renew the treaty when it came due in 1913. Against the advice of the government an immigrant lobby had decided United States foreign policy, and it was the then British Ambassador, Spring Rice, who commented of the Jews, 'They are far better organized than the Irish and far more formidable'.[81] However in 1912 Taft refused to express an opinion on the embryonic question of Zionism because it primarily affected the interests of other countries.[82] Between 1909 and 1913 Taft was also the willing, though naïve, recipient of the attentions of Louis Hammerling whose organization, the American Association of Foreign Language Newspapers, was the vehicle both for Hammerling's self-aggrandisement and for the seduction of the immigrant voter into Republican ranks. He was finally the subject of Congressional investigation in 1919 for his war time activities with foreign language newspapers in support of the Central Powers. [83]

For our purposes, Taft's most interesting encounter with

[80] Bryce to Foreign Secretary, 4 November 1908, *FO* 414/202.

[81] Spring Rice to Sir William Tyrrell, 3 February 1914, Stephen Gwynn, ed., *The Letters and Friendships of Sir Cecil Spring Rice*, Boston; Houghton Mifflin, 1929, v. ii, p. 201. See Alan J. Ward, 'Immigrant Minority "Diplomacy": American Jews and Russia 1901–1912', *Bulletin of the British Association for American Studies*, December 1964, New series, No. 9, pp. 7–23; Naomi W. Cohen, 'The Abrogation of the Russo-American Treaty of 1832', *Jewish Social Studies*, January 1963, v. xxv, No. 1, pp. 3–41.

[82] Taft to Julius Meyer, President of the Zion Literary Society, Boston, 12 February 1912, *Taft MSS.*, Series II, File 2677, Box 479.

[83] *Taft MSS.*, Series II, File 423, Box 374; Robert Park, *The Immigrant Press and Its Control*, New York: Harper, 1922, pp. 376 ff.

immigrant politics was the affair of Luke Dillon. Dillon, a close friend and associate of John Devoy, was an undetected dynamiteer in England in the 1880s and was finally convicted in Canada in May 1900 for attempting to blow up the Welland Canal during the Boer War. The Clan na Gael applied pressure for his release during the election year of 1908 and it was even rumoured that reprisals would be taken on the Prince of Wales during his visit to the Quebec Tercentenary in that year. Special precautions were taken by the police to avert this, although it was probably only a rumour.[84] John Keating and John Devoy of the Clan na Gael also organized, and Devoy actually wrote, an appeal by Dillon's wife for President Roosevelt's intercession, but nothing came of it.[85]

In 1910 Taft received a meorandum on the case from Governor Pothier of Rhode Island, a French Canadian by origin in a state with potent numbers of Irish-American voters. This explained, in reasoned terms, the political nature of Dillon's crime and with a calculated caution set out its Irish-American implications:

The man's environment, his prominent connection with secret organizations, and a mistaken sense of duty, rather than any personal desire to commit crime, were responsible for his activity in the undertaking ... the element of the American population which is especially interested in the liberation of Dillon comprises a very numerous, powerful and progressive factor in our citizenship. Through a chain of organizations, reaching over the country, its influence is tremendous, and there is every reason for the assurance that the successful culmination of the movement to restore freedom to Luke Dillon would arouse the civic spirit in a million American hearts, as no other occurrence at the present time possibly could do.

Pothier renewed his appeal in 1911 and the Secretary of State, Knox, unofficially raised the issue with the Canadian Government. He argued at that time that the coronation of Edward VII and a proposed new Anglo-American arbitration treaty provided an appropriate setting for the removal of any outstanding

---

[84] Bennett, New York to Foreign Secretary, 12 May 1908, *FO* 371/566.

[85] Keating to Devoy, 2 November 1908; undated draft letter from Mrs Luke Dillon to Roosevelt, in Keating's handwriting, and a statement on the Dillon case, O'Brien and Ryan, *op. cit.*, pp. 367–70. Keating to Devoy, 3 November 1908, *Devoy MSS.*, 10, 610.

differences between the USA and the British Empire.[86] In fact, as we shall see, his motive was to secure Irish-American support for the new arbitration treaty.

Taft appears to have first suggested new general arbitration treaties from which questions of national honour should *not* be excluded, in August 1910. He followed this in December with a public statement favouring arbitration of *every* question which could not be solved by negotiation. The British government was very wary. The Foreign Secretary, Grey, instructed Bryce that any initiative had to come from the USA for Britain wanted no repetition of the 1897 and 1905 failures.[87] Bryce, following Taft's example, was optimistic throughout because Carnegie's 'sentimental arbitrationists' and the President's support for the principle of peaceful settlement had had, he felt, a great effect on American public opinion. Furthermore, Bryce argued, there was a 'growing sentiment of Anglo-Saxon solidarity'. This growth was certainly insufficient for economic or military combinations, but obligatory arbitration could, he felt, be the next move towards closer Anglo-American relations. What, however, of the oft-feared Irish vote? Bryce had this to say, 'The American-Irish, who have been anyway losing political influence during the last decade, seem to have lost much of their hostility, although this latter might be revived at any moment by a disappointment in their hopes for an early self-government scheme for Ireland'.[88] Thus, in one respect, the ball was in the British court, but there is no evidence of any special British decisions being made for Ireland with the object of influencing the passage of this arbitration treaty. There is, likewise, no evidence of any British government enthusiasm for the treaty. When Eyre Crowe, Senior Clerk in the Foreign Office at that time, saw news clippings of Irish and German-American opinions, he commented, 'It would be interesting to see what the views of the Irish and German societies would be if they knew that the idea of the arbitration treaty originated with the US and that it was rather embarrassing to HMG'.[89] HMG, in fact, had

[86] Pothier memo enclosed in Knox to Reid, 18 July 1912, *Reid MSS.*, Box 43, and memo enclosed in Reid to Hon. Robert L. Borden, 10 July 1912, *ibid.*, Box 178.

[87] Memo n.d. on the proposed treaties; Bryce to Foreign Secretary, 6 January, 6 February, and Grey to Bryce, 9 February 1911, telegram, *FO* 371/1270.

[88] Bryce to Foreign Secretary, 5 January 1911, *ibid.*

[89] Crowe minute, 15 March 1911 on Bennett, New York, to Foreign Secretary, 28 February 1911, *Ibid.*

certain vital interests, particularly imperial interests, which they would have preferred not to arbitrate with anyone, but a treaty was nevertheless signed in August 1911.

Although the *Irish World* opposed the treaty with Britain as an attempt to bring about an alliance, many of Redmond's other American supporters, with a home rule victory in Ireland in sight, played little part in the opposition. Judge Morgan O'Brien, a moderate, explained that he supported the treaty, though he refused to condemn what he alleged was a small group of Irish 'irreconcilables' for fear of drawing attention to them.[90] Another prominent Irish-American, John Crimmins, was on the platform at a large pro-arbitration meeting at Carnegie Hall in December 1911 which was disturbed and finally broken up by Irish and German-Americans.[91] There were joint Irish and German-American protest meetings throughout the period of public debate on the treaty, but the German-American National Alliance, under the leadership of Congressman Richard Bartholdt, Missouri, who was in the forefront of the peace movement, resolved to support arbitration treaties with all countries at its National Convention in October 1911. Nevertheless, Devoy, together with the United Irish and United German Societies of New York, was able to organize protest meetings with the theme of the danger of entangling alliances even before details of the proposed treaty were known and their opposition was in the nature of preventive medicine.[92] 'Pure Americanism' was the key message of a confidential Clan na Gael circular which came into the hands of Scotland Yard, and which appealed for fifty per cent of the Revolutionary Funds then in the hands of each branch to help fight the 'Alliance'. The treasurer of the Clan, John L. Gannon of Providence, handed out money to fight the treaty and reports of joint Irish and German meetings came in throughout 1911.[93] Bryce's view of the Clan in February 1911 was that 'This organization of old fashionedly ferocious anti-English Irishmen has long been declining in influence', and that no one attached the slightest importance to Irish and German demonstrations. A

90 O'Brien to Andrew Carnegie, 17 February, enclosed in Carnegie to Knox, 20 February 1911, *Knox MSS.*, v. 13.

91 *New York Sun*, 13 December 1911. Choate was in the chair.

92 See *Gaelic American*, 25 February, 21 October 1911.

93 E. Henry, Scotland Yard, to Sir Arthur Nicolson, 16 May 1911, *FO* 371/1270; Gannon to Devoy, 28 July 1911, *Devoy MSS.*, 10, 607.

Foreign Office colleague added in July, 'Much "hot-air" as they would say in the US', but Bryce so frequently dwelt on the declining influence of the extreme Irish faction that one suspects he was playing down its importance. He admitted that the simultaneous signature of treaties with both Britain and France on 3 August was calculated to make it harder for the extreme Irish faction to attack the British treaty.[94]

The Senate, however, had its own instinctive opposition based upon a jealous concern for its authority in foreign relations. The Foreign Relations Committee reported the treaties out late in August with important nullifying amendments, but before acting the Senate adjourned for the year. The President took his case to the country in a speaking tour and seemed to receive overwhelming support, but in March 1912, the Senate finally amended the treaties. These had provided for the arbitration of all 'justiciable' questions including 'vital interests' and 'national honor'. In case of any dispute over the application of a treaty to a particular issue a joint high commission of inquiry was to decide whether it applied. The Senate was to play no part in this Commission. As a result the Senators brutally excluded from arbitration the question of states' debts, thereby covering the Confederate bond problem, the Monroe Doctrine, immigration, and every other issue of importance to the United States. The amended versions passed by seventy-six to three but Taft refused to re-negotiate them with Britain and other countries and the vote was, in fact, a resounding defeat.[95]

The Senate was again fighting for both its power in foreign relations and for the traditional independence of America's foreign policy. Roosevelt fought the treaties on this ground. He did not object to arbitration with Britain, for he considered the need would never arise, but Taft intended to span the world with his treaties and include many interests which Roosevelt believed the USA could never agree to arbitrate – the fortification of the Panama Canal, control of Hawaii, the Monroe Doctrine, and immigration. Roosevelt held that arbitration would have forced Britain out of South Africa and Egypt, would have prevented the

[94] Bryce to Foreign Secretary, 28 February, 13, 21 March, 5 August 1911, *FO* 371/1270, 1271, 1272; Unsigned minute on Consul General Leay, Boston, to Foreign Secretary, 31 July 1911, *FO* 371/1271, a report on Irish-German meetings in Boston.

[95] Fleming, *op. cit.*, Ch. 5; Bailey, *op. cit.*, pp. 589–91.

independence of Panama, and would have left Spain in Cuba, all to the detriment of civilization.[96] After reading one of Roosevelt's attacks Sir Edward Grey, the British Foreign Secretary, commented, 'I believe that Mr Taft at first intended a Treaty with us alone – that was indicated in the speeches in which he launched the idea. Then to turn the flank of Irish and German opposition in the US he threw the door open to all nations. This exposed him to Mr Roosevelt's attack. We ourselves are prepared to conclude a general arbitration Treaty with the US but not with all nations indiscriminately.'[97] This interpretation of Taft's original intention was too narrow in view of the range of countries already covered by the 1908 treaties and the growing movement in the USA dedicated to a new world order based on law. Taft did, however, begin with the British and, as Grey knew, Irish and German-Americans led the opposition.

In August 1911 Bryce attributed the proposed amendments to the Senate's desire to assert its authority. Some Senators, he said, might have been influenced by the pressure of the extreme Irish, but if so, they had carefully concealed it.[98] However, the President was sufficiently impressed by the attitude of Irish-Americans to consider that their pacification would considerably enhance the chances of the passage of yet another arbitration treaty. As the British Acting-Consul General in New York, John Broderick, suggested in August 1911, the majority of Irish-Americans and their organizations still took their political opinions from the *Gaelic American* and the *Irish World*, both of which opposed the arbitration treaty with Britain,[99] and one also has to consider that the most active opponents of the British treaty outside Congress were Irish-Americans who organized mass meetings throughout the country. They were the Senate's most consistent supporters and their vocal opposition, using symbols from traditional American foreign policy, must have influenced public opinion. Taft's support for Luke Dillon was an attempt to mollify them.

On 7 July 1912, Taft directly related Dillon's case to the question of arbitration treaties. He cabled to Ambassador Reid:

[96] Roosevelt to Bryce, 19 May, 2 June, to Mahan, 7 June, to Spring Rice, 22 August 1911, Morison, *op. cit.*, v. 7, pp. 267–8, 275–6, 279–80, 332–5.
[97] Grey minute on Bryce to Grey, 11 September 1911, *FO* 371/1271.
[98] Bryce to Foreign Secretary, 22 August 1911, *FO* 371/1271.
[99] Broderick to Foreign Secretary, 17 August 1911, *FO* 371/1272.

I am very anxious for reasons you will understand but may not realize their far reaching importance to secure the pardon of Dillon of whom the State Department has written you. Borden [the Canadian Prime Minister] is now in London. Could you not see him and urge the wisdom of the release of Dillon. It will help me much in a further attempt at peace treaties to remove the serious opposition which manifested itself on the Senate's last vote.

Reid in fact saw Borden on 10 July and supplied him with a memorandum enclosing the information supplied by Pothier in 1910. He reported that the Premier seemed quite open minded. On 12 July he interviewed Doherty, the Canadian Minister of Justice, who promised prompt consideration of the matter. Doherty said he was aware of the Dillon problem but his own origins (he was from a Northern Irish Catholic family) required him to be 'specially circumspect'.[100]

These overtures were not immediately effective for Dillon was not released until July 1914, at the age of sixty-six. The Clan played a part in this. John Keating visited Ottawa to assist in the arrangements and it is clear that the major concern of the Canadian government was that there should be silence and no fuss surrounding the release. Irish-American publicity had hindered Dillon's earlier release by alerting the anti-Catholic Orange opposition in Canada, which provided Canada's own 'Irish problem'.[101] In the interim Taft's enforced retirement from the presidency in 1912 had ended his arbitration plans.

Some of the extreme American-Irish did believe that an arbitration treaty with Britain constituted a *de facto* alliance. This was untrue, but they intuited the direction in which proponents of the various arbitration treaties with Britain wanted America to move. In that sense, and from their point of view, their opposition was justified. To them, any step towards Britain was a step in the wrong direction. They had, of course, an exaggerated idea of their own influence. Not only did they congratulate themselves in the *Gaelic American* for having defeated the treaties, but they also carried this into their private correspondence and the myth of their power has lived on in the literature of the Irish revolution. The more correct view is that when

100 Taft to Reid, 7 July 1912, telegram, *Reid MSS.*, Box 91; Reid to Borden, 10 July, and to Taft, 24 July 1912, *ibid.*, Box 178.
101 Keating to Devoy, 13 May 1914, O'Brien and Ryan, *op. cit.*, v. 2, pp. 443–4.

the Irish in America chose to support Americanism, and the prerogatives of the Senate, they always found themselves in the ranks of the victorious, and their support contributed substantially to those victories. The defeat of President Wilson's League of Nations was to provide further evidence of this fact.

In addition, Irish-Americans were the primary stumbling block in the path of any attempt to improve Anglo-American relations. They could always be counted on when the issues were easily grasped or easily distorted. They were a great mass, with the lack of subtlety which accompanies such bodies, and when it came to pressure group activities in highly specialized subject areas they could not compare with, say, shipping and sealing interests in the Pacific north-west or fishing interests in the north-east. The Alaskan boundary and pelagic sealing disputes between the USA and the Dominion of Canada, for example, were settled to the satisfaction of quite small US interest groups with particular, precise, and relevant interests. The *Gaelic American* insisted that the complex Alaskan Boundary settlement, which had given the USA all that it could have wished, was a British victory, but effective opposition was impossible because its readers would have found the whole issue uninteresting and rather esoteric.[102] But give them a simple 'alliance' and the mass meetings sprang up over-night, to the absolute horror of successive American governments.

[102] C.S.Campbell, *op. cit.*, passim; *Gaelic American*, 24 October 1903.

4 Preparing for War, 1912–15

*'Some Americans need hyphens in their names, because only
part of them has come over.'*

WOODROW WILSON, MAY 1914

Revolutionary Irish nationalism was dying in 1911 when Ulster
presented it with a new lease of life. The Parliament Act of
August that year had abolished the House of Lords' absolute veto
by providing that any bill passed by the House of Commons in
successive sessions could only be vetoed twice. Since Irish home
rule was assured of majority support in the Commons from the
Liberal-Nationalist coalition it was assumed that it would
become law in 1914 on its third passage, notwithstanding its
anticipated defeat in the Lords. But the leaders of Ulster acted
to block such a victory by non-parliamentary means. At Craig-
avon, in September 1911, 100,000 Ulstermen welcomed Sir
Edward Carson as their leader and vowed their opposition to
home rule. In September 1912 the first of almost 500,000 signatures was appended to the Ulster Covenant which was a pledge
to resist home rule by force if necessary. On the last day of
January 1913, Ulster's leaders published their plan for a provisional government of Ulster and in September the formation of
this government was announced with Carson as Chairman,
ready to assume office at any time. This 'administration' could call
upon the 50,000 men of the new Ulster Volunteer Force, under
their commander Lt-General Sir George Richardson, a retired
British officer. In addition, the Curragh mutiny of March 1914
indicated that the British government could not rely on the
loyalty of large numbers of British officers serving in Ireland.

During these years the Irish problem had become inextricably
tangled in the web of British party politics – the Lloyd George
budget, radical Liberalism and the reform of the House of Lords.
There were, of course, strong emotional bonds between the Conservatives and Ulster, but in addition the Conservative Party
believed that by bringing the government down on the question

70

of Ireland the whole Liberal programme of political and social reform might be destroyed. For Irishmen themselves the issues were probably less complex. To Ulster Protestants, government by Catholic nationalists in Dublin was anathema; to the Irish majority, home rule without Ulster was unthinkable. Both sides were inflexible, the products of generations of emotional in-breeding.

Ulster began to organize and arm itself for resistance in 1911 and the nationalist south and west of Ireland followed its example. Redmond was reluctant to do so and the lead came instead from the labour movement in Dublin. In the autumn of 1913 strikes and lockouts in Dublin produced a heated atmosphere in which the Irish Transport and General Workers' Union, under James Larkin's leadership, decided to create an Irish Citizen Army. Until this time labour had been under attack from the more extreme nationalists for placing the interests of the Anglo-Irish working class above the interest of Ireland, but when the strike collapsed early in 1914 the Citizen Army carried on, ultimately to fight for Ireland in Easter week 1916.[1] It was never strong and a more serious challenge to the Ulster Volunteers came from the Irish Volunteers, initiated by Professor Eoin MacNeill of the National University in October 1913. The IRB co-operated in the creation of a provisional committee for the movement in late November with MacNeill as chairman, but took care not to publicize its sponsorship. By May 1914, 70,000 men had joined and as the membership grew John Redmond became concerned that the Volunteers would not respond to the leadership of the Irish Parliamentary Party. In June he demanded that the provisional committee should seat enough of his nominees to match its existing membership. To avoid a public split in the nationalist movement a majority of the committee accepted this ultimatum but it forced a minority faction, largely of radical IRB men, closer to the Citizen Army. The Irish Transport and General Workers' Union headquarters, Liberty Hall, Dublin, became

[1] J.D. Clarkson, *Labour and Nationalism in Ireland*, New York: Longmans, Green, 1925, Ch. IX. 'Twentieth Century Nationalism'. Sean O'Casey was the first Hon. Secretary of the Citizen Army. For his coloured version of its development see P.O'Cathasaigh (Sean O'Casey), *The Story of the Irish Citizen Army*, Dublin: Maunsel & Co., 1919. For an account of Larkin's work for Ireland, see Emmet Larkin, *James Larkin: Irish Labour Leader, 1876–1947*, London: Routledge and Kegan Paul, 1965.

thereafter the home of the extreme physical force movement in Ireland. After Redmond had supported the British stand in the European war which began that August, the minority, estimated by Denis Gwynn as 12,000 men, made its final break. In September 1914 it seized the administration and declared itself to be the only *Irish* Volunteer force. Some who had hitherto accepted Redmond's demands, for example Eoin MacNeill, also changed sides at this point. Thereafter, the majority, estimated at 160,000, became known as the *National* Volunteers but whereas they were heavily depleted by the loss of men to the British Army, the minority Irish Volunteers, eager to use Britain's disability for Ireland's gain, remained behind and prepared for a rebellion.[2] With their core of IRB men, they had the support of the Clan na Gael and although John Devoy had no illusions about their numbers, for he argued that Redmond had succeeded in 'denationalizing' the majority of the Irish by 1914, he believed that the small minority was more virile and more prepared for battle than ever before.[3]

In June 1914 an Irish National Volunteer Fund was established in America with a Clan veteran, Joseph McGarrity of Philadelphia, as chairman, and a Celtic Press Service in Philadelphia plied the press with stories of Volunteer activities and meetings in the USA. By February 1916 more than $39,000 out of a total of over $44,000 collected by the fund in America had been spent in Ireland or elsewhere for revolutionary purposes,[4] but it was scarcely a large enough sum to support an 'army'. Devoy estimated that between 1913 and 1916 the Clan na Gael donated $100,000 to the revolutionary organization in Ireland, but even if this was true, and it does seem excessive in view of the Clan's financial plight, very little was actually available in the summer of 1914. In June Devoy regretted that funds available to bolster the provisional committee against Redmond's demands were very low. Five thousand dollars were sent direct to Clarke later that month and it was clear that none of this would go to Redmond's nominees, but it fell far short of what Devoy would have liked to

---

[2] The O'Rahilly wrote to John Devoy on 10 November 1914 that the 'Irish volunteers' took £7,000 of the volunteer funds and £500 worth of weapons. John Devoy, *op. cit.*, pp. 414–15.

[3] *Ibid.*, p. 480.

[4] Audited accounts of the Irish National Volunteer Fund, 24 February 1916, *Maloney MSS.*, Box 12.

send.[5] In July, Clarke, anxious for more money, assured Devoy that Redmond would never be allowed effectively to control the Irish Volunteers,[6] but there was no money to send and no way of fulfilling requests for arms and for American officers to lead the Volunteers, even had Devoy and the Clan been able to decide between rival claimants for aid. Both Patrick Pearse, representing those who had opposed Redmond's ultimatum, and Eoin MacNeill, representing those who had reluctantly agreed to compromise in form if not in spirit with Redmond, appealed directly to Joseph McGarrity for aid in July and August 1914.[7] When the Volunteer split first occured in June over Redmond's ultimatum, the *Irish World* established a fund for Redmond's faction but the paper broke from Redmond when he supported Britain in the war. There was at least $10,000 in its fund but it had to be passed to Redmond's supporters in the United Irish League of America when pro-Redmond subscribers threatened to demand their money back.[8]

In December 1913 the British government banned the importation of arms into Ireland because of the growing danger of conflict there. The Ulster Volunteers had had longer to equip themselves but in April 1914 they augmented their already vastly superior stocks by importing more weapons in the illegal Larne gunrunning. In July, at Howth, the Irish Volunteers landed a much smaller supply, only 1,500 rifles and 49,000 rounds of ammunition, as against Ulster's 35,000 rifles and 2,500,000 rounds.[9] As treasurer of the provisional committee of the Irish Volunteers since its inception, Sir Roger Casement played a leading role in the planning of this effort and it was to campaign for desperately needed arms and ammunition, and the money

[5] Devoy, *op. cit.*, p. 393; The money was sent to Clarke although he at first asked Devoy to hold it in New York when the Volunteer committee surrendered to Redmond. See Devoy to McGarrity, 14, 18, 22 June 1914, *Maloney MSS.*, Box 16.

[6] Tom Clarke to Devoy, 7 July 1914, *Maloney MSS.*, Box 14.

[7] Eoin MacNeill to McGarrity, 1 July, 10 August, telegram, 1914, *Maloney MSS.*, Box 13; Patrick Pearse to McGarrity, 17, 28 July, 12 August 1914, in F.X.Martin, *The Howth Gun-Running*, Dublin: Browne and Nolan, 1964, pp. 52–6, 167–8, 190–2.

[8] Dr John G.Coyle to Redmond, 11 December 1914, reported on the pressure applied to the *Irish World* which had yielded $10,017.85 to that date. *Redmond MSS.*, P.C. 262(1).

[9] Martin, *Howth, passim;* Great Britain, *Report of the Royal Commission into the Circumstances Connected with the Landing of Arms at Howth on July 26th, 1914*, Cd. 7631, xxiv, 805, 1914.

to purchase them, that he decided to visit the USA.[10]

In his youth Casement's poetic imagination was fired by Ireland's struggle for national autonomy, but it was later, in 1905–6, between his British Colonial Service postings to Africa and South America, that he became actively involved in it. Even before accepting a knighthood in 1911 he came to hate the British government and to extol Germany. He resigned from the British service in 1913, aged 48, and devoted his life to Ireland. He had already begun to write articles for the nationalist press but until October 1913 he operated under assumed names. In that month he supported Eoin MacNeill's appeal for a nationalist volunteer force and became treasurer of the new organization. Shortly afterwards he wrote to his friend Alice Stopford Green, 'If God grant me life and purpose to end as I hope, I'll do some of the things John Mitchel left undone'.[11]

On 2 July 1914 Casement left Ireland on a circuitous route via Glasgow and Canada for New York. He had two purposes. One was to solicit more American support for the Irish Volunteers and the second was to interest the German government in Ireland. He had last been in America in 1912 for diplomatic discussions on South America, and on that occasion he had been introduced to President Taft as 'a very enthusiastic representative of the Irish party – at least he was before he was knighted in 1911'.[12] Now he arrived with less formality and encountered a cool reception because Clan na Gael leaders were distressed by the success of Redmond's bid for the Irish Volunteers. Casement had already written to John Devoy to explain why he had voted to accept Redmond's terms. He believed the alternative would have divided Ireland at a time when nationalists had to appear united; home rule would have been wrecked and the leaders of

[10] Casement had wanted to travel to America to 'wreck the "Anglo-Saxon Alliance" ', since at least January 1914. See Casement to Green, 16 January 1914, *Maloney MSS.*, Box 3. Reliable books about Casement are available and a detailed discussion of his early life and career are unnecessary here. See particularly René MacColl, *Roger Casement: A New Judgement*, London: Hamish Hamilton, 1956.

[11] Casement to Alice Stopford Green, 2 February 1914, *Maloney MSS.*, Box 3. A number of Casement's articles, dating from 1911, have been conveniently collected in Roger Casement, *The Crime Against Europe*, ed. Herbert O.Mackey, Dublin: C.J.Fallon, 1958.

[12] Memo. from State Department Latin Affairs Division enclosed in Chandler Hale to President Taft, 12 January 1912, *Taft MSS.*, Series 2, File 2537, Box 475

the Irish Volunteers would have been held responsible by the Irish people.[13] On his arrival in New York Casement found that he had still to convince these men, to whom he was a complete stranger, of his good faith. Despite the fact that Clarke, in a letter to McGarrity, had accused him of masterminding the surrender to Redmond, Casement managed to overcome the suspicions of the Irish-Americans and the Clan supported his fund-raising mission.[14]

As the European war got under way in August, Casement's hatred of the British became quite apparent. He drew up model resolutions favouring Germany and was instrumental in seeing them adopted at a number of meetings he attended. He drafted a declaration of Irish-American support for Germany which was signed by the Clan executive and sent to the Kaiser, and he wrote articles for the press.[15] On 5 October 1914 the *Irish Independent* published an open letter in which he declared that any Irishman enlisting in the British army was a traitor to Ireland. The most significant feature of Casement's American visit was not this publicity work, however, but his preparations for a visit he had decided to make to Germany. Through the Clan he submitted a cogently reasoned memorandum to the German Ambassador, Count von Bernstorff, dated 5 September and a week or so later he visited von Bernstorff in Washington with Devoy. In the memorandum he suggested an attack on the British mind and its sense of security. Britain could be weakened, he argued, through India, Egypt, or, most decisively, through Ireland. British morale would be shattered if Ireland could be detached from the Empire.[16] At a meeting with the German Military Attaché, Franz von Papen, Casement introduced the notion of an Irish brigade to be recruited from prisoners-of-war in German camps, although at this time he believed there was very little chance of an ultimate German victory.[17]

[13] Devoy, *op. cit.*, pp. 412–13.
[14] Clarke to McGarrity, 17 July 1914, *Maloney MSS.*, Box 12. Patrick Pearse supported Casement. Pearse to McGarrity, 17 July 1914, Martin, *Howth*, pp. 52–6; Devoy, *op. cit.*, pp. 410–13.
[15] See *Maloney MSS.*, Boxes, 2, 3, 4; Devoy, *op. cit.*, pp. 404–6.
[16] Memo to von Bernstorff, 5 September 1914, *Maloney MSS.*, Box 3; MacColl, *op. cit.*, p. 135.
[17] Franz von Papen to Casement, 18 September 1914, *Maloney MSS.*, Box 2; Casement to Mrs Green, 14 September 1914, *ibid.*, Box 3. In a memo from Brixton prison to Mrs Green and others, n.d., Casement stated that the idea of an Irish

Devoy baulked at the proposed visit to Berlin because he felt, quite reasonably as it transpired, that Casement was temperamentally unfit for the task, but Casement persisted. On 5 October Devoy, Cohalan and McGarrity agreed to pay for the mission from Clan funds and a few days later they met with von Bernstorff to finalize the arrangements.[18] On 15 October Casement left New York for Germany and by 2 November he was in Berlin. There he sought a declaration of support for Ireland from the German government and its co-operation in raising an Irish brigade from prisoners-of-war. Von Bernstorff had already written to his government on 27 September indicating the importance to America of the Irish question:

I do not think it necessary in [the war] to be too much exercised about American public opinion, as we are most likely to find friends here if we give freedom to oppressed peoples, such as the Poles, the Finns and the Irish.... The decisive point seems to me to lie in the question whether any prospect of an understanding with England is now in view, or must we prepare ourselves for a life and death struggle? If so, I recommend falling in with Irish wishes, provided that there are really Irishmen who are prepared to help us. The formation of an Irish legion from Irish prisoners of war would be a grand idea if only it could be carried out.

The Germans moved quite rapidly. On 20 November they issued a declaration supporting the Irish people, and 'on 28 December Casement and the German Under-Secretary of State, Zimmerman, signed what Casement regarded as a treaty. It provided that an Irish brigade was to be formed and equipped by the German government. In fact Irish prisoners were already being assembled in a camp at Limberg, north-west of Frankfurt, in November, and Casement visited them in early December. No volunteer was to receive any payment from Germany.[19]

Devoy was sceptical at the whole idea of the Brigade, for to his mind Ireland needed arms, not men, and indeed the Irish brigade proved to be an abysmal failure. Out of two thousand Irishmen assembled at Limberg, only fifty-five, of very poor quality,

brigade in Germany came from conversations with Major John MacBride who served in the so-called Irish Brigade during the Boer War. *Ibid.*, Box 3.

[18] Devoy, *op. cit.*, p. 417. McGarrity's notes on the 5 and 10 October 1914 meetings are in *Maloney MSS.*, Box 15.

[19] Great Britain, *Documents relative to the Sinn Fein movement*, Cmd. 1108, xxix, 429,1921, pp. 3, 4, 7; MacColl, *op. cit.*, pp. 155–6.

volunteered. For a while, early in January, Casement visited the camp daily but it was a humiliating experience. He tried to see some good in the brigade. 'It will have a deep effect upon the [Irish] national mind,' he wrote to Devoy in April but he had already written to another American, 'I will not return to Limberg to be insulted by a bunch of recreant Irishmen.'[20] Failure was especially hard for Casement because of his own unqualified enthusiasm. He could not conceive that Irishmen might be hostile to his own brand of patriotism but he had overlooked the fact that these particular Irishmen had volunteered for the British army and were loyal to it. His health collapsed and 1915 was an utterly miserable year for him.

Meanwhile Casement's amateurism and eccentricities were worrying the 'professionals' in America. There was first the problem of Adler Christensen, a young Norwegian seaman whom Casement had met quite casually in New York on his first day there, and whom he insisted on taking with him to Germany. The story of their odd relationship and of Findlay, the British Minister in Christiana, Norway, who offered the young man £5,000 to assist in Casement's capture, has been well told by MacColl. It was an incident of little real importance to which Casement reacted emotionally and which took most of his energy and time for several months. When Christensen returned permanently to the USA late in 1915 the suspicions held by the Germans about his moral character, the Findlay fiasco, his financial troubles in Copenhagen *en route*, and other problems, led to Devoy's damning indictment, 'The nurse [Christensen] is an all-round crook and dead beat'.[21] There are records of fairly regular payments from McGarrity to Christensen in the summer of 1916, possibly for work he was doing and probably out of McGarrity's respect for Casement, but he received no help from Devoy and was never active with the Irish again.[22]

Casement also wanted American officers to command the Irish brigade. Devoy asked himself how any self-respecting American officer, with American involvement in the war looming ahead, could go to Germany to command fifty-five men. Since

[20] Devoy, *op. cit.*, pp. 435–8; Casement to Father Nicholson, 16 March 1915, *Maloney MSS.*, Box 2; MacColl, *op. cit.*, pp. 165–6.
[21] Devoy to McGarrity, 13 December 1915, *Maloney MSS.*, Box 16. See also *Devoy MSS.*, 10, 610.
[22] *Maloney MSS.*, Box 12.

no qualified American could be found, Tom Clarke was asked to find a man in Ireland to assist Casement. He secured Robert Monteith, a former NCO in the British Army and a veteran of the Boer War who was then a captain in the Dublin Brigade of the Irish Volunteers. Monteith arrived in New York on 9 September 1915 and quickly made his way from there to Germany with Christensen, who had temporarily returned to America, but his arrival did nothing to bolster Casement's flagging health or spirits.[23]

The Americans were particularly annoyed at the cost of Casement's mission. Casement received over $10,000 from the Clan. He himself lived frugally, but he spent a great deal of money on the Irish brigade and on Christensen, and he asked for more. He failed to understand that the American movement was itself starved for funds. 'You know that a small minority do the work and the vast majority are indifferent,' Joseph McGarrity wrote to him in July 1915, and in his autobiography Devoy noted that 'Casement's notion that we could obtain money from rich Irishmen in America was, of course, a delusion. With a few notable exceptions moneyed Irishmen and Irish-Americans were unfortunately not then interested in the freedom of their motherland.' In July Devoy wrote to McGarrity that their organization was going down instead of up, and that the question of raising money was very serious.[24] However, although Devoy was not aware of it at that time, the position of the revolutionary faction in America was improving because Redmond was rapidly losing his American supporters. To understand why this happened it is necessary to return to Redmond's policy for Ireland when Britain found itself at war in August 1914.

In May 1914 the House of Commons passed the Government of Ireland Bill for the third time, thereby overriding the veto of the House of Lords. The Lords rejected a Government amend-

[23] In his book Devoy argues that had Christensen not tricked the Clan, in some unspecified way, fifty Irish-Americans could have been sent to Germany at Casement's request, but at the time he made it quite clear that the project was impossible. There were no funds available and Casement's mission had been a waste of money. See Devoy to McGarrity, 13 July 1915, *Maloney MSS.*, Box 16; Devoy, *op. cit.*, p. 441.

[24] McGarrity to Casement, 10 July 1915, *Maloney MSS.*, Box 1; Devoy to McGarrity 15 July 1915, *ibid.*, Box 16. Casement took $2,500 with him and received $7,740 thereafter. Casement's receipt plus his Irish Brigade and personal accounts are in *Devoy MSS.*, 10,607. See also Devoy, *op. cit.*, pp. 418–22.

ment to exclude Ulster temporarily from home rule for six years, an offer which would have allowed the judgement of at least one general election before the final settlement of the Irish question, and when they voted for Ulster's permanent exclusion in July 1914, they in fact rejected any settlement on the Government's terms. To have actually implemented home rule at this stage would have led Ulster into civil war, but the British Prime Minister, Asquith, was equally convinced that, having been approved the requisite three times in successive parliamentary sessions, its rejection would have caused a nationalist civil war.[25] The European war which broke out in August conveniently cooled the situation but some form of interim Irish settlement had to be arranged. Home rule was therefore signed into law in September, but was delayed by the application of a Suspensory Bill until the peace settlement in Europe. In the House of Commons, on 3 August, Redmond pledged Ireland's support for the war, and Irishmen flocked to the British army. But speaking for the Irish minority, the IRB supreme council unanimously resolved 'to work for an insurrection in arms against England to be launched at the earliest possible moment, without further provocation by England than her continued Government of Ireland, and the military occupation of Ireland by an English garrison'.[26]

In the United States Redmond's following was very large as home rule appeared certain. The Clan na Gael was at its lowest ebb and its leaders expressed grave concern at their lack of funds and at the success of the United Irish League. The American scene dramatically changed when Redmond opted to support the British government in the war and agreed to the suspension of home rule. The *Irish World*, still edited by the great anglophobe Patrick Ford, withdrew its support from him and the United Irish League of America began to crumble. To avoid an out-right collapse the proposed national convention in December was cancelled with Redmond's approval. When a New York Metropolitan UIL Convention was held that month there were 420 delegates representing eighty-three branches, all committed to Redmond, but as one of the delegates admitted, some of these branches were created out of others for the purpose of inflating

25 Cabinet Memo September 1913, *Asquith MSS.*, Box 38.
26 Le Roux, *op. cit.*, p. 144; Macardle, *op. cit.*, pp. 127-8.

the total.[27] The *New York Times* reported the convention and the *New York World* published a few pro-Redmond articles by Patrick Egan, but Redmond's friends desperately felt the loss of their own newspaper, and they looked for another without success.

By 1915 Redmond was humbled into supporting the UIL from funds in Ireland, a tragic reversal of the normal flow, and added humiliation came with the problem of maintaining the office of the League in Boston and New York. In Philadelphia it was run from his own offices by the President, M. J. Ryan, who made no secret of his personal sympathy for Germany. The Clan na Gael and the Ancient Order of Hibernians took sides with the Central Powers when the European war was declared and lost no members, but for Redmond and the UIL the war brought disaster in America. There were prominent Irish-Americans who supported the Allies, but very few were prepared to voice this support. A notable exception was Bourke Cockran.

A new wave of Irish-American pressure, led by those who were hostile to Redmond, was bound to be applied to Woodrow Wilson and his administration as a result of the war in Europe. The issue for most Irish-Americans, as for Casement and the Irish Volunteers, was quite simple; Britain's time of trouble was Ireland's opportunity. That this was felt more strongly by the Irish in America than by the Irish in Ireland was an unpublicized fact.

Wilson was, of course, elected in 1912 with the aid of the well-organized urban Irish-American Democrats. However, he came into conflict with the Irish-American Senator O'Gorman of New York, a Tammany stalwart, over the distribution of patronage in New York. Tammany and political corruption were discredited in the country at large and Wilson refused to accept O'Gorman's nominees or those of Tammany's 'Boss' Murphy over the nominees of his cabinet members.[28] But though ever ready to support an Irish cause, Irish Democratic Party bosses like Murphy in large cities, New York, Boston and Chicago for example, were not leaders of Irish-American nationalism and Wilson, though

[27] Dr John G. Coyle to Redmond, 18 December 1914. These problems of the UIL are illustrated in detail in *Redmond MSS.*, P.C. 262(1).

[28] Woodrow Wilson to O'Gorman, 20 April, 5 May 1913, *Wilson MSS.*, Series II, Box 35; Wilson to William Jennings Bryan, 19 February 1915, *Bryan MSS.*, Box 43.

hostile to bosses generally, had never been unfriendly to Irish-Americans as such. He had many in his political entourage including his personal secretary from New Jersey, Joseph Tumulty, and William McAdoo, Secretary of the Treasury, who had been active in New York Irish-American affairs for many years. In fact Wilson was subjected to fierce anti-Catholic pressure for having so many Irish-Americans and Catholics around him.[29] He avoided directly antagonizing the Irish but his ambiguity in speeches to Irish-Americans must have perplexed them. In March 1909, when President of Princeton University, he addressed the St Patrick's Day banquet of the New York Friendly Sons of St Patrick and instead of eulogizing the Irish in the conventional, if platitudinous way, Wilson chose to speak of his conception of America in world affairs. 'We have now to think in terms of the world and not in terms of America,' he said. 'We have come out upon a stage of international responsibility, from which we cannot retire.'[30] The unveiling of a monument to the Irishman John Barry, a pioneer of the American navy, was the occasion for another unconventional speech.

Irish-American pressure in Congress had resulted in a $50,000 grant for the Barry monument to be erected in Franklin Park, Washington, and both houses of Congress adjourned for the ceremony on 16 May 1914. The President delivered an address which was, in fact, a veiled attack on the very Irish-Americans gathered around him, as the following extract demonstrates:

John Barry was an Irishman, but his heart crossed the Atlantic with him. He did not leave it in Ireland. And the test of all of us – for all of us had our origins on the other side of the sea – is whether we will assist in enabling America to live her separate and independent life, retaining our ancient affections, indeed, but determining everything that we do by the interests that exist on this side of the sea. Some Americans need hyphens in their names, because only part of them has come over; but when the whole man has come over, heart and thought and all, the hyphen drops of its own weight out of his name. This man was not an Irish-American; he was an Irishman who became an American. I venture to say if he voted he voted with regard to the questions as they looked on this side of the water, and not as they affected the other side, and that is my infallible test of a

29 See *Wilson MSS.*, Series VI, Box 89, File 61, 'Roman Catholic Affairs'.
30 *Gaelic American*, 27 March 1909.

genuine American, that when he votes or when he acts or when he fights his heart and his thoughts are centred nowhere but in the emotions and the purposes and the politics of the United States.[31]

No one can say if this corresponds to the facts of Barry's life, but Wilson had made his point and had presented an attitude towards 'hyphenism' which was to become very important during the coming war.

Wilson's speech was probably influenced by the role of Irish-Americans in the Panama Canal tolls controversy then current in the United States.[32] The canal was nearing completion in 1912 when Congress passed an act governing its operation which exempted US coastal shipping from the payment of tolls. This concession was, as the British immediately argued, a violation of the 1901 Hay-Pauncefote Treaty which forbade discrimination in favour of any country in the administration of the then envisaged canal. President Taft, Secretary of State Knox, Theodore Roosevelt and the Progressive Party, and a large number of Democrats in Congress supported the 1912 Act, and indeed Wilson was elected on a Democratic platform which explicitly favoured the exemption of US coastal shipping from tolls. However, appearing before Congress on 5 March 1914, Wilson accepted the British case and opposed the act. 'We . . . are too big, too powerful, too self respecting a nation,' he argued, 'to interpret with too strained or refined a reading the words of our own promises just because we have power enough to give us leave to read them as we please.'

A fierce battle now followed. Pressure from individuals in each of the three major parties, from shipping lobbyists, the Hearst press, anglophobes of all kinds, and hundreds of petitions from Irish-American organizations, contributed to the campaign against the President. The Irish also began to hold mass meetings. One, in Carnegie Hall on 20 March 1914, was addressed by the Progressive, Bainbridge Colby, later to become Wilson's last Secretary of State, who had organized a committee to agitate on the subject. Joseph McGarrity organized a meeting at the Philadelphia Academy of Music on 30 March which was attended by three thousand people. Although Irish-Americans were not

[31] O'Dea, *op. cit.*, v. 3, pp. 1475–86.
[32] See Arthur S. Link, *Wilson: The New Freedom*, Princeton: Princeton University Press, 1956, pp. 304–14, and Bailey, *op. cit.*, pp. 599–602.

represented on the organizing committee and Wharton Barker, an eccentric Philadelphia publisher, was ostensibly the organizer, McGarrity paid the bill. During hearings before the Senate Committee on Inter-Oceanic Canals, W.Bourke Cockran and other Irish-Americans appeared as delegates of the 'Committee for the Preservation of American Rights in the Panama Canal'.[33]

The President succeeded, however, in having both houses of Congress agree to the repeal of the tolls. He authorized the most blatant use of the patronage instrument by Postmaster General Burleson on wavering Congressmen and he seriously argued that the tolls question impeded his negotiations with Britain on the Mexican problem. The vote in the House, in June, was 247 to 162, and in the Senate 50 to 35. To many Irish-Americans it appeared that the President had betrayed American interests to the British and his conduct when the war broke out in Europe shortly thereafter confirmed this impression in their minds.

The revolutionary Irish faction in the USA was short of both supporters and money during the first year of the war, but this does not mean that they were ineffective. They had already sent Casement to Germany. A small band of dedicated activists can be powerful in almost any setting and America was a very favourable hunting ground in 1914 and 1915. To illustrate why, the general point must be made that the USA was, and is, an immigrant society. As T.A.Bailey so effectively explained:

> From the very outset it was clear that the American people would find it more than ordinarily difficult to avoid taking sides. This was a *world* war; and the United States, the historic asylum of the oppressed, contained a 'menagerie of nationalities'. However much orators might descant on the magic of the melting pot, millions of 'hyphenated Americans' could not completely forget the land of their birth and cultural heritage – German-American, Irish-Americans, Jewish-Americans, and other 'hyphenates'. 'America,' wrote the British Ambassador, 'is no nation, just a collection of people who neutralize one another.'[34]

In his book on the immigrant press, Robert Park made the general calculation about immigrant allegiances that the Germans and the Irish supported Germany, the Swedes inclined to Germany,

---

[33] These and other aspects of the Irish-American campaign are in *Barker MSS.*, Box 20.

[34] Bailey, *op. cit.*, p. 610.

the Poles and Jews opposed Russia, but Lithuanians and Ruthenians opposed the Poles, Yugoslavia opposed both Italy and Austria, while Slovaks opposed Hungary – and so on! Park also noted that the immigrant press was more concerned with the old quarrels of Europe than the native American press and its newspapers were often run, as in the Irish case, by political refugees with very strong feelings. Of the *foreign language* press the German had always been predominant and, although its proportion had dropped as newer national groups moved into the country, by 1914 it still accounted for forty-six per cent of the total and 532 newspapers.[35]

The following table of foreign born and first generation Americans demonstrates the huge numbers involved in the potential problems of allegiance raised by the war. Note particularly the numbers of German and Irish-Americans.

Principal Foreign Elements in the United States Population – Census of 1910
(Total Population of Continental USA 91,972,266)

Country of Origin	Foreign Born	Natives		Total
		2 F.B. Parents	1 F.B. Parent	
*Germany	2,501,181	3,911,847	1,869,590	8,282,618
Austria-Hungary	1,670,524	900,129	131,133	2,701,786
UK (excl. Ireland)	1,219,968	852,610	1,158,474	3,231,052
*Ireland	1,352,155	2,141,577	1,010,628	4,504,360
Russia & Finland	1,732,421	949,316	70,938	2,752,675
Italy	1,343,070	695,187	60,103	2,098,360
Total for *all* foreign countries (incl. those not listed)	13,345,545	12,916,311	5,981,526	32,243,282

Note that these figures do not convey any impression of the complex loyalties of the many ethnic groups represented in the Russian and Austro-Hungarian Empires.

The United States was wide open to propaganda offensives from both sides in Europe and it was absolutely essential to the stability of American life that the government should be seen to be neutral. There were a number of other reasons for a policy of strict neutrality which cannot be debated here – the influence of

35 Park, *op. cit.*, Chs VIII and XVII.

tradition, the geographical and mental isolation of large numbers of Americans, particularly in the mid-west, rival commercial interests, and the desire of Wilson and Colonel House, even before the war began in Europe, to mediate and conciliate. However, the importance of America's ethnic origins cannot be ignored for immigrants were an important element contributing to public opinion which set the limits within which the government was free to operate.

Wilson had won the support of many immigrants in 1914 when, like his predecessor, Taft, he had vetoed literacy test provisions in proposed immigration legislation, but foreign relations involved very different problems.[36] As the war broke in Europe migrants in the USA took sides. Wilson's public statement on the war, issued on 18 August, warned that only neutrality could prevent the division of Americans into hostile groups, and in October he expressed his growing concern in a letter to Ambassador Page:

> More and more, from day to day, the elements (I mean the several racial elements) of our population seem to grow restless and catch more and more the fever of the contest. We are trying to keep all possible spaces cool, and the only means by which we can do so is to make it demonstrably clear that we are doing everything that it is possible to do to define and defend neutral rights.[37]

Wilson reminded the American people of this policy at every opportunity, even though he and many of his closest associates abhorred what they saw as Prussian militarism. No protest was made at the German invasion of Belgium or against the alleged atrocities committed there and the American government ruled that it would only protest when American interests were directly involved. Any other policy might have been construed as support for one side or the other, with serious repercussions at home. Theodore Roosevelt, who wanted US intervention on the Allied side, condemned Wilson's policy in November 1914:

> [Wilson] believes that in the course he has followed he will keep the pacifists with him here at home and placate the German vote and

36 John Higham, *Strangers in the Land: Patterns of American Nativism, 1860–1925*, Brunswick, New Jersey: Rutgers University Press, 1955, pp. 188 ff.

37 Wilson to Page, 26 October 1914, *Wilson MSS.*, Series VII, Box 9, Letter-Book No. 17A, pp. 479–82.

the extreme Irish vote – not the bulk of the Irish vote – which simply wants to harm Britain at any price.[38]

However, Roosevelt's close friend, Henry Cabot Lodge, believed that the combination of German-Americans, pacifists and 'irreconcilable Irish' was a vital factor in American foreign relations and Wilson had to consider it.[39]

The President believed himself to be walking a tightrope between the belligerents but even neutrality proved to have pitfalls because the strict application of the established international laws of neutrality was bound to involve the USA in even closer economic relations with the Allies than had existed before the war. Great Britain controlled the seas and although the United States could offer to trade in contraband of war with each one of the belligerents without legally prejudicing its neutrality, the British could ensure that this meant, in fact, trade with the Allies only. Furthermore, America's trading position required that the Allies, as purchasers, should be granted adequate finance, in the form of loans or credits, by the United States. In August 1914 Wilson and his cabinet were agreed that loans by American banks to belligerents would be inconsistent with the spirit of neutrality, but in October they conceded that Wall Street bankers could extend massive credits to belligerents, a move overwhelmingly advantageous to the Allies. So began the series of credits and loans which were to embroil the USA in the European conflict long before any actual declaration of war.[40]

This apparently pro-Allies bias of the US Government was reinforced by other factors. In London the US Ambassador, Walter Hines Page, was an arch-anglophile and for some time his speeches of praise for England and its contribution to America had been the subject of Irish-American attacks in the press and Congress. When war broke out he immediately identified himself with the Allies. In September 1915, for example, he wrote:

The impression grows that the 'peace at any price' type of man has control of American opinion. . . . Thinking men persist in regarding the United States as a more or less loose aggregation of emptied nation-

[38] Roosevelt to Spring Rice, 11 November 1914, Morison, *op. cit.*, v. 8, p. 841.

[39] Henry Cabot Lodge to Moreton Frewen, 16 August 1915, *Frewen MSS.*, Box 44.

[40] Arthur S.Link, Wilson: *The Struggle for Neutrality, 1914–1915* Princeton: Princeton University Press, 1960 pp. 62–4 132–6, 616–28.

alities without national unity, national aims, or definite moral qualities.

Wilson, very annoyed, added this pencilled note:

> I wish Page could feel a little more strongly that we are acting upon our own convictions and not upon English opinion. Of course they want us to pull their chestnuts out of the fire.[41]

Colonel House, whose informal diplomacy in Europe on behalf of Wilson was a feature of the period, was also sympathetic to the Allies. An extremely frank communication of views passed between the British and American governments via House and British representatives in the United States, notably Sir William Wiseman. Even during the most severe American attacks on Britain's blockade and embargo policies, when American trade in non-contraband of war items with the Central Powers and European neutrals was checked by British sea power, Anglo-American diplomacy, both official and unofficial, was carried on with a degree of trust and friendship quite absent from American dealings with the Central Powers. James Gerard, the US Ambassador in Germany, had no access to the Court and very little access to the German government. He continually complained of his ostracism in Berlin and was completely ineffective. As Arthur Link wrote, 'This former dilettante in Tammany politics was an authentic international catastrophe,' and Wilson himself exclaimed: 'I wish they would hand this idiot his passports!'[42]

Wilson's tolerance of Page's anglophilism contrasts markedly with his intolerance of the pro-German sympathy of the US Consul in Munich, T.St John Gaffney, who had originally been appointed to Dresden by Theodore Roosevelt as a reward for his services as an Irish-American in the 1904 Presidential campaign. Wilson called for Gaffney's resignation in September 1914 because of his well publicized activities in support of the German cause. This support was determined by Gaffney's Irish birth and sympathies.[43]

41 Page to Lansing, telegram, 8 September, and Wilson note, 10 September 1915, *Wilson MSS.*, Supplementary Papers, vol. I. 'I think England will save Europe from itself', Page wrote to Wilson, 23 August 1914, *Wilson MSS.*, Series II, Box 61.

42 Link, *Wilson: Neutrality*, pp. 311 and 657; Gerard to Lansing, 8 September, Gerard to Wilson, telegram, 9 September and Wilson's notes, 10, 11 September 1915, *Wilson MSS.*, Supplementary Papers, vol. I.

43 T.StJohn Gaffney, *Breaking the Silence: England, Ireland, Wilson and the War*, New York: Horace Liveright, 1930, passim; *Wilson MSS.*, Series VI, File 549, Box 356.

When war came in 1914 German-Americans immediately supported Germany and demanded a stricter neutrality. One of the leading agencies for the articulation of this demand was the National German-American Alliance, founded in 1901 and composed of American citizens. In 1914 it was the largest organization of any national minority in the USA with two million members. It could call upon spokesmen in Congress, particularly Representatives Richard Bartholdt of Missouri and Henry Vollmer of Iowa. To its members, it was primarily an alliance of German-American social and cultural societies, but as a political organization it had served the interests of German-American brewers, and it was they, not the German government, who subsidized it. However, when war broke out it was used to mobilize pro-German sentiment, and was joined by the hitherto hostile Roman Catholic Central Verein.[44] There were also powerful United German Societies in many large cities which had existed for several years. German-American opposition to the Boer War and the Anglo-American arbitration treaties, and the formal agreement between the Alliance and the Ancient Order of Hibernians discussed earlier, provided a foretaste of their wartime activities.

German-Americans closed ranks in 1914 and were joined by the revolutionary Irish in America. Some influential Germans had exaggerated ideas about the strength and effectiveness of this combination. In January 1915, for example, Ambassador Gerard in Berlin reported an incredible conversation with the German Under-Secretary of State for Foreign Affairs, Zimmerman. He wrote:

I do not think that the people in America realize how excited the Germans have become on the question of selling munitions of war by Americans to the Allies. . . . [Zimmerman] said that perhaps it was as well to have the whole world against Germany, and that in case of trouble there were five hundred thousand trained Germans in America who would join the Irish and start a revolution. I thought at first he was joking, but he was actually serious.

Wilson hurried this message to House with his own comment, 'Is not the last paragraph amazing?' In September Gerard sent a

44 See Clifton James Child, *The German-Americans in Politics, 1914–1917*, Madison: University of Wisconsin Press, 1939; Richard Bartholdt, *From Steerage to Congress*, Philadelphia: Dorrance & Co., 1930, and Link, *Wilson: Neutrality*, pp. 20–4.

report of a leading article in the *Frankfurter Zeitung* which expressed concern at the possibility of going to war against a country, the USA, which housed millions of people of German blood. Nevertheless, it claimed, 'Germany readily assumes their loyalty . . . We have learned to recognize the value of the sympathies for the fatherland aroused again in the hearts of the countless numbers in America and hope for great results from this sympathy in the future.' Wilson found this 'very significant,' but as von Bernstorff testified some years later, the Germans always expected too much from German-Americans.[45]

The most persuasive argument pressed by Central Power propaganda was that the United States should be neutral in fact as well as in principle. In this view the export of war supplies to *both* sides should have been banned. Since the Allies had control of the seas and monopolized the purchase of war supplies this 'neutral' action would, in fact, have prejudiced their chance of victory. By condoning the arms trade Wilson, in the view of the Central Powers, was violating neutrality. This had been the argument of the South African Republics against the British during the Boer War and it had been rejected on that occasion by the American government.

The organization of a movement to force the United States to institute an embargo on the sale of war supplies and to prohibit loans and credits to all belligerents began in 1914 and Bernstorff is on record as having donated $5,000 to launch it. Irish and German-Americans joined forces in a number of organizations to promote the embargo – the American Embargo Conference, Friends of Peace, American Neutrality League, American Truth Society, and so on. They regularly packed mass meetings throughout the country. One of the first into battle was the German-Irish Legislative Committee of Chicago which organized meetings late in 1914 and sent lobbyists to Washington.[46] In December 1914 Congressmen Bartholdt, Vollmer and Lobeck (Nebraska), and

[45] Gerard to Wilson, 24 January, enclosed in Wilson to House, 28 January 1915, *R.S.Baker MSS.*, Series I, Box 7; Gerard to Wilson, telegram, 4 September 1915, *Wilson MSS.*, Supplementary Papers, vol. I. For a similar report see Link, *Wilson: Neutrality*, p. 332. See also Count J.von Bernstorff, *My Three Years in America*, London: Skeffington, 1920, p. 19.

[46] Arthur S.Link, *Wilson: Confusion and Crisis, 1915–1916*, Princeton: Princeton University Press, 1964, pp. 55–6; Link, *Wilson: Neutrality*, pp. 31–6, 164; Park, *op. cit.*, pp. 422–7.

Senator Hitchcock (Nebraska) introduced resolutions which would have empowered the President to prohibit the export of arms and ammunition from American territory. Late in January 1915, an Embargo Conference in Washington, DC, led to the establishment of the American Independence Union, with Bartholdt as President, to champion Americanism and the German conception of neutrality. In fact the embargo resolutions were pigeon-holed in committees and to that extent the agitation failed but the government was forced to tread very cautiously. An attempt to consider Senator Hitchcock's bill as an amendment to another received an impressive thirty-six votes against fifty-one in February, while 167 of 440 newspapers replying to a *Literary Digest* poll in January favoured the embargo. The mid-west was heavily in favour, and had many Congressmen and Senators not been loyal to the President the issue of an embargo might have gone the other way.[47]

As part of the government's answer to the embargo campaign the Secretary of State, Bryan, issued a reply to a series of complaints listed by Senator Stone, Chairman of the Foreign Relations Committee, which summarized the German-American case against American neutrality policy. In fact Stone's complaints and the reply from Bryan were engineered by the Counsellor to the State Department, Robert Lansing. They were published late in January 1915 and the reply contained a point by point rebuttal of the case for an embargo. It stated that the German government had agreed that as a neutral the United States was legally entitled to trade freely in military supplies, and concluded that it was the task of the belligerent, not the neutral, to prevent these from reaching an enemy.[48]

In December 1915 Page warned Wilson that the British were becoming very suspicious of German influence in the USA and the following month a message from the British Foreign Secretary, Sir Edward Grey, to Ambassador Spring Rice, which was intended for the President, complained about the Congressional

[47] Child, *op. cit.*, pp. 47–57; Bartholdt, *op. cit.*, pp. 369–70, 376–9; Link, *Wilson: Neutrality*, pp. 162–70.

[48] *Ibid.*, p. 163. US Congress, Senate, Committee on Foreign Relations, *Neutrality: Correspondence between the Secretary of State and Chairman, Committee on Foreign Relations, relating to certain complaints that the American Government has shown partiality to certain belligerents during the present European War*, 63 Cong. 3 Session, 1915, Doc. No. 716, p. 20.

discussion and the influence of German societies and the German Ambassador. In Grey's view, embargo legislation would have aided the power which had prepared for war, namely Germany. In fact the United States did not embargo arms for reasons of its own, not as a sop to British pressure, and, in a reply to Grey, Bryan insisted that although German and Irish-Americans were pro-German they did not determine American policy and their embargo policy would not be adopted.[49]

The German case was, in general, at a great disadvantage. The British and French governments controlled the wire services to the USA and most of the foreign news printed in American papers originated in England, very often with English correspondents. A *Literary Digest* poll of 367 editors in November 1914 recorded 20 pro-German, 105 pro-Allies and 242 neutral, but most of the actual information on the war carried by their papers came from England. German attempts to woo or bribe the press were unsuccessful but, as Link argues, the sheer mass of material supplied to the press by the German information service and diplomatic posts meant that some pro-German material did find its way into the American press to soften the impact of pro-allied reporting.[50] The foreign language press, unlike the native American press, was manipulated in favour of Germany for a handsome fee by Louis Hammerling, who had previously used his Association of Foreign Language Newspapers to promote the Republican Party. The hostility of the German and the foreign language press in general caused particular concern to Lansing and the President, but its general tide could not be stemmed and in this respect the German effort was successful. It was certainly augmented by the consistently anti-British Irish-American press.[51]

German agents co-operated with the Irish in America whenever they could. In his book, *My Three Years in America,* von Bernstorff wrote of the activities of one German

[49] Page to Wilson, 15 December 1914, *Wilson MSS.*, Series II, Box 69; Grey to Spring Rice, telegram, 22 January 1915, *House MSS.*, Drawer 9, File 8. Grey also had informally protested against the Hitchcock Bill through Page in December. See Link, *Wilson: Neutrality*, pp. 166, 185.

[50] Child, *op. cit.*, pp. 23–5; Bailey, *op. cit.*, p. 613; Link, *Wilson: Neutrality*, pp. 31–6; Horace C. Peterson, *Propaganda for War*, Norman: University of Oklahoma, 1939, pp. 12–14.

[51] On 22 January 1915 Lansing discussed this problem and ways of remedying it with the editor of the *Milwaukee Germania-Herold*, *Lansing MSS.*, vol. 7. See also Park *op. cit.*, pp. 376 ff.

agent, Dr Dernberg, during the first eight months of the war:

> [Dernberg's] connection with Irish leaders laid the foundation for a
> co-operation which in the following year was of great importance to
> our position in the United States, and which with a somewhat more
> intelligent backing by our government departments at home might
> have been more fruitful still.[52]

According to John Devoy, Irish-American liaison with the
German government, largely through the German Military
Attaché, von Papen, was arranged at a meeting between the Clan
na Gael executive, von Bernstorff, von Papen, and another
German, von Igel, in the German Club, New York, soon after the
war began in Europe. It was there that the Irish-Americans
expressed their hope that the war might be used to establish
Ireland's independence. The point was very firmly made that the
Irish needed military aid, not money, and that a rebellion in
Ireland would benefit Germany by diverting British troops from
the front in Europe.[53] In addition, of course, von Bernstorff and
the Clan collaborated in Casement's mission.

In his book Devoy insisted that the Clan accepted no German
money, and there is no evidence that sums of any importance
found their way into the Clan funds or to Ireland from German
sources. Similarly, although the British and American governments made great play of a dispatch intercepted from the German
General Staff, dated 26 January 1915, in which Casement was
alleged to have suggested that Joseph McGarritty of Philadelphia,
John P.Keating of Chicago, and Jeremiah O'Leary of New York
could recommend persons for tasks of sabotage, there is no
evidence that they either committed or organized such acts.[54]
However, on platforms and in newspapers throughout the
country the Irish spoke for Germany, some individuals certainly
did receive German money, and the Irish co-operated in organizations, the American Embargo Conference for example, which
received German subsidies. James K.McGuire, who was an
Irish-American Democrat, a former mayor of Syracuse, and the
owner of several newspapers, dedicated his book, *The King, the*

---

[52] Von Bernstorff, *op. cit.*, pp. 47–8.

[53] Devoy, *op. cit.*, Ch. LIV, 'First Interview with von Bernstorff'.

[54] John R.Jones and Paul M.Hollister, *The German Secret Service in America*,
Boston: Small, Maynard, 1918, pp. 171–2. Great Britain, *Documents re. Sinn
Fein*, p. 8.

Kaiser and Irish Freedom, in March 1915, to the German-Americans 'who form the bulwark of American civilization'. He was particularly scathing in his attack on Redmond's policy during the war, and Ireland's real hope, he concluded, lay not in Redmond's parliamentary agitation, but in Germany's victory. It was not revealed until 1919 that the German government had underwritten McGuire's activities with $22,000.[55] A similar tone was adopted by the American Truth Society, founded in 1912 by the Irish-American Jeremiah O'Leary of New York, which began issuing pamphlets on the war in 1915. It advocated 'true' neutrality and non-intervention, and opposed arms shipments or loans to the Allies. In March 1916, O'Leary founded the pro-German journal *Bull*, which he claimed reached a circulation of 48,000 and he probably received aid from the Germans.[56]

These Irish propagandists joined with German-Americans whenever possible, and the Friends of Peace organization was a fine example. It co-ordinated a large number of pro-German groups and among the Honorary Vice-Chairmen of the committee for its National Convention in Chicago in September 1915 were M.J.Ryan of the UIL, Robert Ford, who had taken over editorship of the *Irish World* when his father died, John Devoy of the Clan na Gael and the *Gaelic American*, Jeremiah O'Leary of the American Truth Society, Daniel Cohalan of the Clan na Gael, Mary McWhorter of the Ancient Order of Hibernians Ladies' Auxiliary, and many others of German and Irish extraction. This organization grew out of a mass meeting organized by German and Irish-Americans in Madison Square Garden, New York, in June 1915, and from the Eighth National Convention of the National German-American Alliance in San Francisco in August.[57]

Without real evidence, but with evident concern, Ambassador Spring Rice wrote of a 'German Party' in February 1915:

> They are organized for un-American and purely German purposes. They propose to put pressure on all candidates for office and to carry

---

[55] James K.McGuire, *The King, the Kaiser and Irish Freedom*, New York: Devin-Adair, 1915, p. 269; US Congress, Senate, Sub-committee on the Judiciary, *Hearings, Brewing and Liquor Interests and German Propaganda*, 65 Cong. 2 and 3 Sessions, 1919, v. 2, pp. 1392, 1396–8, 1504.

[56] Jeremiah O'Leary, *My Political Trial and Experiences*, New York: Jefferson Publishing Co., 1919, Part I.

[57] Child, *op. cit.*, pp. 80–4; Jones and Hollister, *op. cit.*, p. 251.

out their policy by the intimidation of Congressmen and Presidents, either actual or would be. Their meetings are held all over the country. The Irish leaders, who are paid by the German organization, take part in these movements. . . . There is also an atmosphere of hatred. For it is inconceivable that the formation of a strong and compact State within the State should not create a reaction.

In January 1916 Spring Rice wrote again:

A most active propaganda is going on and all the enemies of England have been marshalled against us. There are unfortunately a good many and the Irish have lent their unequalled power of political organization to [German and Russian] Jews, Catholics, and Germans. . . . The best politicians in the country are the Irish, and the professional Irish politician is against us.

By 'professional Irish politician' Spring Rice did not mean 'Irish Democratic politician'. The professionals were rather Devoy, Ford, Cohalan and their kind. In March he wrote, 'The Clan na Gael have captured the majority of the New York Irish although not Tammany. The St Patrick's day procession showed that the Redmondites are a small minority.'[58]

The peace propagandists included many who opposed war in principle, and others who genuinely opposed American participation, in any form, in purely European wars, but, as is so often the case, they were frequently manipulated and used as a 'front' by people with partisan interests. One who fell prey was the Secretary of State, William Jennings Bryan. He resigned in June 1915 over the issue of the severity of the second Lusitania note and on 24 June he addressed the mass meeting in Madison Square Garden, organized by the United German and United Irish Societies of New York, from which the Friends of Peace originated. Bryan's message was one of peace and non-involvement in the war, but the motive of the meeting was propaganda and a resolution favouring an arms embargo was endorsed. Bryan recognized the trap too late and agreed to address the Chicago Convention of the Friends of Peace in September only on condition that he could disassociate himself from an embargo resolution, and this he did. He was just as opposed, he wrote, to helping one side as the other. Resolutions carried at the June and September meetings con-

58 S. Gwynn, *Spring Rice*, v. 2, pp. 254, 309; Spring Rice to Sir Horace Plunkett, 23 March 1916, *Plunkett MSS*.

demning the arms trade and loans to the Allies were, of course, attacks on Bryan's own policy as Secretary of State.[59] His actions were widely misrepresented as support for Germany, and the mischief was compounded when an article was circulated, ascribed to Bryan as Secretary of State, attacking British rule in India. In fact it was written before he held office and as part of his general opposition to imperialism. Spring Rice made this clear to the British government but the damage was being done in America.[60] Bryan, who had resigned on a point of principle, now found himself distrusted by the President for his lack of discretion.[61]

The British were not defenceless in the publicity field and their approach was very successful. In his book on British propaganda during this war, James D.Squires argued that the British began slowly but learned from von Bernstorff and the Germans exactly what *not* to do, and that although British propaganda reached torrent proportions it was always veiled. The Allies' advantages included their monopoly of cable services after the German cable was cut, British domination of American overseas press sources, the anglophile character of the American 'upper crust' society and intellectuals, and the fact that, in the words of George Viereck, the pro-German editor of *Fatherland*, 'The shock troops of Allied propaganda were invariably American volunteers.' The various 'preparedness' groups, for example, which campaigned for rapid American military and naval growth, quite explicitly directed their campaigns against Germany. Much of the eastern press, which generally supplied information and opinions to the rest of the country, implicitly or explicitly favoured the Allies.[62] In an article in *Harper's Monthly* dated March 1918, the director of the British propaganda effort in the USA, Sir Gilbert Parker, described the British approach in America. It involved regular contacts with American correspondents in London, articles and pamphlets distributed informally to a huge number of recipients, personal contacts with university leaders and scientists, and so

[59] Bryan to Henry Wiseman, 27 August 1915, *Bryan MSS.*, Box 30; Child, *op. cit.*, pp. 75–83; Link, *Wilson: Confusion*, pp. 30–3.

[60] Spring Rice to Bryan, 20 August 1915, *Bryan MSS.*, Box 30.

[61] Wilson to House, 20 September 1915, *R.S.Baker MSS.*, Series I, Box 7.

[62] James D.Squires, *British Propaganda at Home and in the United States, 1914–1917*, Cambridge, Mass.: Harvard University Press, 1935; Peterson, *op. cit.*, *passim.*; George Sylvester Viereck, *Spreading Germs of Hate*, New York: Horace Liveright, 1930.

on. In addition, prominent politicians, including Lloyd George, Balfour, Law, Chamberlain, and John Redmond, gave regular interviews to the American press.[63]

Some Americans, Theodore Roosevelt for one, were eager that the British should do more to advertise their cause in the USA, and the English poet John Masefield, then working on British propaganda, advised, in early April 1916, 'It is most important that some authoritative loyal Irish member, preferably a Catholic, should go over as soon as may be . . . to silence the Irish-American part who exude poison from every pore.'[64] This question had already been discussed by the government several times. Here, for example, is part of a cable from Sir Edward Grey to Spring Rice dated 13 August 1915:

> Certain American friends and Englishmen who say they represent the American point of view tell me that the agitation which is being conducted in the United States against our restrictions with trade against Germany is increasing in force and effectiveness. . . . They lay particular stress on what they conceive to be the necessity of sending out a Roman Catholic Home Ruler in order to investigate and report on the trend of feeling among the American Irish and if possible to establish an organization in order to inform and direct that feeling.
>
> This view which is being pressed on me implies a radical change of policy. We have as you know made absolutely no attempt of this nature and have avoided any sort of interference with the natural course of public opinion in the United States.[65]

Spring Rice, following the examples of his predecessors during the Boer War and the arbitration treaty periods, had already opposed an active British propaganda in America and he replied to Grey's cable that the US public was becoming more sympathetic to the Allies as news of Germany's subversive activities in the USA became known, and as the German 'danger' came closer to America. On Ireland he added:

> Some of your friends seem to think that there is need of an energetic propaganda on our side. A distinctive English propaganda would be a great mistake. It would, however, be perhaps useful if someone

[63] Sir Gilbert Parker, 'The United States and the War', *Harper's Monthly*, March 1918, v. 136, pp. 521–31.

[64] Peterson, *op. cit.*, p. 241.

[65] Grey to Spring Rice, telegram, 13 August 1915, *House MSS.*, Drawer 9, File 8.

could be found who could persuade the Irish that the English Government are not, as is said here, going back on their promise as to Home Rule and that the Irish in Ireland desire to maintain good relations with the English for the sake of Ireland.

How this could be achieved he did not suggest although, in October 1914, he had written, 'The Irish, on the whole, are with us, but I wish you would tell the censor to let some racy details escape him as to the Irish regiments.' In another letter to Grey in June 1915, he had written, 'It is evidently of very great importance that no action should be taken in England which would arouse a strong anti-British sentiment among the Irish here. Our friends view with undisguised alarm the news of a quarrel between Unionists and Nationalists.' In his view it was even more important to American public opinion in general than to the Irish in America that Britain be seen to be united in self-sacrifice.[66] If only home rule could have been completed in 1914 there would have been no question of American hostility to Britain because of Ireland.

Plenty of British information did come before the American public and the 'soft sell' was the British order of the day. Squires tells us that Gilbert Murray's pamphlet, *The United States and Britain*, written in 1916, was propaganda, although it absolved the USA from any obligation to enter the war on the side of the Allies. Squires also lists several publications by Redmond which were sent to the United States as propaganda.[67] Typical of these was *The Irish Nation and the War*, a collection of speeches dating from 3 August 1914, which committed Ireland to the war, praised Irish unity and the gallantry of its soldiers, and alleged that home rule, albeit suspended, had succeeded in making Ireland 'the strongest arm in the defence of the Empire'. In a similar vein was S. Parnell Kerr's book, *What the Irish Regiments Have Done*. These and similar items can be found in the Library of Congress and in other libraries in America, very often inscribed, 'A gift from Sir Gilbert Parker.' There is no indication, however, that Irish-Americans were influenced by this material, whatever may have been the effect on others.

[66] Spring Rice to Lord Newton, 21 October 1914, Stephen Gwynn, *Spring Rice*, v. 2, p. 239; Spring Rice to Grey, 10 June, *ibid.*, v. 2, p. 273, and 19 August 1915, *ibid.*, pp. 278–9.
[67] Squires, *op. cit.*, p. 72 and appendix.

What probably helped British propaganda most were the activities of the agents of the Central Powers themselves during 1915. The sinking of the Cunard liner *Lusitania* by a German submarine in May 1915, with the loss of 124 American lives, had a great effect on American public opinion. Bernstorff himself reported, 'Our propaganda in this country has, as a result of the *Lusitania* incident, completely collapsed,'[68] but even worse was to come. Papers belonging to a German agent, Dr Albert, were intercepted by the American government in July. Some of their contents were deliberately leaked to the *New York World* which in August published accounts of German undercover operations – the subsidizing of newspapers, the financing of German and Irish-American organizations, the purchase of a munitions plant in Connecticut, and so on. The activities of Franz Rintelin, involving sabotage of shipping, the fomenting of a counter-revolution in Mexico, and the organization of the pro-German Labour's National Peace Council, were uncovered by the British and Americans and published between September and December 1915. In October the Austro-Hungarian Ambassador, Dumba, was expelled for un-neutral activities and in December, as the result of revelations at the trial of four Hamburg-Amerika Line employees for un-neutral conduct, Captain Boy-Ed and Captain von Papen, the German Naval and Military Attachés respectively, were required to leave the country.[69] As a result of these activities a wave of anti-German feeling swept the country, fanned wherever possible by anti-Germans. A book using much of the new information, *German Conspiracies in America*, by William Skaggs, was published in London in October 1915 and found its way to the United States very quickly as British propaganda.

The war in Europe and the divisions in America had obviously presented a severe challenge to the notion of the American 'melting pot', the mixing of races into a new American stock, and in 1915 the United States witnessed the beginnings of a public counter-attack on 'hyphenated Americans'. Theodore Roosevelt was in the vanguard of this agitation as was the *New York Times*, a long-term enemy of Irish-American hyphenism. On 1 February

[68] Bernstorff, *op. cit.*, pp. 25–6. See also Link, *Wilson: Neutrality*, pp. 377–99.

[69] *Ibid.*, pp. 554–6, 561–4, 645–50; Link, *Wilson: Confusion*, pp. 56–9; Konstantin Dumba, *Memoirs of a Diplomat*, trans. I.F.D.Morrow, London: Allen and Unwin, 1933, pp. 255–69.

1915, during the embargo struggle in Congress, an editorial declared, 'Never since the foundation of the Republic has any body of men assembled here who were more completely subservient to foreign influence and a foreign power and no one ever proclaimed the un-American spirit more openly.' These were strong words addressed to the Irish and German-Americans from a paper which Spring Rice had thought pro-German, presumably because neutral, only a few months before.[70]

On 19 November 1915, with fresh revelations on German activities in America appearing regularly, Joseph Tumulty, Wilson's secretary, wrote to the President, 'I do not like to alarm you but there is no mistaking the fact that the country is dissatisfied with our seeming attitude of indifference toward the propaganda initiated by our hyphenated friends.'[71] Secretary of State Lansing identified hyphenism as the cause of the difficulty in arousing the American people to the problems of the European war. In a private memorandum on 9 January 1916 he wrote, 'We are not yet ready to meet the submarine issue squarely. Our people are not aroused to a sufficient pitch of indignation at the barbarism of the Germans.' Drastic action would not be authorized by Congress, he felt, because of the success of German propaganda with the pro-Germans and anti-British (synonyms for German and Irish-Americans), and he added, 'This country is very different from other countries in that our people are not united by ties of blood. We are a mixture of many races and lack as a whole nationality in its ethnological sense. We are still too young a nation to have assimilated and amalgamated the various nationalities which compose our population.' It was Lansing's hope that the USA could stay out of the war until it was ready to fight as a united country.[72]

One way of mobilizing the vast mass of unaroused Americans was to direct their attention to 'disloyal' elements in their midst, and this was done in an anti-hyphen crusade in 1915 and 1916. Before the US Congress on 7 December 1915, the President launched a savage attack:

There are citizens of the United States, I blush to admit, born under other flags but welcomed under our generous naturalization laws to

70 Spring Rice to Chirol, 13 November 1914, Stephen Gwynn, *op. cit.*, p. 242.
71 Tumulty to Wilson, 19 November 1915, *Tumulty MSS.*, Box 1.
72 Private memo 9 January 1916, *Lansing MSS.*, Box 2, v. 1, p. 37.

the full freedom and equality of America, who have poured the poison of disloyalty into the very arteries of our national life; who have sought to bring the authority and good name of our government into contempt, to destroy our industries, wherever they thought it effective for their vindictive purposes and to strike at them, and to debase our policies to the uses of foreign intrigue....[73]

As if by prearrangement, in November and December the *New York World* and *New York Times* carried stories of both Wilson's address to Congress, with its attack on disloyal foreign-born citizens, and of the subversive activities of the German agent Franz Rintelin. News was also carried of the loss of a US tanker in the Mediterranean, sunk, it was said, by an unknown submarine. The reading public could conclude what it might from these stories as the attack on hyphens went from strength to strength in pro-Allied newspapers and journals such as the *Atlantic Monthly*.

From mid-1915 'Americanization' drives were launched with campaigns directed at foreign-born Americans. German-Americans were consistently rated as good citizens prior to 1914, but their activities in support of an embargo on trade and against Americans travelling abroad in belligerents' ships which might be sunk, were now used to discredit them. Suspicion of them quickly grew and as Higham noted in his book on American nativism, the war produced the 'most strenuous nationalism and the most pervasive nativism' that America had ever known.[74] The climax was reached when the USA entered the war, but the process was set in motion in 1915. Of course German-Americans bore the brunt of this attack, but in the press, in the public debate, and in the letters of prominent men of the time, the Irish were always identified as pro-Germans, and to many this was synonymous with disloyalty. Those who backed the Allies, or a pro-Allies neutrality, escaped such public denunciations although they, and indeed the denouncers, were very often guilty of their own kind of hyphenism. Many were, whether they recognized it or not, British-Americans. To them, war with Great Britain was unthinkable, but using a different set of ideological spectacles, war with the Central Powers was certainly acceptable.

---

[73] Child, *op. cit.*, p. 90. Link, *Wilson: Confusion*, pp. 34–7.
[74] Higham, *op. cit.*, p. 195.

5 Sir Roger Casement and the Easter Rising, 1916

'We execute a worthless rebel, and for Ireland a heroic saint emerges from the felon's grave.... "The Fifteen" will be framed upon the walls; and if our Law Courts add Roger Casement as a sixteenth, he will stand in the centre. Instead of being regarded as a well-intentioned but crack brained set of people they will be enshrined under that Necromancy or Magic of the Dead which is both the treasure and the plague of their country.'[1]

H.W.NEVINSON, 1916

Roger Casement landed in Tralee Bay on the west coast of Ireland just before dawn on Friday, 21 April 1916. The small craft in which he and two companions had landed was soon discovered and early that afternoon he was captured by police in the nearby ruins of the ancient McKenna's Fort, his companions by this time having made their way to Tralee, a dozen miles away. He possessed incriminating evidence including, incredibly, a German code and a German railway ticket.

Casement had actually come to stop the Irish rebellion which was planned for Easter 1916. His experiences in 1915 had led him utterly to distrust the Germans and their promises of aid. 'So full of good-will,' he wrote, 'they are swine and cads of the first order.'[2] He was recuperating in Bavaria from a physical and mental breakdown when the news of the planned rebellion was first brought to him early in March and he was immediately horrified at Germany's refusal to send adequate aid, both officers and machine-guns, to help the rising. In the privacy of his diary he wrote:

---

[1] H.W.Nevinson, 'Sir Roger Casement and Sinn Fein', *Atlantic*, v. 118, August 1916, pp. 242–3.

[2] Note by Casement on Monteith to Casement, 2 February 1916, *Maloney MSS.*, Box 2.

The only object this Government has in now offering us this meagre and belated help is to continue the fooling of the Irish in America and a possibly far off hope that we may create some little complication for England in Ireland.[3]

The Germans knew of Casement's opposition to a rising yet they agreed to help him return to Ireland, against the advice of John Devoy who wanted him kept out of the way in Germany.[4] On 12 April he sailed in a German U-boat for Ireland with two companions, Robert Monteith, who had been sent from Ireland to help him in Germany, and one of the Irish brigade, Daniel J. Bailey, who was apparently included in the party at Monteith's request.[5] This was a bad move for although Monteith managed to evade arrest in Ireland and escaped to America, Bailey was captured and turned King's evidence. *En route* the submarine developed engine trouble and but for this Casement would have arrived two days earlier. Nevertheless he arrived on 21 April, Good Friday, with still two days in which to delay, if he could, the rebellion which was set for Easter Sunday.

For a year and a half Casement had been an amateur playing a game for professionals and the complex Irish, Irish-American, and German negotiations for a rising had by-passed him almost completely. The Irish in Ireland had decided on the revolt themselves, although Ireland was prospering during the war, its thoughts far from revolution. In many ways – in land ownership and agricultural productivity, in local government, old age pensions, housing and social services – Ireland had never been more prosperous and when John Redmond committed his countrymen to the war in August 1914 even Devoy was moved to admit to the 'almost universal approval of John's pledge. . . . The moral rottenness at home is the worst part of it.'[6] But a series of

[3] 'The Last Page', Casement's Diary of his last few months in Germany, p. 25, *Maloney MSS.*, Box 7. (The Original is in the National Library of Ireland.) The diary tells a great deal of Casement's negotiations with the Germans from January to April, and also states that he sent an American, John McGoey, to Ireland to stop the planned rising. McGoey either did not arrive or was ineffective. Casement made a detailed note of his meeting with members of the German General Staff on 16 March 1916, on the back of a telegram, Monteith to Casement, 14 March 1916, *ibid.*, Box 2.
[4] 'The Last Page', *ibid.*, Box 7; Capt. Karl Spindler, *The Mystery of the Casement Ship*, Berlin: Kribe-Verlag, 1931, pp. 248–50.
[5] Gaffney, *op. cit.*, p. 159.
[6] John Devoy to Joseph McGarrity, 27 August 1914, *Maloney MSS.*, Box 16.

incidents and blunders played into the hands of the extremists. Home rule was suspended in 1914 in response to Ulster's threats, and Redmond accepted this as a war measure. His own suggestion that the Nationalist and Ulster Volunteers should combine for the home defence of Ireland was rejected, and his unofficial promise to the Irish that the British Government would arm the Nationalist Volunteers was never honoured. In June 1915 Redmond attributed the loss of Irish sympathy for the war to the Government's refusal to blend Irish units from the north and the south, while the lack of nationalists suitably equipped for commissions also led to a disproportionate number of Ulstermen as Irish officers.[7] It may not have been Lord Kitchener's job as Secretary of State for War to consider the political implications of his recruiting programme, but it certainly was the Cabinet's, and in Irish eyes they failed. In addition, when the coalition government was formed in May 1915, Carson, who a year before had been ready to lead a rebellion, accepted the important post of Attorney General, and when he resigned in October he was succeeded by his Unionist colleague, F.E.Smith. Redmond, honouring the nationalist's pledge to remain independent, refused to join the government. In April 1915 Sir Matthew Nathan, the Under-Secretary for Ireland, admitted to the existence of a large body of anti-English feeling in Ireland which was producing Irish indifference to the war. A minority, he claimed, was pro-German but the majority had shown a tendency to join them whenever conscription, taxation, or other demands threatened their interests. When conscription for Ireland was being mooted in the autumn of 1915, for example, the Irish Volunteers grew in number. Resistance to conscription was, indeed, the *raison d'être* of the organization for many men.[8]

The merits of these issues cannot be discussed here, but the overall image presented to nationalists in Ireland was a disturbing one and extremists were steadily making inroads into the bulk of the 'loyal' Irish. Seditious journals were regularly suppressed

[7] Redmond to Prime Minister Herbert Asquith, 5 June 1915, *Asquith MSS.*, Box 36. See also John Redmond, *The Irish Nation and the War*, Dublin: Sealy, Bryers and Walker, 1915.

[8] Sir Matthew Nathan to Col. J.Eustace Jameson, 8 April 1915, *Wilson MSS.*, Series VI, Box 558, File 3926. See also, J.O.Hanney, 'Recruiting in Ireland', *Nineteenth Century*, v. 79, pp. 173–80, January 1916, and Great Britain, *Report of the Royal Commission on the Rebellion in Ireland*, 1916, Cd. 8279, xi, 171, p. 7.

by the British government and anti-recruiting posters appeared overnight on walls throughout the country. There were still recruits from the nationalist sector of Ireland but they fell short of the number required, and the tide was slowly moving in favour of the extremists. It was, for example, becoming impossible to secure convictions for seditious activities from a great many Irish juries, although Asquith resisted the pressure to abandon trial by jury.[9] In May 1915 the IRB Supreme Council was replaced by a Military Committee, and later a Military Council, to weld the IRB, Irish Volunteers, and Sinn Fein into a viable revolutionary instrument. The Gaelic League also came under Irish Volunteer control when MacNeill replaced the pioneer, Douglas Hyde, as President. In the summer of 1915 Joseph Plunkett went to Germany to report on the revolutionary movement to the German government and in an audacious gesture John Devoy, in America, and Tom Clarke, in Ireland, stage-managed a funeral for the old revolutionary, O'Donovan Rossa, who died in America on 29 June 1915. The Irish marched with his coffin in New York, he was shipped to Ireland and lay in state in Dublin's City Hall, and he was buried with Republican pomp and ceremony in Ireland on 1 August 1915. It was less a funeral than a Republican demonstration staged under the noses of the British. Then, early in 1916, the Irish Citizen Army joined forces with the non-labour revolutionaries and the stage was set for action.[10]

The revolutionaries in Ireland owed their survival over the years to the United States and the Clan na Gael, but it was they who actually made the decision to act. Devoy had impressed upon them the difficulty of supplying German help but they went ahead and asked him for money and aid in December 1915.[11] In early February, 1916, Tommy O'Connor, their messenger who worked for the White Star Line, brought news to Devoy and the Clan Revolutionary Directory that the date for a rising had been decided. Devoy was surprised. In his view the war situation was unfavourable and he wrote in his autobiography:

[9] *Ibid.*, pp. 7, 10. Secret Memorandum on Ireland, 2 May 1916, *Asquith MSS.*, Box 42.

[10] F.X.Martin, 'Eoin MasNeill on the 1916 Rising', *Irish Historical Studies*, v. xii, 1960–1, pp. 228–9; Le Roux, *op. cit.*, pp. 159–67; Macardle, *op. cit.*, pp. 139–42; Clarkson, *op. cit.*, pp. 310–12.

[11] MacDermott ('J.Flynn') to Devoy, 12 December 1915, *Maloney MSS.*, Box 9.

They did not ask our advice; they simply announced a decision already taken; so, as we had already recognized the right of the Home Organization to make this supreme decision, our plain duty was to accept it and give them all the help we could.

A week later Philomena Plunkett, the sister of Joseph Plunkett, arrived in the USA to confirm plans for the rising and to transmit code signals for German vessels bringing arms.[12]

Four men in America, other than German officials, were fully informed on the planned rising; the three members of the Clan Revolutionary Directory, Devoy, John Keating and Joseph McGarrity, plus Judge Daniel Cohalan. They arranged for Clan na Gael funds to be sent to Ireland and it was also their task to communicate Irish requests to Germany, through the German Embassy in Washington and German agents in New York. Devoy therefore sent a message for the Irish to Germany on 10 February 1916 which read:

Unanimous opinion that action cannot be postponed much longer. Delay disadvantageous to us. We can now put up an effective fight. Our enemies cannot allow us much more time. The arrest of our leaders would hamper us severely. Initiative on our part is necessary. The Irish regiments which are in sympathy with us are being gradually replaced by English regiments. We have therefore decided to begin action on Easter Saturday. Unless entirely new circumstances arise we must have your arms and munitions in Limerick between Good Friday and Easter Saturday. We expect German help immediately after beginning action. We might be compelled to begin earlier.

On 4 March the German government offered the Irish 20,000 rifles, ten machine guns, ammunition and explosives to be landed at Fenit Pier, Tralee Bay.[13]

This offer was a disappointing one. In the informal code which the Irish at home and in America used when transmitting messages to each other, Devoy, alias James Digby, wrote about his new 'position', 'The salary is not as big as I expected, but it is a living wage and I am certain I would get a raise soon when they saw I could make good.'[14] Casement felt that the arms offer was totally inadequate and he knew that on 16 February Devoy

12 Devoy, *op. cit.*, pp. 458–60.
13 Great Britain, *Documents re. Sinn Fein*, pp. 9–10.
14 Devoy ('James Digby') to unknown, 9 March 1916, *Maloney MSS.*, Box 16.

had appealed for 100,000 rifles, plus artillery and German officers![15]

The Irish at home were prepared to act, irrespective of the size of the German contribution, but the cumbersome avenue of communication, via New York and then often via Amsterdam or Berne, caused even the small German contribution of weapons to be wasted. On 14 April Miss Plunkett returned to New York with the instruction that it was imperative that arms should *not* arrive before nightfall on Sunday, 23 April, and that a force of Germans, no matter how small, should follow at once. The Irish also hoped for a diversionary German naval and air attack on England at the time of the arms landing. Her message probably reached Berlin on 15 April and reminders followed a few days later, but the arms ship had left on 9 April, without radio, and expected to rendezvous as already planned, off Tralee, during the night of 20–21 April.[16] Even Casement had set off on 12 April. The arms ship, the *Aud*, arrived on time, waited twelve hours before putting to sea again, and was intercepted by the British on 21 April. She was escorted to Queenstown where her crew very effectively scuttled her on 22 April.[17]

The Irish also confused each other. Eoin MacNeill, Chairman of the Irish Volunteer executive and its Chief of Staff, knew nothing of the rising planned by the new Military Council until the Thursday preceding Easter. He had consistently opposed a rising during the war, favouring a steady growth of the revolutionary movement so that by the end of the war the British government, faced by a resolute body of Irish Volunteers, could not resist their demands. If forced into action prematurely he believed in staging a guerilla war, not an attack on Dublin. MacNeill decided to stop the rising and on Easter Saturday evening he countermanded the orders issued by the Military Council in his name for a rising to begin on Sunday. The news of the capture of the *Aud* and Casement had been published in Saturday's newspapers and reinforced his pessimism, but he appears to have received no message from Casement to abandon

---

[15] 'The Last Page', *Maloney MSS.*, Box 7.

[16] Great Britain, *Documents re. Sinn Fein*, p. 12. This does not include a cable dated 15 April 1916 concerning Miss Plunkett's mission. This message had been handed to von Papen, the German Military Attaché for transmission on 15 April 1916. *Von Igel MSS.*, and Devoy, *op. cit.*, pp. 462–3.

[17] Spindler, *op. cit., passim.*

the rising.[18] In the confusion caused by the contradictory orders the rebellion finally began on Easter Monday, 24 April, the work of one faction of the revolutionary Irish Volunteers led by IRB men, plus the Irish Citizen Army. They had decided on Sunday to go ahead, despite MacNeill's instructions and come what may. Five or six hundred Volunteers and two hundred members of the Citizen Army turned out in Dublin but in only a few places outside the city did Volunteers respond. By 29 April the rebellion in Dublin had ended and in a few more days the whole of Ireland was quiet again.[19]

How much did the British actually know about the rising in advance? In 1921 the British government published *Documents Relative to the Sinn Fein Movement* which contained items of major correspondence between Ireland and Germany on the planning of the rising and illustrated the intermediary role played by the Irish-Americans and the German Embassy in the United States. These intercepted messages dated from 1914 and included everything the British government needed to anticipate the rising. The sources, however, were undisclosed, and one cannot assume that the British actually intercepted them as they were being sent, or assume that they were able to decipher and understand them had they done so. Furthermore, how much information was passed to the British by the American government's intelligence services, either before or after the USA joined the war, is unknown.

Some writers have pointed to the von Igel raid of 18 April as evidence of Anglo-American collusion in suppressing the Easter rising. On that day four American Secret Service agents raided the office of a German diplomat, Wolf von Igel, ostensibly an advertising agency in New York. In Devoy's words, this was 'contrary to recognized international procedure', and Tansill also accuses the American government of un-neutral activity.[20] But what the raid revealed was that the German Embassy and German diplomats were involved in Indian and Irish revolutionary plots, in conspiracies to destroy American merchant shipping, and in attempts to destroy the Welland Canal in Canada. Notes were discovered giving details of the proposed rebellion in Ireland

[18] Martin, 'Eoin MacNeill', *op. cit.*, *passim.*

[19] Estimates vary as to how many men turned out. See Macardle, *op. cit.*, p. 172, (1500), Denis R.Gwynn, *De Valera*, London: Jarrods, 1933, p. 34 (700). The numbers increased as the week progressed.

[20] Devoy, *op. cit.*, p. 463; Tansill, *op. cit.*, pp. 196–8.

including a draft of the following cable implicating Daniel Cohalan, signed by von Skal, a German agent responsible for liaison with the Irish. It was sent to Berlin by the German Embassy two days *after* the raid:

Cohalan requests me to send on the following: The Irish revolt can only succeed if assisted by Germany, otherwise England will be able to crush it, although after a severe struggle. Assistance required: There would be an air raid on England and a naval attack timed to coincide with the rising, followed by a landing of troops and munitions and also of some officers, perhaps from an airship. It might then be possible to close the Irish harbours against England, set up bases for submarines and cut off food export to England. A successful rising may decide the war.

Later, the British claimed that the request had been, in part at least, fulfilled, for Zeppelin and naval raids took place on the English East Coast on 24 and 25 April.[21] When a selection from the von Igel documents was finally published in America in 1917, the US government gave this reply to charges that it had betrayed Casement to the British:

When the von Igel papers were seized in New York the district attorney and his assistants busied themselves in a search for information to sustain the indictments which they had obtained against von Igel, and overlooked for the time being the great mass of other evidence which pointed incriminatingly to others. Department of Justice officials admit that the papers relating to Casement were sent to Washington the night before Casement's arrest was reported, but they were not received by the Attorney General until the afternoon of the day upon which the British authorities picked up the Irish leader, and were not presented to the State Department until 7 o'clock that evening. Meanwhile Casement had spent several hours in an Irish prison.[22]

The quite chance capture of Casement and the lack of British preparation for the rising suggest that the USA did not inform the British of Casement's arrival. In any case, the von Igel papers indicate that very little, if anything, was known in America about

[21] *Von Igel MSS.* The von Igel papers in the National Archives are not complete, either through loss or censorship. Some which remain were published in Great Britain, *Documents re. Sinn Fein*, pp. 12–13, and it is possible that some of the missing papers were among others included in this collection.

[22] US Committee on Public Information press release for Sunday, 23 September 1917, *von Igel MSS.*

Casement's quite sudden plan to travel by submarine. The first information about the von Igel papers to arrive in Britain appears to have been a cable from Spring Rice dated Sunday, 23 April, which paraphrased Cohalan's message to the Germans and made no mention of Casement. It arrived too late to affect the capture of Casement or the *Aud* or even to prepare for the original date set for the rising, Easter Sunday.[23]

The American statement in 1917 referred only to Casement and made no mention of any betrayal of the German arms shipment, which Tansill claimed was intercepted as a result of the von Igel raid. However, the evidence will not bear the weight of Tansill's interpretation. Information that an arms ship and two sub-marines (Casement's first one broke down) had left Germany for Ireland had actually been in the hands of the General Officer commanding Queenstown on 16 April, two days before the raid, so the British could at least have anticipated an arms shipment. The lack of preparation looks even worse when one considers that on 22 March 1916 the British Division of Military Intelligence informed the GHQ Home Forces that a reliable informant had forecast a rising to begin on 22 April, that the Irish had asked for arms to be delivered, and that acting on similar information the Admiral, Queenstown, had ordered stringent patrolling of the Irish coast. However, Dublin Castle authorities played down the possibility of a rising, Casement was captured quite by chance, the *Aud* went undetected for a day and the militia was far below strength on 24 April when the rising finally began. General Friend, the C-in-C, Ireland, was on leave in England, and the bulk of the British officers stationed in Dublin were at the races. Both the Cabinet and Dublin Castle were completely surprised by the rebellion.[24] Given the first Spring Rice telegram of 23 April and

[23] Captain (later Admiral) Hall, Chief of the Admiralty Intelligence Dept., was present at Casement's interrogation at Scotland Yard, London. He told Casement of the von Igel raid on Monday, 24 April. The news appeared to have arrived very recently for Casement was brought in specially to be told at 11 p.m. See secret memo on Ireland, 2 May 1916, *Asquith MSS.*, Box 42 for details of the Spring Rice cable. H.Montgomery Hyde, ed., *The Trial of Roger Casement*, London: William Hodge, 1960, p. xxxvii.

[24] Secret memo on Ireland, 2 May 1916, and R.H.Brede for Army Council, to Field Marshal C-in-C, Home Forces, 28 April 1916, demanding an explanation. The general intelligence confusion was demonstrated in the reply in May (n.d.) which, like the Royal Commission, blamed no one. *Asquith MSS.*, Box 42, and Great Britain, *Rebellion in Ireland*.

this state of affairs in Ireland, to suggest an American 'betrayal' is to infer altogether too much. Spring Rice outlined what he, in America, knew of the rising in a letter to Sir Horace Plunkett dated 4 May 1916:

This Irish business is heartbreaking. The arrangements seem to have been made here with a combination of secrecy and openness. Such a thing was talked of and was the subject of public meetings and was openly advocated in public but the private arrangements were kept moderately secret although many people announced they knew all about them. John Devoy probably did know a good deal and a great deal of money must have passed through his hands. The Germans certainly knew a good deal but I doubt whether they even thought the movement was likely to be successful. The object was probably only to keep troops from going to France. It is a good instance of a thing which everybody talked about until nobody believed that it could ever happen. Now it has happened, everyone said it was inevitable and wonder why it didn't happen before. It seems strange looked at from here why the government was not better prepared. On the other hand, it must look strange from over there why we were not better informed here.[25]

The Dublin rising ended in the afternoon of Saturday, 29 April, and various actions in the provinces were quelled by 1 May. Martial Law had meanwhile been declared and on 3 May Thomas Clarke, the first of the rebels to be condemned by court martial, was executed by a firing squad in a courtyard at Kilmainham Jail, Dublin. Fourteen more leaders of the rebellion were soon to be executed after secret trials. The government chose to commute the death sentences on seventy-five others, but of the three thousand five hundred people arrested, almost two thousand were interned without trial in English prisons. The retribution had been swift and severe for this had been a civil uprising in the middle of a great war and conspiracy with the enemy had clearly been established. The rising itself had led to 450 deaths and 2,614 wounded. It had lasted for a week and had diverted troops and ships from important war duties.[26] There seems to be general agreement that the rising was unpopular in Ireland. The Government was quite aware that the Irish Volunteers, though growing, were still a very small minority, and it understood that the rising

25 Sir Cecil Spring Rice to Sir Horace Plunkett, 4 May 1916, *Plunkett MSS.*
26 Great Britain, *Documents re. Sinn Fein,* pp. 14–15.

had not been widespread outside Dublin. Even there the number involved as insurgents was no more than 1,500 to 2,000. In the House of Commons on 27 April John Redmond expressed his horror at the rising and from Ireland came reports that the majority of Irishmen supported him. By early June, however, even British authorities were agreed that Irish opinion was turning against them. Sinn Fein was growing in strength and was using the martyrdom of the dead rebels to win support. Even pro-Redmond nationalists were being forced to espouse the martyrs in an attempt to deny Sinn Fein any gains at their expense.[27] What had happened in the intervening months to cause this reaction? There had been the secret trials and executions of the leaders, thousands had been deported, and there had been the senseless killing of Francis Sheehy Skeffington, a nationalist but a pacifist, on the orders of an officer later adjudged insane. Skeffington had only recently, in December in fact, returned from a lecture tour of the United States and was well known to the Clan na Gael and many other Irish-Americans.[28] These actions were taken in the name of the government which, as yet, had released very little information to indicate the extent of the conspiracy with Germany. In the light of this repression the people of Ireland turned against the British in ever growing numbers, but more significant, from the standpoint of this story, was the indignation voiced in the United States. The proclamation of the 'Provisional Government of the Irish Republic', published on the day of the rising, had claimed the support of Ireland's 'exiled children in America' as well as her 'gallant allies in Europe' – the Germans. Until Easter week the only American friends of an outright revolution were the Clan na Gael, but now greater numbers were to be mobilized.

The *New York Times*, which had championed the Allies from the start of the war, declared that the British executions were 'incredibly stupid', and added its condemnation to many other newspapers and journals throughout the country which had

[27] Report by N.Chamberlain, Inspector General, Royal Irish Constabulary, 6 June 1916, *Asquith MSS.*, Box 44, and memo by General Maxwell, 16 June 1916, *ibid.*, Box 42.

[28] See Major Price to the General Officer, C-in-C, HM Forces in Ireland, 12 May 1916, *Asquith MSS.*, Box 43. See also, Great Britain, *Report of the Royal Commission on the Arrest and Subsequent Treatment of Skeffington, Dickson, and McIntyre.* 1916, Cd. 8376, xi, 311; Macardle, *op. cit.*, p. 189.

condemned the rising whilst advocating lenient treatment for the offenders.[29] Correspondence from a wide range of writers normally favourable to the British insisted that the executions had been wrong or unwise. Theodore Roosevelt, for example, wrote:

> Two years ago Carson and the Ulstermen were openly talking of armed resistence to the Imperial Government, and some extremists among them were not obscurely hinting that they would under certain circumstances not look askance at a possible understanding with the Emperor of Germany. Under these circumstances I wish your people had not shot the leaders of the Irish rebels after they surrendered.[30]

In New York an Irish Relief Fund opened, with Thomas Addis Emmet as president, the three American cardinals as honorary presidents, and forty archbishops and bishops as patrons. In fact the open support of great numbers of American churchmen for a radical, and even revolutionary, settlement of the Irish question dated from this time. Redmond's programme was no longer adequate. President Wilson also provided valuable ammunition for an Irish-American agitation by his public proclamation of the principle of self-determination on 27 May.[31] Spring Rice wrote from the USA in June of the effect of the rising on American opinion:

> The attitude towards England is changed for the worse by recent events in Ireland. I think we might adopt a benevolent attitude towards the distribution of funds for the sufferers by the revolt. If we are able in some measure to settle the Home Rule question at once, the announcement will have a beneficial effect here, although I do not think that anything we could do would conciliate the Irish here. They have blood in their eyes when they look our way.[32]

General Maxwell, who had been given the unenviable task of quelling the disturbances in Ireland, dismissed Spring Rice's letter by arguing that although this Irish-American feeling would be bitter it was not a matter of great importance to either Britain

[29] Spring Rice to Foreign Secretary, 4 May 1916, *FO* 115/2073; Wittke, *op. cit.*, p. 281.

[30] Theodore Roosevelt to Arthur Lee, 7 June 1916, Morison, *op. cit.*, v. 8, p. 1054. See also Roosevelt to Plunkett, 9 July 1916, *Plunkett MSS*.

[31] Macardle, *op. cit.*, pp. 198–9. Arthur S.Link, *Wilson: Campaigns for Progressivism and Peace, 1916–1917*, Princeton, N.J.: Princeton University Press, 1965, p. 25.

[32] Spring Rice to Sir Edward Grey, 16 June 1916. S.Gwynn, *Spring Rice*, v. 2, p. 338.

or the United States.[33] Maxwell had shown some awareness of the need to stabilize public opinion in Ireland[34] but now he dangerously ignored the importance of the 'Greater Ireland' overseas. In the USA even the most sympathetic newspapers to the British cause were shocked by the image of savage repression.

Lloyd George, then Minister of Munitions, did recognize the importance of America in the Irish situation. 'The Irish-American vote', he is reported as saying of the forthcoming American elections, 'will go over to the German side. The Americans will break our blockade and force an ignominious peace on us, unless something is done even provisionally to satisfy America.' In the Cabinet both Balfour and Grey supported this view.[35] Asquith himself returned from an inspection of Ireland in May convinced that home rule had to be implemented, in some form, to satisfy the Irish and Lloyd George took on the impossible task of finding an acceptable formula. In July, after two months of confused negotiation, Redmond and the nationalists rejected his scheme which guaranteed the immediate application of home rule on condition that the six Ulster counties were excluded pending a new bill. The strong evidence that temporary exclusion would have become permanent was confirmed by a government bill introduced on 25 July which failed to gain acceptance.[36] Neither Irish nor American public opinion was influenced by this British gesture. On the contrary, the controversy surrounding Casement's trial eclipsed the home rule issue.

The Cabinet and General Maxwell held the belief that the rebellion would have been more widespread had Casement not been captured.[37] He was not only deemed guilty of treason, but was seen as the leader of the rising, and they were determined to put him on trial. Spring Rice warned against this from the very start, for in April, before any executions at all, he wrote:

The attitude of public opinion as to the Irish rebellion is on the

[33] General Maxwell to Asquith, 11 July 1916, *Asquith MSS.*, Box 37.

[34] *Ibid.*, 5 June 1916.

[35] Michael MacDonagh, *The Life of William O'Brien*, London: Ernest Benn, 1928, p. 225. See also Balfour to Grey, 29 May 1916, Link, *Wilson: Progressivism and Peace*, pp. 14–15; Cabinet minute by Asquith for the King, 27 June 1916, *CAB.* 41/37 (24).

[36] Denis R. Gwynn, *The History of Partition, 1912–1925*, Dublin: Brown and Nolan, 1950, pp. 144–57.

[37] Maxwell to Lord French, 13 May 1916, *Asquith MSS.*, Box 44; Maxwell to Asquith, 28 May 1916, *ibid.*, Box 37.

whole satisfactory. The press seems to be agreed that the movement is suicidal and in the interests of Germany alone. The attitude of the majority of the Irish is uncertain, but if the movement spreads the effect here will be very serious indeed. All are agreed that it will be dangerous to make Casement a martyr.

In May he added:

The great bulk of American public opinion, while it might excuse executions in hot blood, would very greatly regret an execution some time after the event. . . . It is far better to make Casement ridiculous than a martyr.

This astute advice was tendered at least a dozen times and was consistently ignored by Asquith and his colleagues.[38] On 29 June, before the Court of Kings Bench in London, Casement was found guilty and sentenced to martyrdom by death.[39] Prosecuting for the Crown was the Attorney General, Sir F.E.Smith, a leader of the Ulster Volunteers in 1914. As Casement pointed out in court, Ulster's leaders had taken the path to the woolsack, while he had taken a path he knew would lead to the dock. Smith must surely have been one of the 'Ulster rabble' listed for arrest in April 1914 before the government abandoned plans it had made to prosecute Ulster's leaders, but now he stood as prosecutor.[40] Casement represented the disintegration of both the Union and the Empire to him. The sentence was upheld on appeal on 18 July and the execution was set for 3 August, but during July the Cabinet was intensely concerned with the interest Casement had aroused at home and abroad. American newspapers had given a fair account of the trial and most of them accepted that treason had been technically proven, but the wisdom of pursuing the case through to a hanging was very much in dispute.

Irish-Americans were represented at the trial by M.F.Doyle, the Philadelphia lawyer, who travelled to England in June with $5,000 from the Clan na Gael to finance Casement's defence when an amount raised in England and Ireland proved inadequate.[41]

[38] Spring Rice to Grey, 28 April, 30 May 1916, Stephen Gwynn, *op. cit.,* v. 2, pp. 331, 335; *FO* 115/2073.

[39] For Casement's trial see Hyde, *op. cit., passim;* MacColl, *op. cit.,* pp. 227 ff.

[40] Discussed in letters and telegrams to and from Asquith, Birrell and Redmond in April 1914, *Asquith MSS.,* Box 41.

[41] Getrude Bannister, Casement's cousin, appealed to Devoy for money on 17 May 1916. *Devoy MSS.,* Box 10,607. Doyle's receipt for $5,000, 3 June 1916, is in *Maloney MSS.,* Box 12.

He assisted Casement's counsel, Serjeant A.M.Sullivan, and his solicitor, George Gavan Duffy. Doyle, however, was a good Democrat and a devout supporter of the President. He took the case because Mrs Agnes Newman, Casement's sister who had been in the USA since 1915, asked him to and he explained his action in a letter to Wilson's Secretary, Tumulty, in April. He had accepted, he wrote, on condition that Mrs Newman would avoid giving newspaper interviews and would keep herself free from any association with people 'disregarding the President's strict orders of neutrality'.[42] It was clear that Doyle was very wary of pro-German elements in the Irish-American ranks, but he nevertheless did carry Clan na Gael money for Casement's defence to England when he left in June.

Doyle did what he could, but in London Casement's defence was a confusing affair. Doyle preferred to plead the truth, that Casement had come to stop the rising, whilst G.B.Shaw, in whose house many of the meetings of the defence counsel were held, argued that Casement should plead not guilty to treason and demand to be held as a prisoner of war.[43] Casement himself refused to plead that he returned to stop the rising, for he believed he would weaken whatever benefit had accrued to Ireland from it, but in his interrogation, begun at Scotland Yard before he knew the rising had started and completed long before he knew it had failed, he quite frankly admitted that he saw it as a 'most hopeless enterprise' and had come to stop it. In court, however, his defence, at Sullivan's insistence, was almost exclusively based on a challenge to the prosecution's interpretation of the Treason Act of 1351. Casement did not enter the witness box to challenge the Attorney General's charges that he was a recent convert to Irish nationalism, that he had been associated with the *Aud* in a plot to land arms and that he planned to lead a rebellion, all of which were false.[44]

In the USA Agnes Newman began her campaign on behalf of her brother very soon after his capture. On 27 April, with the aid of Doyle, she saw the Acting Secretary of State, Polk, but was

---

[42] Michael F.Doyle to Joseph P.Tumulty, 29 April 1916, *Wilson MSS.*, Series VI, Box 520, File 3085.

[43] Doyle's report on the trial, 1 August 1916, *Devoy MSS.*, Box 10,607. See also G.B.Shaw, *The Matter with Ireland*, ed. D.H.Green and Dan H.Laurence, London: Rupert Hart-Davis, 1962, pp. 114 ff.

[44] Hyde, *op. cit.*, pp. xxxiii–xxxvi, lxxix–lxxxi.

told that the American government could do nothing. She later saw Spring Rice but there is no evidence that his advocacy of clemency owed anything to her pleas. On 20 April she addressed an emotional letter to the President, citing Casement's service to humanity as grounds for compassion. This did reach Wilson, who instructed Tumulty, 'We have no choice in a matter of this sort. It is absolutely necessary to say that I could take no action of any kind regarding it.'[45]

The State Department took the orthodox stand that the USA had no legal ground for intervention in British courts save in cases involving American citizens. As an act of courtesy the US Embassy in London was asked to give Doyle any assistance it could properly render him, but no official encouragement or sympathy was tendered to his cause.[46] Wilson did not compromise as pressure for clemency in Casement's case grew. In July Doyle wrote to Tumulty, 'John Redmond and Lord Northcliffe both told me the President's word would save [Casement],' but Wilson's instruction to Tumulty was unequivocal, 'It would be inexcusable for me to touch this. It would involve serious international embarrassment.'[47] He had similarly refused to intercede on behalf of four Bohemian national leaders sentenced to death by the Austro-Hungarian government.[48] One appeal which gave the administration something to think about was submitted in May by the San Francisco Knights of St Patrick, who supplied details of precedents where the government of the United States had intervened to plead for the lives of *foreigners* abroad. These ranged from Jefferson's appeal to France to release Lafayette in 1793 and Seward's appeal to Mexico in 1867 for clemency in the case of Emperor Maximillian, to the many representations made by the United States on behalf of the Jews in Russia.[49] Nevertheless Wilson took the view that there was no legal case for inter-

[45] Spring Rice to Foreign Secretary, 28 July 1916, telegram, *FO* 115/2073; Agnes Newman to Wilson, 30 April 1916, and Wilson to Tumulty, 2 May 1916, *Wilson MSS.*, Series VI, Box 520, File 3085.

[46] Frank Polk, State Department, to Tumulty, 2 June 1916, *ibid.*

[47] Doyle to Tumulty, 6 July, and Wilson's note, 20 July 1916, *Wilson MSS.*, Series VI, Box 520, File 3085.

[48] Discussed in *Wilson MSS.*, Series VI, Box 528, File 3271 'Bohemian Leaders'.

[49] The discussion on the Knights of St Patrick memo involving Wilson, Tumulty, Polk and Senator Phelan (California) is in *Wilson MSS.*, Series VI, Box 521, File 3152, 'Knights of St Patrick', and the *Polk MSS.*, Drawer 77, File 134, 'Ireland. Political Prisoners'.

vention, although he might from time to time make strictly informal approaches to the British. He told one visitor in July that it was well known in Britain that Americans were greatly interested in Casement's case and the feeling in Washington was that the sentence would be commuted.[50] Washington, or Wilson, was very wrong!

The United States Congress was less reticent than the President. For many years until 1916 Congress had shown only minor interest in Ireland. Resolutions of support for home rule had been introduced into the House of Representatives in 1908, 1909 and 1913 but these were not even discussed in committees and died. From the Easter rising onwards, however, the number of petitions and resolutions grew quickly. The 'martyrs' of 1916 certainly succeeded if their object was to act as a catalyst. Individual Senators and Congressmen began to take a greater interest in Ireland. Senator Borah, of Idaho, for example attacked the suppression of the Irish in a speech to the Senate in May and to constituents he explained that his concern was not with Britain's rights, but with her methods; 'Drumhead Courts are supposed to be out of date.'[51] In July he sent an appeal on behalf of Eamon De Valera, who was captured in the rising, to the State Department and received the reply, from Assistant Secretary of State Alvey A. Adee, that the Department had investigated this case after similar requests from other Members of Congress and had concluded that De Valera was convicted by court martial after a fair trial. Adee added that the fact of De Valera's possible American citizenship was no reason for clemency in his case.[52]

The suggestion has often been made that Eamon De Valera, though sentenced to death in May 1916, was saved because of his alleged American citizenship and the intervention of the US government, but there is no evidence for this. He was born in Brooklyn, New York, in 1882, the son of a Spanish born father and an Irish born mother, but when his father died in 1884 he was sent to Ireland to live with relatives. He was born an American but by not

---

[50] The visitor was a German-American, Franz H. Krebs, who sent a copy of his record of the interview to Tumulty, 7 July 1916, *Wilson MSS.*, Series VI, Box 520, File 3085.

[51] Senator William Borah, Idaho, to Edward R. Lewis, 20 May 1916, and to Jesse Hawley, 10 July 1916, *Borah MSS.*, Box 179.

[52] Alvey A. Adee to Borah, 11 July 1916, *ibid.*, Box 173.

living in the United States for a sufficient period as a minor he lost his American citizenship. His status was therefore unclear because he never applied for British citizenship.[53] He commanded a Dublin unit in the rising but was not a signatory to the proclamation issued in the name of the Provisional Government of the Irish Republic. However, neither were eight men who had already been executed before the death sentences passed on De Valera and Thomas Ashe were commuted on 10 May. After that date only James Connolly and Sean McDermott were executed and both had signed the proclamation. It seems, as Macardle claimed, that clemency was granted to all those still under sentence of death who had not signed the proclamation of the Provisional Government. This was probably the effect of a Cabinet decision, made on 5 May, that only 'ring leaders and proved murderers' should be executed.[54] There is on record an instruction from Sir Edward Grey, the Foreign Secretary, to the Irish military administration that United States or neutral citizens should not be executed without reference to the British government, but it was sent twelve days *after* De Valera's reprieve. The reply from Dublin was that the *only* US citizen court-martialled had been Jeremiah (Diarmuid) Lynch, who was not executed.[55] Lynch was a naturalized American who had returned to Ireland. There was no mention of De Valera, or of Thomas Clarke, although the latter had also become an American citizen. The general confusion of those immediate post-rebellion days must explain the poor state of information about the rising then available.

Senator Martine, Democrat of New Jersey, brought the US Senate into the Irish problem by introducing a controversial resolution. As debated on 22 July 1916, it read:

Whereas the Senate of the United States have heard with deep regret that the sentence of death has been pronounced upon Sir Roger Casement after a hasty (so-called) trial: Therefore be it *Resolved*, That the President of the United States be, and is hereby, requested to ask

[53] Gwynn, *De Valera*, pp. 21–2. In 1919 the British considered refusing De Valera re-admission from the USA because he was not a British subject. Curzon to Grey, telegram, 28 September 1919, *FO* 115/2514.

[54] Macardle, *op. cit.*, p. 193; Cabinet minute by Asquith for the King, 6 May 1916, *CAB*. 41/37 (19).

[55] Sir Eric Drummond to B.Carter, 22 May 1916, and J.Bryan (Richmond Barracks, Dublin) to B.Carter, n.d., *Asquith Mss.*, Box 37.

a stay in the execution of said sentence in order that new facts may be introduced.[56]

The only 'new fact' was that the Senate of the United States was taking an interest in the case. The Senate Foreign Relations Committee had to consider a number of other resolutions on this subject but on 29 July it reported the majority opinion that it was deemed inexpedient for the Senate to adopt any of the resolutions at that time, and that they would not accomplish their purpose. In the debate which followed Senator Phelan quoted the precedents supplied to Wilson by the Knights of St Patrick, and he added new information which cannot yet be verified. According to him, only three hours before the scheduled execution of Lynch, Senator O'Gorman of New York pointed out to the President that the condemned man was an American citizen and Wilson immediately sent a protest to the British. Lynch was not executed and was specifically mentioned in the letter from Ireland to Sir Edward Grey cited above. This claim by Phelan was certainly plausible, but another was less so. He claimed that two 'citizens of New York', Volera [*sic*] and Kilannan, were also saved as the result of the direct intervention of the President. As we saw above, this is highly unlikely.

On 29 July, Senator Pittman of Nevada introduced a resolution which read:

Resolved, That the Senate expresses the hope that the British Government may exercise clemency in the treatment of Irish political prisoners and that the President be requested to transmit this resolution to that Government.

This made no mention of Casement and the wording was comparatively mild, but there were still a number of Senators, of both parties, who opposed it. Senator Williams, Democrat of Mississippi, made it clear that the Foreign Relations Committee was in full agreement that Casement should not be executed, but was divided on the means of conveying this sentiment, and Senator Lodge added that the majority of the Committee felt that any resolution would do more harm than good for Casement. However, Pittman's resolution passed comfortably by a vote of 46 to 19, with 30 abstentions, and Martine's was dropped.

[56] The debates on Casement and clemency for Irish political prisoners discussed here are in US *Congressional Record*, 64 Cong., 1 Session, 1916, v. 53, pt. 11, pp. 11429 ff., and pt. 12, pp. 11773 ff.

The resolution was then forwarded to the White House where it was unaccountably held for several days before being sent on to the State Department for cabling to London. As a result it arrived a few hours after Casement's execution on 3 August. This proved embarrassing to the American government when Irish-Americans insisted that the delay had cost Casement his life. However, the Senate debate was not secret and the British were fully informed. The Acting Secretary of State, Polk, discussed the case with Ambassador Spring Rice several times before the Senate vote was taken, and in October, when the delay in the White House was still being investigated, he wrote to Tumulty:

The night before Sir Roger Casement was executed, Wednesday August 2, the British Ambassador read me a message from his Government in which it was stated that after considering the Casement case and the Senate resolution the British Cabinet had reached the conclusion that it could not grant clemency in this case.[57]

The British Cabinet's final discussion on Casement, a very long one, was indeed on 2 August when appeals were considered 'from authorities and friendly quarters in the United States'. American opinion probably figured as a factor in each of the Cabinet meetings at which the execution was discussed and there were at least five such discussions.[58]

On 2 September, Secretary of State Lansing reported that no official reply had yet been received from Britain concerning the resolution but on 28 August Grey had sent a long letter to Colonel House which included the following extract:

We are not favourably impressed by the action of the Senate in having passed a resolution about the Irish prisoners, though they have taken no notice of outrages in Belgium and massacres of Armenians. These latter were outrageous and unprovoked, whereas the only unprovoked thing in recent Irish affairs was the Rising itself which for a few days was a formidable danger. I enclose a short summary that was drawn up here as relevant to the Senate resolution though we have not yet sent it to the President. The natural question

[57] Polk to Tumulty, 5 October 1916. This and the rest of the extensive correspondence on the issue of the delay in the White House, involving Wilson, Tumulty, Lansing, Polk, Phelan, Doyle and others, is in *Wilson MSS.*, Series VI, Box 520, File 3085. See also *Foreign Relations*, 1916 Supplement, pp. 870–71; *Lansing MSS.*, v. 21.
[58] *CAB.* 41/37 (25, 26, 27, 28, 29). See also Roy Jenkins, *Asquith,* London: Collins, 1964, pp. 403–4.

on the action of the Senate is 'why if humanity is their motive do they ignore outrages in Belgium, etc.?'

The enclosed summary stated that the Irish rose without provocation at a time when Ireland was free of coercion and martial law, and that no one had been sentenced without proof of his responsibility for wanton and cruel bloodshed; 1,272 prisoners had already been released and a remaining 569 would be freed when this could be done without disturbance.[59]

No attempt was made to solicit American sympathy by publishing this letter, but even before his trial the British government had instigated a campaign to destroy any sympathy for Casement based upon his diaries. These were found soon after his arrest in trunks which he had left in London years before. They contained very detailed accounts of regular homosexual activities. René MacColl and H. Montgomery Hyde both discuss the authenticity of the diaries at length in their books on Casement and conclude, categorically, that they were Casement's. In addition, Serjeant A. M. Sullivan, Casement's Chief Counsel, in 1954 confirmed the fact that the Attorney General wanted Sullivan to use the diaries to support a defence plea of insanity. The government did not want to hang Casement, Sullivan said, in view of American feelings.[60] Thomas Artemus Jones, another of Casement's counsel, in a letter to W.J.M.A. Maloney in 1933, confirmed that the Attorney General had suggested a plea of guilty but insane and had offered photographic copies of the diaries for the defence.[61]

On 5 July the Cabinet submitted copies of the diaries for psychological analysis. Asquith himself recorded that a Cabinet split existed, with several, including Grey and Lansdowne, in favour of Casement's confinement in an asylum rather than allowing him to be considered a martyr in Ireland and America. When the psychologist's report arrived it confirmed that though abnormal, Casement was certainly not certifiably insane.[62]

Meanwhile, steps had already been taken to use the diaries to so discredit Casement in the eyes of his supporters that he could be

[59] Lansing to Tumulty, 2 September 1916, *Wilson MSS.*, Series VI, Box 520, File 3085; Grey to House, 28 August 1916, *House MSS.*, Drawer 9, File 8.
[60] MacColl, *op. cit.*, p. 228.
[61] Thomas Artemus Jones to W.J.M.A. Maloney, 4 March 1933, *Maloney MSS.*, Box 19. See also Hyde, *op. cit.*, p. lxvi.
[62] Cabinet minutes by Asquith for King, 5, 14 July 1916, *CAB.* 41/37 (25, 26); Jenkins, *op. cit.*, pp. 403–4.

disposed of with a minimum of protest. Ambassador Page was told of them and when, in early July, the State Department asked if the US government should transmit an appeal to the British government from Casement's sister, he replied:

I fear that a request made to the British Government in this matter will produce very disagreeable impression. Not only does Casement, a British subject, stand convicted of treason but I am privately informed that much information about him of an unspeakably filthy character was withheld from publicity. If the Government will permit me to deliver his sister's telegram they will permit Doyle. I respectfully suggest that she can send it to Doyle. Thus the same result will be accomplished and our Government will not become the channel of communication. If all the facts about Casement ever become public it will be well that our Government had nothing to do with him or his case.[63]

Whether this was the first the American government knew of Casement's diaries is unknown, although Spring Rice had been told on 10 May.[64] In any case Page's advice went unheeded. Mrs Newman's letter was sent to the US Embassy for transmission to the British government.

Through June, July and even into August, after the execution on the 3rd, copies of selected pages from the diaries found their way into a large number of British and American hands. Casement's character and his diaries were mentioned in the British press soon after his trial and early in June Captain, later Admiral, Hall of British Naval Intelligence showed copies of selected pages to American and British journalists.[65] In America the medical editor of the *New York Herald* was provided with typewritten copies of the diaries by, he claimed, the British Foreign Office, and no doubt other newspapers were also involved.[66] In fact Spring Rice requested copies on 19 July for his use in confidentially quashing sympathy for Casement.[67] The agent responsible for the dissemination of copies of selected pages from the diaries, both typed and photographed, in America was the British Naval

[63] Page to Lansing, 3 July 1916, *Wilson MSS.*, Box 520, Series VI, File 3085.

[64] Grey to Spring Rice, 10 May 1916, *FO* 115/2073; Spring Rice spread the news in a letter to W.Bourke Cockran, 14 May 1916, *Cockran MSS.*, Box 18.

[65] Hyde, *op. cit.*, pp. lxv, cxx; MacColl, *op. cit.*, pp. 289–90.

[66] James J.Walsh, formerly medical editor of the *New York Herald*, to W.J.M.A. Maloney, 3 August 1938, *Maloney MSS.*, Box 20.

[67] Spring Rice to Foreign Secretary, 19 and 20 July 1916, *FO* 115/2073.

Attaché, Guy Gaunt, and he continued for three weeks after Casement's death.[68]

The British continued to ply the US government with just-ifications for Casement's execution until it was done. On 1 August Page lunched with Asquith and made this note of the meeting:

One does not usually bring away much from [Asquith's] conversa-tions, and he did not say much today worth recording. But he showed a very eager interest in the Presidential campaign, and he confessed that he felt some anxiety about the anti-British feeling in the United States. This led him to tell me that he could not in good conscience interfere with Casement's execution in spite of the shoals of telegrams that he was receiving from the United States. This man, said he, visited Irish prisoners in German camps and tried to seduce them to take up arms against Great Britain – their own country. When they refused the Germans removed them to the worst places in their Empire and, as a result, some of them died. Then Casement came to Ireland in a German man-of-war (a submarine) accompanied by a ship loaded with guns. He spoke of the unmentionable Casement diary, which shows a degree of perversion and depravity without parallel in modern times. 'In all good conscience to my country and to my responsibilities I cannot interfere.' He hoped that thoughtful opinion in the United States would see this whole matter in a fair and just way.

Asquith then added, wrote Page, 'After any policy or plan is thought out on its merits my next thought always is how it may affect our relations with the United States. That is always a fundamental consideration.'[69]

The deliberate act of character assassination, quite irrelevant to the crime of treason, swayed very few people but it did create the myth of the 'forged diaries' to add to the case of the Piggot forgeries which were used against Parnell. This has figured in a number of books, and Yeats even enshrined it in verse.[70] On 4 August the London *Times* turned and attacked the attempt which had been made by the government to use the press to discredit Casement, and it seems incredible that the Cabinet, in view of its

---

[68] John Quinn to Patrick McCartan, 31 January 1919, *Maloney MSS.*, Box 21.

[69] Page memo, 1 August 1916, *Wilson MSS.*, Series II, Box 105.

[70] W.B. Yeats, *Collected Poems*, London: Macmillan, 1958, 'Roger Casement', pp. 351–2.

division on the Casement issue and its hours of anguished debate over his execution, should have authorized it. Nevertheless it is known that Sir Ernley Blackwell, Legal Adviser to the Home Office, recommended such a course in July, and the Cabinet must be held responsible.[71]

It was clear in July that, despite the campaign against Casement's character, some members of the Cabinet believed that he had in fact returned to stop the rising. Their resistance was broken by the presentation to the Cabinet, just a few days before the execution, of confidential papers intercepted between Casement and his solicitor, G.Gavin Duffy. These included the text of Casement's 'treaty' with the Germans from which the Cabinet learned that provision had been made for the Irish brigade to fight in the Middle East with Turkey if it became impossible to transport it to Ireland. There was also a damaging confession, or more properly a stupid piece of ego-mania, in which Casement swore that had he been younger the arms would have been landed, 'and I should have freed Ireland, or died fighting at the head of my men'.[72] This statement, quite contradicting the evidence now available and his own story under interrogation, the transcript of which was available to the Cabinet very early in May,[73] yet absolutely fitting the heroic role cast by Smith during the trial, was very likely the final nail in Casement's coffin.

That the Cabinet was divided is certain although on 19 July, five days after they had considered the psychological report, the Cabinet's decision to hang Casement was minuted as unanimous.[74] Mrs Asquith insisted that the 'damned old Tories' in the Cabinet were determined to use the case to attack her husband, no matter what the outcome,[75] and in his introduction to G.B.Shaw's *Discarded Defence of Roger Casement*, in 1922, Clement Shorter wrote, 'Shortly before Roger Casement was hanged I met Mr Edwin Montague, then Minister of Munitions, at a luncheon at the Savoy. He said, "I have an idea we shall hang Roger Casement and shall be sorry for it afterwards".' The British government was indeed to be sorry for having denied clemency. Casement was an

71 Hyde, *op. cit.*, pp. cxxi–cxxii.
72 *Ibid.*, pp. cxxii, cxxvii–cxxviii.
73 Printed Cabinet Document, May 1916. Sent to Spring Rice by Eric Drummond, 3 May 1916, *FO* 115/2073.
74 Cabinet Minute by Asquith for King, 19 July 1916, *CAB*. 41/37 (27).
75 Page memo, 1 August 1916, *Wilson MSS.*, Series II, Box 105.

unsuccessful eccentric who was distrusted by both the Germans and his erstwhile Irish-American allies. By his trial and execution he became a martyr to the Irish who were hitherto almost totally unaware of his existence. In February 1965 his remains were belatedly transferred to a martyr's grave in Ireland, but from the year of the rising and his execution, the tide turned ever increasingly against the British, in Ireland and Irish-America.

6 The United States on the Eve of War

'Fighting for the Allies would be fighting for the combined subjection of Ireland, India and Egypt to English rule.'

IRISH-AMERICAN CONFERENCE RESOLUTION,
NEW YORK, FEBRUARY 1917

The Irish revolutionary movement mustered far fewer followers in America than the United Irish League until World War I produced a dramatic change. In October 1915, leaders of the Clan na Gael began to organize an 'Irish Race Convention' and when this was held the following March approximately two thousand representatives of Irish-American organizations attended. From the meeting emerged a new organization, the Friends of Irish Freedom, proposed by Robert Ford of the *Irish World*, seconded by John Devoy of the *Gaelic American*, supported by the Ancient Order of Hibernians, and dominated by members of the Clan na Gael. Its task was greatly simplified by the almost total collapse of the United Irish League of America. From now on the Clan operated largely through this new organization, although it retained its separate identity. It was the Clan's own Revolutionary Directory, for example, which handled the Irish-American contribution to the Easter rising in 1916. In the hands of John Devoy, Daniel Cohalan, and the Clan na Gael, the Friends of Irish Freedom became the most efficient and effective propaganda and activist organization in Irish-American history. Its declaration of principles attacked the 'Anglo-Saxon' myth, expressed loyalty to America, attacked Britain's garrison in Ireland, and argued that a free Ireland would mean freedom of the seas. It alleged that not only had Britain violated American rights during the war but that the British were poised for an attack on the USA! The organization stood for an embargo on food and military supplies to the belligerents and the denial of US protection to Americans travelling on belligerent ships.[1]

The Friends grew quickly after the suppression of the Easter rising. Many protest meetings were held which drew attention to Ireland's case. One, in Carnegie Hall, was addressed by Bainbridge Colby, a Roosevelt Progressive in 1912 who later became Wilson's Secretary of State. His attack was sharp. The 'votive offering' of fifteen Irish lives on the altar of liberty, he argued, had doubled or trebled the number of Irishmen in the world; Irishmen not of birth, perhaps, but Irishmen in principle and sympathy.[2] Colby's own stand on the rising was unequivocal, but he was wary of the direction that Irish protests were taking. A few days after this meeting, on 20 May 1916, he wrote to Cohalan on the subject of an Irish-American protest committee:

> The accounts in this morning's papers of the Hoboken meeting last night rekindle all the doubts I have expressed to you as to the advisability of my becoming a member of the committee – at least for the present.
>
> The fact that German speakers were on the program, that the band from the German steamship 'Vaterland' furnished the music, and that the German national anthem was received with what one of the papers described as 'a joy that became almost delirious!' is discouraging to one, who, like myself, feels that the attempt to marshall America's deep sympathy for the principle of liberty and the right of every nation to self-government, will be compromised if the cause of Ireland is confused in the public mind with the hyper-zeal of the German propagandists among our citizens. The principle of genuine home rule in Ireland deserves recognition for its own sake, and not as a mere implement for the service of German hostility to England, inevitable as that feeling doubtless is among those of German extraction.[3]

Colby's suspicion was justified for, until the USA entered the war, the new sympathy for Ireland felt by Irish-Americans, and a great many other Americans, was turned at every opportunity into opposition to Britain and her cause. 'The Dublin executions,'

---

[1] Tansill, *op. cit.*, pp. 188–90; Devoy, *op. cit.*, Ch. LX; Great Britain, *Documents re. Sinn Fein*, p. 9. The president, composer Victor Herbert, secretary, treasurer, three vice-presidents, fifteen of the seventeen on the Executive and thirty-seven of the fifty-two directors, were members of the Clan na Gael.

[2] Extract from Colby's speech, 14 May 1916, *Colby MSS.*, Box 8.

[3] Bainbridge Colby to Daniel Cohalan, 20 May 1916, *Colby MSS.*, Box 2.

reported the *New Republic*, 'have done more to drive America back to isolation than any other event since the war began.'[4]

Irish-Americans were certainly very active in this period. The widow, Mrs Sheehy Skeffington, was in the USA for eighteen months from December 1916 lecturing to them on British militarism in Ireland.[5] The Friends of Irish Freedom published pamphlets arguing that Britain's defeat was necessary before any final Irish settlement, while Jeremiah O'Leary's American Truth Society kept up the propaganda in articles, meetings, and through such subsidiaries as the United Food Society of New York, which campaigned for a food embargo on belligerents. The Ancient Order of Hibernians at its national convention in Boston, in July 1916, congratulated Germany on its war effort and expressed the belief that Germany would be the liberator and defender of small nations.[6] In January 1917 a new American Sinn Fein organization was launched from the offices of the Friends of Irish Freedom with a varied collection of officers, including John and Jeremiah O'Leary of the American Truth Society, Peter Golden, Dennis Spellissy and John D. Moore of the Friends of Irish Freedom, Robert Monteith, then in the USA having evaded capture in Ireland, and James Larkin, the founder of the Irish Citizen Army, also then living in America. On 4 and 5 February 1917, a national conference of twelve hundred or so Sinn Fein supporters met in New York under the chairmanship of Cohalan and offered this advice to America:

> Fighting for the success of the Allies would be fighting for the combined subjection of Ireland, India and Egypt to English rule. It would be a war against America as well as against Germany and keep Ireland, whose sons fought for America in their way, under the heel of England.[7]

Of more direct embarrassment to the British government was the Irish Relief Fund established in New York to supply money to those who had suffered from the suppression of the rising. By July 1916, $50,000 had already been raised for relief and more was to follow.[8] That month the British government detained the fund

[4] Quoted in Link, *Wilson: Progressivism and Peace*, p. 14.
[5] She met Wilson in January 1918, *New York Times*, 12 January 1918.
[6] *Boston Herald*, 22 July 1916.
[7] Great Britain, *Documents re. Sinn Fein*, pp. 27–8.
[8] *Gaelic American*, 29 July 1916.

treasurer, Thomas Hughes Kelly, his wife, and an assistant, Joseph Smith, in Liverpool on their way to Ireland with a large sum of money. President Wilson and the State Department soon came to know of the anger this provoked in the USA when they received appeals from Cardinal Farley of New York, Mayor Curley of Boston, and many others.[9] On 26 July, the Acting Secretary of State, Polk, instructed the London Embassy to investigate the case and to help Kelly and Smith. He claimed that Kelly had never been connected with Irish politics, was a trustee of St Patrick's Cathedral, and, presumably referring to the three honorary presidents of the fund, that he was a friend of three American cardinals.[10] But the British certainly knew that Kelly was national treasurer of the Friends of Irish Freedom. They had also discovered a printed invitation to a dinner for Smith, signed by Mayor Curley, who had claimed that Smith had been selected by the Friends of Irish Freedom to distribute relief funds and gather data on the rebellion. Finally, they had probably already intercepted a message, which they published in 1921, from von Bernstorff to the German Foreign Office dated 14 July 1916. This discussed the reorganization of the revolutionary forces in Ireland and money which had been sent from the United States for this purpose. It also said, 'In the near future, the Committee here will proceed to Ireland, taking with them the money which has been collected for the poor, and will then be in a position to get more accurate information.' From this it seems clear that Kelly and his companions were involved in Irish politics and were, if not carrying money for revolutionary purposes, certainly prepared to gather information on the revolutionary scene in Ireland. Efforts to induce the British to admit them failed and they returned to the USA in August. However another party, comprising John Archdeacon Murphy of Buffalo, and John Gill, President of the Bricklayers' Union, was admitted to Ireland with relief funds.[11]

Irish-American and German co-operation continued in 1916 despite the failure of the rising and the capture of incriminating documents in the raid on von Igel's office. In fact, for reasons

9 *Wilson MSS.*, Series VI, Box 521, File 3152.

10 Frank Polk to American Embassy, London, 26 July 1916, *Polk MSS.*, Drawer 77, File 133.

11 Circular signed by Curley, n.d. and Grey to Spring Rice, 24 July 1916, *FO* 115/2073; Great Britain, *Documents re. Sinn Fein*, pp. 16–17.

which will be examined in the next chapter, von Igel was free to continue much as before. In August 1916 von Bernstorff reported the following in a message to his government which was intercepted by the British:

Von Igel and von Skal ... keep up relations with the Indians and Irish respectively since von Papen left. The consul general asked me not to expose him in this respect to any risk of being compromised in view of his instructions from you. For that reason von Papen [the Military Attaché] took the business on himself and then transferred it to von Igel. Von Skal maintains relations with the Irish, for which he has special qualifications in his many relationships in those circles and has their complete confidence.[12]

In September and December 1916 the Irish Revolutionary Directory in America again asked the Germans to land arms and men in Ireland, and the German government did offer arms to be landed in the west of Ireland in February or March. They went as far as to send the codes for the operation to America, but in January their proposition was rejected by the Irish-Americans who argued, probably on instructions from Ireland, that without German troops a rising would fail. The British learned of the plans very early in February and any landing would certainly have been intercepted efficiently this time.[13]

In December 1916, before the German offer of arms was made, Wilson asked the belligerents to state their peace terms. The German government complied but von Bernstorff reported to them that the Irish felt deserted by Germany's proposals for a peace conference because Irish independence was not a German condition for a settlement.[14] The German offer of arms, whether sincere or not, was probably the German government's way of expressing its support to the Irish privately, without having to make a public commitment to a peace settlement acceptable to Ireland. Von Bernstorff was not satisfied with this and on 22 January 1917 he cabled the following to his government:

I request authority to pay out up to $50,000 in order, as on former occasions, to influence Congress through the organization you know,

12 *Ibid.*, p. 21.
13 *Ibid.*, pp. 22–3, 26–8.
14 At its meeting in Boston, 20 December 1916, the executive council of the Friends of Irish Freedom demanded that Germany should declare its position on Irish independence, *ibid.*, pp. 25–6.

which can perhaps prevent war [probably the Friends of Peace]. I am beginning in the meantime to act accordingly. In the above circumstances a public German official declaration in favour of Ireland is highly desirable in order to gain the support of Irish influence here.[15]

An opportunity to help Ireland came very quickly. That same day, 22 January, Wilson addressed the US Senate on the subject of 'Peace Without Victory', and on 31 January von Bernstorff wrote to the Secretary of State that the German government agreed with most of Wilson's suggested war aims. He added, however:

> These principles especially include self-government and equality of rights for all nations. Germany would be sincerely glad if in recognition of this principle countries like Ireland and India, which do not enjoy the benefits of political independence, should now obtain their freedom.

He aimed another dart at Britain, one equally consistent with Wilson's declared principles, when he wrote of Germany's support for the freedom of the seas. This message lost all its impact, however, for attached to it were two memoranda detailing German arrangements for the resumption of unrestricted submarine attacks on shipping, both belligerent and neutral, supplying the Entente powers. Within days the USA had broken diplomatic relations with Germany and war was certain.[16] This naturally helped the British, although they lost a valuable chance to win further American approval. On 21 December 1916, the War Cabinet decided to release all Irish political prisoners, giving two reasons. First, they recognized that failure to do this earlier had been largely responsible for the defeat of conscription proposals in the 1916 Australian referendum by a campaign organized by Irish-Australians. Secondly, in view of Wilson's peace note, they wanted to impress on America that the British government was determined to settle the Irish question. For some reason this important decision was not implemented.[17] Prisoners were held until June 1917.

The President and government of the United States struggled with the wartime problem of ethnic minorities long before the

15 *Ibid.*, p. 27.
16 *Foreign Relations*, 1917, Supplement 1, pp. 97–102. Wilson's 22 January speech to Congress is pp. 24–9.
17 War Cabinet Meeting 14, 21 December 1916, *CAB.* 23/1. See also Meeting 24 (11), 1 January 1917, *ibid.*

USA became a belligerent and their problem did not end with the declaration of war on 6 April 1917. Britain was to be no more popular with Irish-Americans as an ally than before. In March 1917 Arthur Balfour, the Foreign Secretary, asked Ambassador Page why the British were so unpopular in the USA and was told, simply, 'It is the organized Irish. Then it's the effect of the very fact that the Irish question is not settled.'[18] Spring Rice expected the Irish question to make a considerable impression on Wilson and he wrote, in April 1917:

> The Irish party are of very great importance at the present moment. The question is one which is at the root of most of our troubles with the United States. The fact that the Irish question is still unsettled is continually quoted against us, as a proof that it is not wholly true that the fight is one for the sanctity of engagements or the independence of small nations. The President is by descent an Orangeman and by education a Presbyterian. But he is the leader of the Democratic party in which the Irish play a prominent part, and he is bound in every way to give consideration to their demands.[19]

There is no evidence that Wilson thought in these terms about Irish-American Democrats and there is little evidence of an organized Irish lobby working through the Democratic Party. Spring Rice was thinking in the categories of the 1880s when Cleveland, for example, was forced to yield to the Irish, whereas Wilson's personal attack on hyphenated Americans was unrestrained by considerations that he would offend the Irish and hence damage his party. On the contrary, he divided the Irish into two, the 'loyal', whom he refused to court by crude attacks on the British, and the 'disloyal' whose support he positively shunned. His attitude brought him into conflict with Irish-American leaders in the 1916 Presidential election.

Before the National Democratic Party Convention began in June 1916, Tumulty warned Wilson that the issue of the 'hyphen' would be critical and advised the President to take a firm stand. The Secretary of the Interior, Lane, backed Tumulty, arguing that the quicker the government could attack what he argued was the German-American dominance over the Republican Party,

18 Page memorandum, 27 March 1917, Burton J.Hendrick, *The Life and Letters of Walter H.Page*, London: William Heinemann, 1924, part II, p. 251.
19 Sir Cecil Spring Rice to Lord Robert Cecil, 13 April 1917, S.Gwynn, *Spring Rice*, v. 2, p. 393.

the better.[20] On 17 June, the *New York World* headlined its Democratic Convention article of that day, 'Democrats adopt anti-hyphen issue: adjourn sure of a Wilson victory,' and an editorial commended the platform for its 'Americanism'. The foreign-born were not mentioned in the Democratic platform, but its message was clear.

> The Democratic party ... summons all men of whatever origin or creed who would count themselves Americans, to join in making clear to all the world the unity and consequent power of America. This is an issue of patriotism.... Whoever, actuated by the purpose to promote the interest of a foreign power, in disregard of our own country's welfare or to injure this Government in its foreign relations or cripple or destroy its industries at home, and whoever by arousing prejudices of a racial, religious or other nature creates discord and strife among our people so as to obstruct the wholesome process of unification, is faithless to the trust which the privileges of citizenship repose in him and is disloyal to his country.... We charge that such conspiracies among a limited number exist and have been instigated for the purpose of advancing the interests of foreign countries and to the prejudice and detriment of our own country.

On the other hand the Republican platform was sufficiently ambiguous in its espousal of an 'honest neutrality' to appeal to many pro-Germans as the lesser evil. If many extremist Irish-Americans were annoyed at the anti-hyphensim of the Democrats' platform there was still something to appeal to them in it. Spring Rice made the point that the Allies would surely look with suspicion at a programme which, by espousing freedom of the seas, would cripple British sea power and, by applying the principle of national self-determination, would recognize Irish and Polish independence.[21]

The National German-American Alliance supported Charles Evans Hughes, the Supreme Court Justice and former governor of New York State, who was the Republican candidate for President. In November 1915 Theodore Roosevelt had written that he could not run for the office because too many Irish and German-Americans, pacifists and 'mollycoddles' were against

[20] Joseph Tumulty to Wilson, 13 June 1916, and Franklin K.Lane to Wilson, n.d. *Tumulty MSS.*, Box 1.

[21] Spring Rice to Sir Edward Grey, 16 June 1916, S.Gwynn, *Spring Rice*, v. 2, pp. 337–8.

him.[22] Of course, Roosevelt was not a candidate for other reasons too. He had, after all, bolted the Republican Party in 1912, but the groups he mentioned were certainly not a negligible factor in the opposition to his candidacy. In fact a German-American newspaper delegation visited the Republican national chairman and issued an ultimatum against Roosevelt or Senator Elihu Root for the Republican nomination because of their support for the Entente powers.[23] Louis Hammerling, who was at that time in the pay of the German government, handled the foreign-language newspaper advertising for the Republican National Committee in 1916 as he had in 1908 and 1912.[24] Although Hughes was not pro-German he courted German-Americans whenever he could during his campaign. How to do this, while at the same time retaining the support of Roosevelt and the many Republicans who had come to distrust hyphenated Americans, was a sophisticated exercise in political agility.

Hughes was balancing on a tightrope. In 1912 either the Republican Taft or Roosevelt the Progressive could probably have beaten Wilson, had one of them withdrawn, and Hughes now needed the support of the Progressives if he was to think of winning. Roosevelt's position on military preparedness, Americanism and, at least implicitly, the hyphen, had to be respected in some way. Roosevelt was prepared to meet Hughes half-way because of his contempt for Wilson and in June 1916 he declared his support for Hughes. In his reply to the endorsement of the Progressive National Committee, Hughes declared in favour of all-round military preparedness, and added:

> We strongly denounce the use of our soil as a base for alien intrigues, for conspiracies and the fomenting of disorders in the interests of any foreign Nation, but the responsibility lies at the door of the Administration.[25]

In the context of Roosevelt's position, this was an attack on German and Irish-American conspiracies, and it was wishful thinking on their part to suppose that it referred to the British. Ambassador von Bernstorff certainly disassociated himself from

[22] Roosevelt to Lodge, 27 November 1915, Morison, *op. cit.*, vol. 8, pp. 991–2.
[23] Child, *op. cit.*, Ch. VI, 'The Election of 1916'.
[24] Park, *op. cit.*, pp. 380 ff.
[25] Charles Evans Hughes to O.K.Davis, Secretary, Progressive National Committee, 26 June 1916. *Hughes MSS.*, Box 3B.

any support for the Republican Party because of Roosevelt. In early October he reported that a Wilson victory looked likely despite the combined opposition of German-Americans, Irish-Americans, and Roosevelt. He himself could find no evidence to suggest that Hughes would be better for Germany than Wilson. 'As all pacifists are on the side of Wilson,' he wrote, 'I should myself prefer to see him elected. It is moreover doubtful whether Mr Hughes will succeed in shaking off the influence of Mr Roosevelt.'[26]

One can only suppose that over the previous two years German-American agitators had gone too far in their campaign against Wilson's brand of 'neutrality' for them to change course at this stage, to vote Democratic and adopt von Bernstorff's view. Furthermore, the extreme Irish were not interested in mediation or compromise, which was what the Ambassador wanted. They were interested only in the defeat of Great Britain, and if the USA had maintained a strict neutrality, by their definition, and had traded with neither side, this might have come about. Wilson, the Democrat, had failed in their eyes and of the potential Republican nominees Hughes was the least pro-ally, and the least disposed to intervene in Europe. Patrick McCartan wrote that the weight of the Friends of Irish Freedom organization and its fifty directors throughout the USA was thrown behind Hughes, but this was contradicted in another account by John J.Splain, National Vice-President of the organization. There was no general Irish-American campaign to defeat Wilson, he wrote, and although there was widespread suspicion of the President there was even more suspicion of Hughes and Roosevelt.[27] This latter view was probably correct, for the Friends of Irish Freedom organization was as yet still young and unable to command its followers. It gained its maximum strength when the war ended. In 1916 the candidates were relatively undifferentiated from an Irish viewpoint. The *bulk* of the Irish were traditionally Democratic and they preferred to remain so.

[26] Von Bernstorff to German Foreign Office, Berlin, 5 October 1916, intercepted by the British and sent to Wilson by Page, 3 December 1917, *Wilson MSS.*, Series II, Box 131. See also von Bernstorff, *op. cit.*, pp. 256–7.

[27] Patrick McCartan, *With de Valera in America*, Dublin: Fitzpatrick, 1932, p. 17; John J.Splain, 'The Irish Movement in the United States since 1911', in William G.Fitz-Gerald, ed., *The Voice of Ireland*, London: John Heywood, 1924, p. 229.

Many of the leading members of the Friends of Irish Freedom in later years, people like F.P.Walsh, Governor Edward Dunne of Illinois, and Justice Victor Dowling of the New York Supreme Court, were supporters of Wilson in 1916. Bainbridge Colby, a friend and spokesman for Irish causes, chose, as a Progressive, to campaign for Wilson rather than Hughes, and, as Link demonstrates, the great majority of the Progressive leadership did likewise.[28] There were Irish-Americans like Daniel O'Connell, long active in California, who chose not to desert the Democratic Party but initially tried to nominate W.J.Bryan before accepting the choice of the party.[29] Bryan also campaigned for Wilson and thereby legitimized the President in many critical eyes, reinforcing the favourable impression made by the new 'hard line' both Wilson and Congress were taking in regard to British violations of American rights. Bryan himself suggested that he should campaign in German-American areas, and he spoke widely in the West.[30] Wilson had been in conflict with a number of Democrats, Senators and Congressmen, over neutrality, men such as Senator Gore and Representative McLemore who were unsympathetic to any special relationship with Britain or the Entente. Their support for the party, its platform, and implicitly for Wilson's leadership assisted in his re-election.

What is clear is that the now familiar leaders of the extremist Irish-American faction were opposed to Wilson – the leaders of the Clan na Gael, the United Irish Societies, O'Leary and the American Truth Society, the leaders of the Ancient Order of Hibernians, plus the *Gaelic American* and the *Irish World*. Wilson did not want their support. His attacks on un-American hyphenism in 1915 and 1916 were directed at such people. When Jeremiah O'Leary attacked Wilson for 'truckling to the British Empire' and threatened that large numbers of voters would desert him, the President replied:

Your telegram received. I would feel deeply mortified to have you or anybody like you vote for me. Since you have access to many

[28] Link, *Wilson: Progressivism and Peace*, pp. 124–6.
[29] William Jennings Bryan to Daniel O'Connell, 17 March 1916, *Bryan MSS.*, Box 31.
[30] Bryan to John Burke, US Treasury Department, 14 August 1916, in Burke to Tumulty, n.d., *Wilson MSS.*, Series vi, Box 491, File 2400.

disloyal Americans and I have not I will ask you to convey this message to them.[31]

Wilson was, of course, supported and encouraged by his Irish-American Secretary, Tumulty, in his Americanism and in these attacks on the Irish, but that is not to imply that Tumulty was hostile to Ireland. Far from it. The problem, as he discussed it with Lansing, was how to help Ireland without offending the British or encouraging people he held to be disloyal to America. He felt that Ireland had more to gain from Wilson than from Germany and he believed that Ireland would gain from the general campaign for the independence of small nations.[32]

Very late in the campaign Hughes was trapped on the hyphenate issue when the Democratic National Committee published reports that at a secret meeting between Hughes and members of the American Independence Conference, representing German and Irish-Americans, Hughes had agreed to attack Britain's embargo policies. In fact the meeting, with Jeremiah O'Leary and three others, did take place, but there is no indication that Hughes agreed to any 'deal'. Rather his outspoken opposition to British infringements of American shipping rights and his seemingly more 'aggressive' neutrality satisfied the delegation, while Wilson's position did not. However, the Democrats had issued three statements on the subject in as many days by 25 October and Hughes was forced to reply that his would be an 'American administration' and that alien intrigues and divided allegiances would not be tolerated in America.[33]

When the results of the election were in, Wilson had defeated Hughes by 9,129,606 votes to 8,538,221 and 277 electoral college votes to 254. He had done extraordinarily well to increase his vote by almost three million since 1912, and had won convincingly in the west, from Kansas to the Pacific, where physical and psychological isolation lent support to his plea that he 'kept us out of war'. Wilson was clearly the 'peace' candidate and this

[31] O'Leary, *op. cit.*, pp. 45–6.

[32] Tumulty to Robert Lansing, 19 and 20 April 1917, *Lansing MSS.*, Vols 26, 27.

[33] Link, *Wilson: Progressivism and Peace*, pp. 137–9. The issue was discussed in a memo drawn up by Henry C. Beerits in 1933–4, under the supervision of Hughes, 'The Presidential Campaign of 1916', *Hughes MSS.*, Box 168. Apart from this, scarcely a trace of the campaign remains in the heavily edited Hughes papers.

certainly helped him, for the returns to the House of Representatives, where Republicans gained a majority, showed that Democratic Congressmen, fighting on local issues, were having less success than the President. In any case the election at all levels was a very complex one. In Indiana, for example, one writer has described the following issues in the campaign – the war, higher taxes from 'progressive' legislation, business opposition to regulatory laws and to tariff cuts, prohibition, and Mexico. Indiana Democrats lost nine of the eleven seats they held in the previous Congress and German districts showed marked swings to the Republicans. A Republican ousted the Indiana Democratic Senator. Overall, however in the Presidential vote for a state which Wilson won in 1912 but lost in 1916, the Democratic proportion of the total vote *grew* from 43 per cent to 46.5 per cent. This pattern of Democratic gains was very widespread.[34]

When one looks closely at some of the data available the difficulty of making claims, particularly that the Irish deserted the Democrats, becomes clear. The Republicans took New York, Massachusetts, New Jersey and Pennsylvania, all states with large Irish populations, but the Democratic proportion of the total vote in each grew, by from 1.5 per cent in New Jersey to 11 per cent in Massachusetts. Similar patterns emerge in counties with large Irish, and often German-American, populations, for example New Haven County, Kings County (Brooklyn, New York), Philadelphia County, and Providence County, Rhode Island. Democratic gains in these ranged from 4 per cent to 9 per cent. In some Irish areas the Democrats lost, notably in Cook County (Chicago) where their proportion of the total vote fell dramatically from 46.6 per cent to 22.1 per cent, and in New York City as a whole, which voted for Wilson, his majority fell below what was normal for a Democrat. The British Consul General, Broderick, attributed this in large part to the German and Irish-American campaigns, although he was impressed by the general nation-wide failure of Irish-American leaders to guide their

[34] Cedric C.Cummins, *Indiana Public Opinion and the World War, 1914–1917*. Indianapolis: Indiana Historical Bureau, 1945, pp. 208 ff. Voting figures are taken from Edgar Robinson, *The Presidential Vote, 1896–1932*, London: Oxford University Press, 1934. Demographic characteristics were determined from information supplied in US Department of Commerce, Bureau of the Census, *Fourteenth Census of the United States taken in the Year 1920*, Vol. II, 'Population, 1920', Chapters VI, VII, IX.

flocks away from the Democrats.[35] However, Broderick failed to note that the Republican vote also fell in New York City and Wilson's proportion of the vote there was the highest for any Democrat since 1896.

Using both county and ward statistics for selected areas with large Irish-American populations, William M.Leary concluded that, in general, the higher the percentage of Irish in an area, the higher the Democratic proportion of the vote. Unfortunately he made no analysis of the redistribution of the large Progressive Party vote of 1912 or to the voting behaviour of German-Americans who very often exceeded the number of Irish-Americans in high density Irish areas. How far Progressives voted with the Democrats to offset possible Irish and German defections from the Democratic Party is unknown, although in any case German-Americans were traditionally more closely identified with the Republican Party. What emerges from the available election data, however, is the clear impression that there was no dramatic swing away from Wilson in the majority of areas with large Irish populations. On the contrary, neither his anti-hyphenism nor his policies of neutrality and peace appeared to damage him seriously at the polls. Leary concluded, 'Although it is necessary to speculate about the reasons why Irish-Americans voted for Wilson, one thing is clear: they responded to American issues and not to those of Ireland.' He suggests that the American issues were Wilson's economic and social policies, and his commitment to peace.[36] But the most compelling explanation must be the role of the Irish-American politicians in local Democratic politics. Their interests, power, patronage, and careers depended on turning out a vote for the Democratic candidate, not for Ireland, and they did this in 1916 as they had so many times before. It is not that the Democrats gave up any hope of capturing the Irish vote, as Leary suggests, but rather that they took the 'loyal' Irish vote for granted and therefore did not mount the special campaign to secure it which he seems to have expected. Irish-American 'leaders', that is those in the forefront of the campaign for Irish independence, cannot be equated with

35 Memo by Consul General Broderick, New York, 19 January 1917, enclosed in Spring Rice to Foreign Secretary, 22 January 1917, *FO* 115/2244.
36 William M.Leary, Jr., 'Woodrow Wilson, Irish Americans, and the Election of 1916,' *Journal of American History*, v. LIV, No. 1, June 1967, pp. 57–72.

Irish-Democratic politicians. These latter were not primarily interested in Ireland or in American foreign policy. They were concerned with political power which they were able to protect by delivering the Irish vote.

In his comments on the election results, Consul General Broderick warned that although the Irish-American press and the leaders of the Clan na Gael *et al.* had not been able to determine how the Irish would vote in 1916, almost all of the Irish in America followed the lead of these people in their general attitudes towards Britain and could be relied on to support any anti-British movement. In fact, the election results aside, in 1916 Irish-Americans were organizing a very active anti-British propaganda which was going to be the most powerful in Irish-American history. Their failure to influence the 1916 presidential election must certainly not be interpreted as evidence of impotency.

7 The United States Enters the War, 1917–18

*'If the people of the United States could feel that there
was an early prospect of the establishment for Ireland
of substantial self-government a very great element of
satisfaction and enthusiasm would be added to the
co-operation now about to be organized between
this country and Great Britain.'*

WOODROW WILSON TO DAVID LLOYD GEORGE,
10 APRIL 1917

The Irish in America fought long and hard against US entry into
World War I. John O'Dea, the historian of the Ancient Order of
Hibernians, recorded, 'The tide of events swept the United States
into war on the side of England in spite of the most strenuous
exertions of the Irish citizens to prevent it.' Writing only of
Indiana, but in fact reflecting a much broader picture, another
writer concluded that Irish-Americans were second only to
German-Americans in their opposition to the war. Only in the
last days of peace did they change their tactics and begin to
argue for an independent American war against Germany.
The United States severed diplomatic relations with Germany
on 3 February 1917, and by 6 April had become a belligerent
power.[1]

Ireland had become very popular in the USA in 1916 but when
war was declared the *Gaelic American* was only saved by the
donations of friends, so quickly did support and subscriptions
decline.[2] Irish-Americans now had two objectives to pursue.
Since the war was being fought for America's defence and for
American interests, their loyalty to America had to be un-
questioned. But secondly, they sought to have Irish independence

[1] O'Dea, *op. cit.*, v. 3, p. 1493; Cummins, *op. cit.*, *passim*.
[2] Wittke, *op. cit.*, pp. 279–80.

made a condition of the peace settlement. These two objects, involving loyalty both to America and Ireland, were not thought to be contradictory and Daniel Cohalan and others supported the policy at the 1917 New York commemoration of the Easter rising.[3] The Friends of Irish Freedom organized a petition with an alleged 500,000 American signatures, pleading that Ireland should be treated as one of the small nations for whom the President had said the United States was fighting. In California Irish Freedom stamps were sold for a dollar bearing Wilson's own phrase, 'We shall fight for the rights and liberties of small nations.'[4] Americanism and Irish freedom were thus blended.

Lord Northcliffe, who was in the USA for the British government from June to November 1917, detected overt Irish-American hostility to Britain and wrote in September, 'There is no German propaganda against the French. The whole Irish and German propaganda is to the effect that we are getting all the money and are doing little of the work.' This was also T.P.O'Connor's view in July, soon after he began his most difficult tour of America in the face of fierce Irish-American opposition.[5] Northcliffe is reported to have told Sir Horace Plunkett in January 1918, 'I wanted copper – Thomas F.Ryan [an Irish-American industrialist] gave me cigars a foot long but no copper until the Irish question is settled.'[6] There was also evidence that some at least of the Irish in America were conspiring with Germany during the war. Patrick McCartan became the American envoy of the 'Provisional Government of Ireland' in the summer of 1917 and he and Liam Mellowes, who escaped to America after the Easter rising, were involved in negotiating a new Irish rebellion with the Germans. McCartan was actually *en route* to Stockholm in October 1917 for consultations with the German government when he was arrested in Halifax, Nova Scotia, travelling on a false passport, and was returned to the USA. Mellowes was

[3] *New York Times*, 9 April 1917.

[4] Petition enclosed in John D.Moore, National Secretary, FOIF, to Tumulty, 25 June 1917. *Wilson MSS.*, Series VI, Box 558, File 3926. See also Circular letter from Rev. A.Anderson, San Francisco, 15 August 1917, *ibid.*, Box 520, File 3926.

[5] Charles Seymour, *The Intimate Papers of Colonel House*, London: Ernest Benn, 1926–8, v. 3, p. 96; T.P.O'Connor to Lloyd George enclosed in Spring Rice to Foreign Secretary, 13 July 1917, *FO* 115/2244.

[6] Margaret Digby, *Horace Plunkett, An Anglo-American Irishman*, Oxford: Basil Blackwell, 1949, p. 231.

arrested in New York as he was planning to leave for Ireland on a forged passport.[7]

In Berlin, in February 1917, the Irish-American T.St John Gaffney was one of the founders of a German-Irish Society which had three hundred members by December 1917. It published a monthly journal, *Irische Blatter*, and Gaffney and the Secretary, George Chatterton-Hall, represented the Irish case at the International Socialist Peace Conference in Stockholm in June 1917. However, the Society seems to have performed only a publicity, and not a conspiratorial function. The Germans, in fact, were peculiarly inept at this kind of conspiracy. There were, in Berlin, representatives of a host of disaffected 'nations', each an Achilles heel to the Allies – Algerians, Egyptians, Indians, Flemings, Finns, and so on – but one has the impression that Germany distrusted revolutionaries and certainly failed to understand or exploit them.[8] Nationalism was, of course, a dangerous commodity to her ally, Austria-Hungary.

In the United States the majority of Irish-Americans tried to make their loyalty demonstrably clear. The Ancient Order of Hibernians, for example, at its biennial National Convention in 1918, attacked the treason and sedition 'which is currently being openly conducted under the guise of Irish patriotism'.[9] On 2 February 1918 the *Literary Digest* in an article, 'Where Irish-Americans Stand in the War', reviewed a large section of the Irish-American press and found it to be largely opposed to any Sinn Fein interference with Britain's conduct of the war, though there were exceptions, including the *Gaelic American* and the *Irish World*, which supported Sinn Fein. When the Second Irish Race Convention, organized by the Friends of Irish Freedom met in New York in May 1918 it was strongly tempered with moderation, despite the election as National Secretary of Diarmuid Lynch, a Sinn Fein deportee from Ireland whose death sentence in 1916 had been commuted. Radical resolutions were defeated and Cohalan took the side of the moderates. He closed the convention with an address which emphasized the true Americanism of the Irish race in America.[10]

[7] Great Britain, *Documents re. Sinn Fein*, pp. 27–8.

[8] *Ibid.*, pp. 9. 29, 38, 56–8; Gaffney, *op. cit.*, p. 195 and Ch. xix, 'The Stockholm International Peace Conference (1917) and the Irish Question'.

[9] Wittke, *op. cit.*, p. 285.

[10] Tansill, *op. cit.*, pp. 270–2; Wittke, *op, cit.*, p. 287.

Despite their new policy of caution, the Irish and German-Americans had to face a wave of ultra-Americanism when the USA entered the war. Perhaps German-Americans invited accusations of disloyalty. They had been overconfident and bellicose in the years before 1917; their highly organized campaigns for American neutrality and for embargoes on arms and loans had contrasted very markedly with the gentle, but more persuasive, British propaganda. In addition, the American government had encouraged Americanism and anti-hyphenism as an antidote to the potential fragmentation of the American population caused by the war in Europe. In 1915, 4 July was celebrated as Americanization Day with a special appeal to the foreign-born, but having encouraged Americanism it was difficult to stop it getting out of hand. For example, anti-hyphen sentiment was used by Congress to override Wilson's veto of literacy test provisions which had been written into the US immigration legislation passed in February 1917, and in 1918 when the Senate decided to investigate the activities of the National German-American Alliance, it did so with a conspicuous lack of objectivity. No attempt was made to distinguish between pro-German propaganda which preceded US entry into the war and German-American loyalty to the United States which followed that decision. One-seventh of all American schools, in fourteen states, dropped the teaching of the German language as groups dedicated to Americanism campaigned with evangelical fervour and unmitigated bigotry.[11] Leading them all was the American Defense Society, whose Honorary President from January 1918, Theodore Roosevelt, had always insisted in the past that it was wrong to judge people solely by the accident of birth. Now his attacks on 'professional' German-Americans, and his suggestions that leading Irish-Americans should be interned as enemy aliens, provided grist for the bigots' mills.[12] German-Americans kept very quiet and apologists or spokesmen for their loyalty were few.

The test of disloyalty, Irish or German-American, was arrests and charges for sedition or treason, and there were remarkably

[11] Higham, *op. cit.*, pp. 203, 208; Child, *op. cit.*, Ch. vii, 'The Decline and Fall of the Alliance'. Wilson was disturbed by this extreme reaction to German-Americans. See *Wilson MSS.*, Series vi, Box 572, File 4182.

[12] *New York Times*, 26 May 1918.

few of these. The German government was implicated, and its employees sentenced, for organizing Indian revolutionary activities from America, but charges against American citizens were rare.[13] The US government was far more concerned with the spread of anarchist and socialist ideas and journals than of Irish and German-American activities, and a list, dated 8 May 1918, of forty-four publications whose second class mail privileges had been withdrawn after hearings concerning violations of the Espionage Laws contained only one 'Irish' journal, *Bull*, banned in August 1917. This was a journal founded by Jeremiah O'Leary, of the American Truth Society, which he subsequently suspended in October 1917 although its circulation had grown, he claimed, to 48,000.[14] The *Gaelic American, Irish World,* and *Freeman's Journal* were far less suspect than *Bull* but were all banned from the mails at times later in the war for attacks on America's ally, Britain. The *Gaelic American* finally lost its second class mail privilege for the remainder of the war in September 1918 after it had published a notice urging 'Citizens of the Irish Republic' to register with representatives of the Irish 'Provisional Government', but the paper was not barred until the British and American governments had consulted together and discounted any really adverse consequences from public opinion.[15]

Questions of sedition arose from time to time over public meetings but were still very rare. Patrick McCartan, himself engaged in revolutionary conspiracy, later wrote, 'The Irish were the only element in the United States that persisted throughout the War in holding meetings not in furtherance of it.'[16] But of course the line between legitimate attacks on British policy in Ireland and harmful attacks on the entire Allied war effort was very difficult to draw. The American Defense Society held that

[13] Jones and Hollister, *op. cit.,* Ch. xvi, 'Hindu-German Conspiracies'; *von Igel MSS, Foreign Relations, 1917,* Supplement 1, pp. 579–85; Great Britain, *Report of the Committee Appointed to Investigate Revolutionary Conspiracies in India,* 1918, Cd. 9190, viii, 423, Ch. vii, 'German Plots'.

[14] *Burleson MSS.,* v. 20. See also US Department of Justice, *Classified World War One Records,* particularly Class 9–12–0, 'Critical Publications', National Archives. See also O'Leary, *op. cit.,* pp. 35–6, 49, and Park, *op. cit.,* pp. 433 ff.

[15] Wittke, *op. cit.,* pp. 284–5. The Anglo-American discussions are described in William Wiseman to Col. Arthur Murray, 19 September 1918, *Wiseman MSS.,* Drawer 91, File 107; Lansing to British Chargé Barclay, 28 October 1918, *FO* 115/2398.

[16] McCarton, *op. cit.,* p. 41.

Irish-American meetings on street corners in New York were seditious, while the Friends of Irish Freedom hotly denied this. In fact, the only prominent Irish-American to be prosecuted for sedition was Jeremiah O'Leary, but he absconded on bail and when he was finally brought to trial in 1919 only the bail charge had any real meaning.[17]

Wilson abhorred Irish-American 'disloyalty' but he would not be drawn out in detail on his attitude to Ireland either before or after the USA became a belligerent in April 1917. He formally acknowledged most of the appeals for Irish freedom which reached him but to some appellants, if they were influential, and if they were known to be sympathetic to his administration, he would add a private and non-commital note. To John D. Crimmins of New York, for example, it read, 'Confidentially (for I beg that you will be careful not to speak of or intimate this) I have been doing a number of things about this which I hope may bear fruit.' This was attached to a more formal reply signed by Tumulty, but virtually dictated by the President, which said, 'Let me assure you of the President's keen interest in this matter, and of the fact, that, in every way he properly can, he is showing his sympathy with the claims of Ireland for Home Rule.'[18]Tumulty's letter found its way into the *New York World* on 12 May 1917, probably with his approval, but had Wilson in fact tried to do anything for Ireland? There is evidence that he had.

When the United States entered the war Wilson immediately recognized that Ireland would be a major barrier to efficient and effective co-operation with the British. On 10 April 1917, therefore, he personally typed the following message to Lansing:

My dear Mr. Secretary,

The recent debates on the war resolution in Congress leads me to suggest that you send the following confidential message to Ambassador Page in London:

Take an early opportunity in conversation with the Prime Minister to convey to him in the most confidential manner the information that

[17] Cleveland Moffett, American Defense Society, to Wilson, 16 August 1917, and John D.Moore, FOIF to Wilson, 17 August 1917. Attorney General Gregory to Wilson, 22 August 1917, argued that there were no federal statutes to cover street corner oratory of this kind at the time. Amendments to the Espionage Act were made in 1918 to limit freedom of expression. *Wilson MSS.*, Series VI, Box 575, File 4244. See also O'Leary, *op. cit.*, pp. 73 ff.

[18] Tumulty to John D.Crimmins, 5 May 1917. *Tumulty MSS.*, Box 2.

the only circumstance which seems now to stand in the way of an absolutely cordial co-operation with Great Britain by practically all Americans who are not influenced by ties of blood directly associating them with Germany is the failure so far to find a satisfactory method of self-government for Ireland. This appeared very strikingly in the recent debates in Congress upon the war resolution and appeared in the speeches of opponents of that resolution who were not themselves Irishmen or representatives of constituencies in which Irish voters were influential, notably several members from the South. If the people of the United States could feel that there was an early prospect of the establishment for Ireland of substantial self-government a very great element of satisfaction and enthusiasm would be added to the co-operation now about to be organised between this country and Great Britain. Convey this information unofficially of course but as having no little significance. Successful action now would absolutely divorce our citizens of Irish birth and sympathy from the German sympathisers here with whom many of these have been inclined to make common cause.

Page now knows the Prime Minister well enough to know how to say these things to him frankly, and if a way could be found now to grant Ireland what she has so often been promised, it would be felt that the real program of government by the consent of the governed has been adopted everywhere in the anti-Prussian world.

A telegram was sent to Page to this effect on 11 April and in his reply to Lansing on 18 April he described his discussion with David Lloyd George, who had become Prime Minister in December 1916:

> I took up this subject in a confidential conversation with the Prime Minister at my house last night. He instantly understood and showed me that he already knew the facts that I presented and was glad that the President had instructed me to bring the subject up. He had had the American situation in mind during the whole discussion of home rule and he was doing his best. Then he asked me to request the President to give his views to Mr Balfour as soon as possible after his arrival. Our country has no better English friend than Mr Balfour and he belongs to the party that before the war opposed home rule. The enlistment of his influence would be a great help and the Prime Minister feels sure of a good result of a frank explanation to him by the President. I am on my own account, without mentioning the President's instructions expressed [*sic*] my private opinion to the same effect to other influential members of the Government.

This was Page's formal reply through the State Department, but in his report to Wilson he presented a more intimate version of the interview:

> A little while ago [Lloyd George] dined with me, and after dinner I took him to a corner of the drawing room and delivered your message to him about Ireland. 'God knows I'm trying. Tell the President that. And tell him to talk to Balfour.' Presently he broke out – 'Madmen, madmen – I never saw any such task,' and he pointed across the room to Sir Edward Carson, his First Lord of the Admiralty – 'madmen. But the President's right. We've got to settle it and we've got to settle it now.' Carson and Jellicoe came across the room and sat down with us. 'I've been telling the Ambassador, Carson, that we've got to settle the Irish question now – in spite of you.'[19]

Balfour, the new British Foreign Secretary, arrived in the USA late in April to discuss Anglo-American co-operation in the war and with particular instructions to report to the War Cabinet on the importance of the Irish question in the United States.[20] When Balfour saw Secretary of State Lansing he was told that although there existed a traditional American hostility to Britain, the effect of the Irish question on American opinion was the more significant cause of the current hostility.[21] Sir Horace Plunkett, who was then in America, also arranged for Balfour to meet a group of Irish-Americans on 3 May. These were all moderates in the Irish cause, committed to home rule, and firm supporters of Wilson's war policy; the former New York Supreme Court Judge, Morgan O'Brien, Colonel Robert Temple Emmet of New York, the former mayor of Boston and former US Congressman, John F. Fitzgerald, grandfather of President Kennedy, John Quinn, a New York lawyer, and Lawrence Godkin, a well-known journalist. Plunkett wrote later, 'I warned [Balfour] against pulverising these men who would no doubt display ignorance.' A long unsigned memorandum in Plunkett's papers describes the two-hour meeting. The Irish-Americans stressed that Americans would not accept partition as a solution to the Irish problem and they explained that Redmond's support in America had dwindled

[19] Wilson to Lansing, 10 April 1917, Page to Lansing, telegram, 18 April 1917, 'Confidential for the President', *State Department*, 841d. 00/103, 105a, 106; Page to Wilson, 4 May 1917, *Wilson MSS.*, Series II, Box 118.

[20] War Cabinet meeting 116, (23), 10 April 1917, *CAB.* 23/2.

[21] Robert Lansing, *War Memoirs*, New York; Bobbs-Merrill, 1935, p. 277.

owing to the repeated postponements of home rule. Balfour, in his turn, was sympathetic. He understood, he said, the importance of Ireland in Anglo-American relations, but he stressed the very real problem of forcing home rule upon a loyal Ulster in the middle of the war.[22] Of course the most active and successful Irish-American agitators, those behind the Clan na Gael and the Friends of Irish Freedom, were not present at the meeting and condemned the constitutional road to home rule as a sham. It is improbable that Balfour appreciated the importance and strength of their dissent when he cabled to the Cabinet on 5 May, 'The [Irish] question is apparently the only difficulty we have to face here, and its settlement would no doubt greatly facilitate the vigorous and lasting co-operation of the United States Government in the war.'[23] This was exactly the sense of Wilson's message on 10 April.

It was clear that Balfour had been told very seriously that an Irish solution, more than any other factor, would remove barriers to effective Anglo-American co-operation in the war and at a speech in the Guildhall on 27 April Lloyd George supported this view. His words prompted a cablegram from 140 members of Congress who confirmed that nothing would produce greater enthusiasm for the war in America than freedom for Ireland in accordance with Wilson's principle of respect for the rights of small nations.[24] Lloyd George could not have been more aware, then, of the state of official American thought on Ireland when, in May, he announced the decision to call an Irish convention at which parties to the Irish dispute could meet to hammer out a formula acceptable to them all. The War Cabinet took the first step in this direction on 22 March but it took two months to work out the details. The decision had been taken because overseas opinion was important in the effective conduct of the war, because Liberal and Labour members of the coalition government were anxious for an immediate home rule settlement, and because the government wanted to gain the full support of the eighty Irish nationalists still sitting in Parliament. Which of these was the most

[22] Unsigned memo, 2 June 1917, *Plunkett MSS.*, File in 'MA.–O'; Digby, *op. cit.*, p. 205.
[23] Balfour to Lord Robert Cecil for Lloyd George, 5 May 1917, *FO* 115/2244. For a summary of the press reaction to Balfour's mission see, 'Ireland a War Factor', *Literary Digest*, 12 May 1917, v. 54. p. 1400.
[24] US *Congressional Record*, 65 Cong., 1 Session, v. 55, Appendix, p. 161.

important consideration is impossible to say, but none of them was insignificant.[25]

Lloyd George had no positive Irish policy in mind and could see no way out of the morass but he knew that the proposed Irish convention could serve him in three ways. First, though most improbably, it might discover an acceptable solution. Secondly and more probably, it might improve Britain's image overseas, particularly in the USA. Later he argued for the benefit of Americans that the Irish had been given the opportunity of self-determination at this convention and had failed to accept it. Both the *Irish World* and the *Gaelic American* interpreted this another way. To them the convention was designed to force Irishmen into responsibility for England's failure to keep her word to Ireland. Thirdly, of course, a convention, particularly one held in secret, could effectively place the Irish question and its associated problems at home and overseas 'on ice' for six months or more even if it failed. Lloyd George knew of Redmond's opposition to partition, he knew the terms of the only temporarily suspended 1914 home rule act which provided for a *united* Ireland, and he knew of the inflexible opposition of Ulster to anything but partition. His own efforts in 1916 had met with failure so what could this convention really have done other than provide breathing space? The Chairman, Sir Horace Plunkett, was nevertheless optimistic. For him, the most important reason for a settlement was the state of Anglo-American relations. Like Colonel House and a number of his other correspondents, he had hopes of a new age of world order led by an Anglo-American alliance dedicated to peace. Ireland, of course, barred the way to such a plan by preventing Anglo-American co-operation but Plunkett believed a reasonable Irish settlement was possible.[26]

The Irish convention first met in July 1917 and in June De Valera and others still imprisoned or detained from the Easter rising were released to create a favourable atmosphere in Ireland.[27]

[25] War Cabinet 101 (1 and 2), 22 March 1917 and other meetings in *CAB*. 23/2; Trevor Wilson, *The Downfall of the Liberal Party, 1914–1935*, London: Collins, 1966, pp. 107–8.

[26] See Digby, *op. cit.*, Ch. VIII, 'America and the War of 1914–1918'. Digby, primarily using Plunkett's papers, overstates his influence, but illustrates his character and motivation.

[27] War Cabinet meeting 143 (2) 22 May 1917 and 145 (11) 24 May 1917, *CAB*. 23/2. The Irish convention is discussed in Digby, *op. cit.*, pp. 218–38, and D. Gwynn, *Partition*, Ch. VI.

The released men immediately wrote to Wilson and to the US Congress. They quoted Wilson's own message to the new provisional government of Russia which had said, 'No people must be forced under a sovereignty under which it does not wish to live,' and they claimed this right for Ireland. Frank Polk of the State Department supported Wilson's own inclination by advising, 'I think the best thing to do would be to file the papers and not reply,' and no reply was sent.[28]

Sinn Fein and its newly released leaders had no intention of co-operating with the convention and although the Irish Parliamentary Party was represented, it was still smarting from the government's policy of consistently yielding to Ulster's pressure. Redmond himself argued that the convention was designed simply to pacify Ireland during the war and he had already appealed directly to the USA and the Dominions to see that the principle of self-determination was applied to Ireland.[29] William O'Brien claimed that the convention was rigged in favour of partition and refused to participate.[30] It was, moreover, absolutely clear that Lloyd George would have to refuse both nationalist and Sinn Fein claims for an undivided Ireland if his coalition was to survive, because Ulster, and consequently the Unionists, had to be satisfied. In March 1918 the convention predictably collapsed in the face of Sinn Fein's non-participation, Ulster's absolute refusal to compromise on its exclusion from home rule, and the nationalists' refusal to be intimidated by Ulster into concessions.

The American government, at the President's own request, was continuously informed of the progress of the convention, or, more correctly, of Plunkett's optimistic view of it. Plunkett's secret reports to the King were sent to Wilson and House but if the Americans accepted the reports at their face value they were seriously misled. For example, Plunkett insisted in April 1918 that a Dominion form of home rule for a united Ireland, his own plan, had been virtually accepted when, in fact, both Sinn Fein and Ulster were utterly opposed to it.[31] The fact that Plunkett's

[28] Great Britain, *Documents re. Sinn Fein*, pp. 30–3; Frank Polk to Tumulty, 8 August 1917, *Wilson MSS.*, Series VI, Box 558, File 3926.

[29] Digby, *op. cit.*, p. 228; John Redmond to Mayor John Mitchel, New York, n.d. (received 25 April 1917) *Mitchel MSS*, Box 12.

[30] William O'Brien to Moreton Frewen in Frewen to Plunkett, 25 June 1917, *Plunkett MSS*.

[31] Plunkett to House, 26 April 1918, *Plunkett MSS*.

scheme was published in April as the majority report of the convention was irrelevant.

Although Wilson was very interested in an Irish settlement he maintained his attack on 'disloyal' Irish-Americans who were, in fact, those identified with Sinn Fein in Ireland. He had already savagely attacked them in the 1916 presidential election campaign, but he saved his most telling ammunition until September 1917 when the facts concerning the von Igel raid of April 1916, discussed in Chapter 5, were released to the US public at a time and in a manner deliberately calculated to wreck Irish-American activity during the war. The day following the raid Devoy had commented on the captured papers in the double-talk often used by the Irish when communicating with each other, 'We were very anxious for a whole day, but when the firemen got through with their work of salvage we found we had no cause for worry.'[32] His conclusion was completely unwarranted, given the evidence now available.

The raid took place on Tuesday, 18 April 1916, six days before the Easter rising began, and initially the American government took a strong line. Lansing refused to return the captured documents when the Germans insisted on von Igel's diplomatic immunity, and from a survey of them Leland Harrison of the State Department concluded that the German government was aware of Indian revolutionary plots in America, that orders to assist these plots had been issued from the German Foreign Office via the German Embassy and German consulates in New York and San Francisco, that large payments had been made to the Indians, that Germany was also assisting in a planned Irish rebellion, and that communications with Irish revolutionaries were made possible through the German Embassy in Washington. It appeared, therefore, that the German Ambassador and his staff had either violated US neutrality statutes or had been implicated in such violations. There was certainly enough evidence, Harrison concluded, to render them *personae non gratae*. He added that the papers concerning the Irish revolution were not to be published.[33] He gave no reason for this but press publicity would certainly have harmed German interests and Wilson had

[32] Devoy to McGarrity, 19 April 1916, *Maloney MSS.*, Box 16.
[33] Memo signed 'H', n.d., *Von Igel MSS.*; *Foreign Relations*, 1916, Supplement, pp. 807–15; *Foreign Relations: The Lansing Papers, 1914–1920*, v. 1, pp. 95–9.

already recognized by 23 April, when he wrote to Lansing, that it would be possible to argue that the USA had begun to co-operate with the Allies.[34] However, the British Embassy was supplied with details from the raid before 23 April, when Spring Rice cabled them to London, and some news did leak out in America. On Easter Monday the *New York Evening Post* reported that the raid on von Igel's office, which had been reported in most newspapers, had revealed German involvement in a conspiracy concerning a rising in Ireland, but it gave no details. A few days later the press carried a statement by John Devoy that the American government had betrayed information discovered in the von Igel papers to the British and that this had led to the capture of Casement. Lansing vigorously denied this on 28 April. Again the public was denied details although the State Department would not deny that there was Irish material in the captured papers and assorted federal officials said this was so.[35] The von Igel case remained in this state until September 1917. Having begun in a threatening way and having declared that von Igel would be prosecuted, the United States postponed his arraignment and any diplomatic reprisal it had originally planned against Germany. In August 1916 von Bernstorff advised his government that it was in Germany's interest not to raise the question with the American government until after the presidential election. Germany could not afford to have its activities in the United States become an election issue, but in the meantime von Igel and von Skal, another German implicated by the captured documents, continued their work with the Indian and Irish revolutionaries. Von Bernstorff warned that this could only continue if US-German relations were smooth, 'The authorities would not hesitate to attack any member of the Embassy, if internal politics rendered it desirable.'[36]

Ambassador Dumba and others had already been expelled for un-neutral activities in America, but the key to the exceptional developments in the von Igel case was the precarious balance in US-German relations in 1916. The von Igel raid had been launched on the day of the final American note concerning the *Sussex* case

[34] Wilson to Lansing, 23 April 1916, *ibid.*, pp. 98–9.
[35] *New York Times*, 27, 28 April 1916.
[36] Bernstorff to German Foreign Office, 26 August 1916, *Harrison MSS.*, Box 106, File M.22, 'Intrigue of Bernstorff'.

and unrestricted German submarine warfare and it supplied the USA with an important weapon in that context. In the note Wilson issued a clear ultimatum that the USA would sever diplomatic relations with Germany if the submarine campaign was not abandoned. Publication of the captured documents would, as the Germans well knew, have strengthened the anti-German forces in America during the tense days of these negotiations. On 4 May the Germans yielded to American demands that German attacks on unarmed merchant shipping should cease and on 14 May Bernstorff told House that Germany would welcome the USA as a mediator in the war if a period of quiet was first allowed and if each government would stop nagging the other. He mentioned the still unresolved *Lusitania* and von Igel disputes as cases in point.[37] An explanatory letter from Lansing to the US Attorney General, Gregory, in September 1916 made it clear that the United States wanted to avoid a diplomatic rupture with Germany and that the von Igel papers should not be published.[38]

For nine months following the submarine settlement in May 1916 United States tension with Germany eased and Americans were able to focus on the deteriorating state of Anglo-American relations where several things stood out. Wilson summarized them in a letter to House on 16 May:

> The at least temporary removal of the acute German question has concentrated attention here on the altogether indefensible course Great Britain is pursuing with regard to trade to and from neutral ports and her quite intolerable interception of mails on the high seas carried by neutral ships. Recently there has been added the great shock opinion in this country has received from the course of the British Government towards some of the Irish rebels.[39]

The British went from bad to worse. On 18 July they published a blacklist of eighty-five American persons and firms having dealings with the Central Powers with whom British citizens were forbidden to trade. Wilson termed this 'the last straw', and considered prohibiting loans and restricting exports to the Allies. A

---

[37] House to Wilson, 14 May 1916, *Wilson MSS.*, Series II, Box 97; *Foreign Relations, 1916*, Supplement, pp. 232–4; Link, *Wilson: Confusion and Crises, passim*.

[38] Lansing to Attorney General Thomas W. Gregory, 21 September 1916, *Lansing MSS.*, v. 21.

[39] Link, *Wilson: Progressivism and Peace*, pp. 20–1.

very strong note was sent condemning the arbitrary interference with neutral trade.[40] On 8 August Bernstorff was able to report to Berlin that American feelings towards Germany were notably more friendly as a result of the blacklist and the execution of Roger Casement.[41]

The US government had never wanted to clash with Britain but in October Bernstorff correctly observed, 'If peace does not take place serious Anglo-American differences are to be expected.' He forecast that Wilson would make new peace overtures after the November elections in an attempt to offset this problem, and Wilson did exactly as forecast.[42] On 18 December he asked the belligerents for their peace terms and on 22 January 1917 outlined his proposed peace conditions and the League of Nations in a speech before the Senate. He advised the belligerents to accept a 'peace without victory', a course totally unacceptable to the Allies, but on 31 January the Germans solved the problem of the growing Anglo-American discord by resuming unrestricted submarine warfare; America was on the road to war.

Not until the USA had been in the war for several months were the von Igel papers published, and then they were used to attack not the Germans but the Irish, particularly Judge Cohalan and John Devoy. These two were arch conspirators but had been conspicuous by their patience and restraint since the USA entered the war and had not been associated with sedition or with any public activity which could be seen as harmful to American interests. The Committee on Public Information released copy for publication on Sunday, 23 September 1917, under the heading, 'German Intrigue in America. Official Exposé.'[43] It described the von Igel raid and the seizure of documents which proved that German officials in America had violated US laws, had engaged in sabotage of merchant shipping, had assisted Irish revolutionary plots, had financed propaganda, had maintained a spy system under commercial covers, and had fomented industrial unrest. Messages sent by John Devoy to Germany dated 8 and 15 April, and the telegram sent by von Skal on behalf of Cohalan were reported without any embellishments. There was no mention of

[40] Wilson to House, 23, 27 July 1916, *R.S.Baker MSS.*, Series 1, Box 7.

[41] Bernstorff to German Foreign Office, 8 August 1916, intercepted by Britain and enclosed in Page to Wilson, 3 December 1917, *Wilson MSS.*, Series II, Box 131.

[42] *Ibid.*, 20 October 1916.

[43] A copy of the press release is in *von Igel MSS.*

the German collaboration with Indian nationalists which was actually documented far more fully than the Irish conspiracy in the seized documents. Nothing was done to detract from the government's attack on the Irish and, as anticipated, the story was big news. As a typical example, the *Denver Post* of 23 September published in bold type:

Daniel F.Cohalan charged with Being Go-Between in Sir Roger Casement Conspiracy, the funds for which were Handled Thru the German Embassy – Every Neutrality Law Violated in Friendly Country.

No attempt was made to explain that the Irish plot had preceded the American entry into the war by almost a year or to account for the sixteen-month delay in publishing the records.

The American government had no intention of charging Cohalan or Devoy with any offence and instead the revelations became ammunition in the general campaign against disloyalty and hyphenism. Sir William Wiseman, then in New York acting for the British government, wrote:

The whole incident has created an excellent impression as far as we are concerned. It was the biggest newspaper sensation since the [Zimmerman] note, and I think it has been particularly useful to us in two ways – one, it has helped the President and his administration by silencing the criticism that he was too hard on the Germans because they really meant no harm to the American people. Second, it has helped to make the pro-Germans and their activities here very unpopular.[44]

To stir up the brew still further, the British government, with the approval of the State Department, supplied the *New York World*, which had savagely attacked Cohalan day after day since the revelations, with a copy of a message it had intercepted between von Bernstorff and the German Foreign Office. In it von Bernstorff suggested that at the Vatican Germany should support Daniel Cohalan's clerical cousin of the same name for the vacant bishopric of Cork.[45] This letter was published on 4 October and two days later a *World* editorial tied it to Cohalan's message on the rising as evidence of his conspiracy with Germany, al-

[44] William Wiseman to unknown (probably House), 7 October 1917, *Wiseman MSS.*, Drawer 90, File 64.
[45] *Ibid.*

though the two incidents were four months apart and were quite unconnected.

The British hoped to offset the gains Sinn Fein was making in the USA. Richard Hazleton, MP, then in the USA with T.P. O'Connor rather unsuccessfully soliciting funds for the Irish Parliamentary Party, expressed the hope that the von Igel revelations would restrain Sinn Fein activity in America and assist his mission because, as Hazleton noted, money 'was never so much needed or so hard to get'. In fact, as O'Connor observed in December, Sinn Fein did come increasingly under attack and his own position improved considerably as he received numerous invitations to speak, though very little money.[46]

In Ireland the growth of Sinn Fein was demonstrated in July 1917 when Eamon de Valera contested the East Clare seat formerly held by Capt. William Redmond, who had been killed in action. He won by a two to one majority over the nationalist candidate, and refused to take his seat.[47] Other Sinn Fein election successes followed in 1918. In October 1917 De Valera was elected President of Sinn Fein with Arthur Griffith, the founder, as Vice-President, and plans were laid for the organization of quasi-government departments for military, political, educational, financial and foreign affairs. Sinn Fein's intention was to follow the classic campaign proposed long before by Griffith, to render English rule in Ireland impotent by establishing a *de facto* Irish government. The Irish Volunteers were also re-organized, again under De Valera's presidency, so that the 'Republic' had its own army.[48]

The next crisis in Ireland came in April 1918, following the collapse of the Irish convention, when Lloyd George announced that conscription was to be extended to Ireland, a move which Irish revolutionaries had anticipated with relish for many years. The O'Rahilly, who was killed in the rising, had written to Devoy in November 1914, 'When conscription comes, as it will, you will hear from us,' and in November 1915, Joseph McGarrity had

---

[46] Hazleton to Shane Leslie, 26 September 1917, *Cockran MSS.*, Box 18; O'Connor to John Redmond, 22 December 1917. Intercepted by the British censor and a copy sent to Spring Rice by the Foreign Office, 22 December 1917, *FO* 115/2244.

[47] D.Gwynn, *De Valera*, pp. 47–8. Joseph McGuiness, when in Lewes Prison, had already won the Longford by-election for Sinn Fein, *ibid.*, p. 44.

[48] *Ibid.*, pp. 51–2; Great Britain, *Documents re. Sinn Fein*, pp. 36–8, 47–55.

written to Casement, 'I pray for conscription as I believe that will start the fight in Ireland.'[49]

In February 1917, Lord Riddell recorded a conversation in which Lloyd George expressed very clearly the problems he then associated with conscription:

The soldiers say to me 'It is your business to find the men.' I have said to them, 'Show me where the men can be got without sacrificing other essentials.' They say, amongst other things, 'Apply conscription to Ireland.' What would be the result? Scenes in the House of Commons, a possible rupture with America, which is hanging in the balance, and serious disaffection in Canada, Australia and South Africa, They would say, 'You are fighting for the freedom of nationalities. What right have you to take this little nation by the ears and drag it into the war against its will?' If you passed the act you would only get 160,000 men. You could only get them at the point of the bayonet, and a conscientious objection clause would exempt by far the greatest number. As it is these men are producing food which we badly need. The soldiers will not see that.[50]

These problems still existed in April 1918 when the government, desperate for men, under pressure from the military and Unionists, and convinced that the exemption of Ireland would mean a breach of faith with those already or about to be drafted elsewhere, decided on Irish conscription in the full knowledge that this could provoke civil war. All the advice from Ireland, from Lord Wimborne, the Lord Lieutenant, H.E.Duke, the Chief Secretary, General Byrne, the Head of the Royal Irish Constabulary, Sir James Campbell, the Unionist leader, and Sir Edward Carson, was that conscription would lead to chaos and disaster.[51]

Lord Reading, who had succeeded Spring Rice as British Ambassador, warned that the effect in America would be bad and the War Cabinet agreed that Balfour should put the British case to Reading and Colonel House. On 2 April Balfour sent a cable to House in which he outlined Britain's manpower problem, and the risk to British industry of diverting still more men to the battlefield. He asked his advice in the following way:

[49] Devoy, *op. cit.*, pp. 414–15; McGarrity to Casement, 9 November 1915, *Maloney MSS.*, Box 1.

[50] George A.Riddell, Baron Riddell, *Lord Riddell's War Diary, 1914–1918*, London: Ivor Nicholson and Watson, 1933, p. 239.

[51] War Cabinet meetings 374 (12), 375 (2), 376 (5), 27, 28 March 1918, *CAB.* 23/5.

The severity of sacrifices that would be imposed on England and Scotland are obvious and to ask this island to bear added burden while Ireland bears no burden of conscription at all seems almost an insult. At this moment Ireland has not only suffered less than any European belligerent she has suffered less than any European neutral. Would England and Scotland tolerate not merely continuance of this unfair distinction but its serious aggravation? On the other hand, objections from a practical point of view to including Ireland in a measure of conscription are manifest. It is certain that the law can only be enforced at cost of riotings and possibly bloodshed. It is not certain that the 150,000 troops we may expect to obtain will prove useful and trustworthy. Against conscription will be united priests, Parliament, nationalists and Sinn Feiners, and the only scheme for mitigating their objections which we can advise may not impossibly alienate Ulster and all that Ulster and shipyard Belfast means for the effective conduct of the war. For this scheme consists in associating a bill for giving immediate effect to the forthcoming report of the Irish Convention with a bill for extending conscription to Ireland. The report will be out this week. Unionists and England and Scotland may accept it but it is far far from certain that Ulster will. It is even doubtful if it will satisfy Irish Nationalists, for there is a powerful nationalist minority on the Convention including all the Roman Catholic Bishops who want more than the report proposes to give them. If, therefore, we quarrel with the North of Ireland over one of these associated measures and with the South over the other, or over both, what [sic] position (to put it mildly) will not be improved. I have troubled you with this long story of our domestic difficulties because I am afraid they may not prove to be purely domestic. I have never felt competent to measure the exact importance of the Irish Question in American politics and I feel less competent now than ever. I should, therefore, be most grateful if you let me know with the same fullness and freedom which I have used in this telegram how you think the policy which I have just outlined would from the American standpoint affect conduct of the war.

House's reply was the one most feared by the British. He wrote:

I am not able to advise intelligently as to the effect of conscription upon your domestic situation but I feel certain that it would accentuate the whole Irish and Catholic intrigue which has gone hand in hand in some quarters of this country with the German intrigue.[52]

[52] *Ibid.*, 379A (2) 1 April 1918, *CAB.* 23/14; Balfour to House, 2 April 1918, *Wiseman MSS.*, Drawer 90, File 69; House to Balfour, 3 April 1918, *ibid.*, File 64.

As if they were searching for some way to justify conscription in the light of House's pessimistic response, the Government asked Wiseman on 5 April whether he had spoken with House or the President on the subject and what his own views were. Wiseman's reply, cabled the same day, gave them all they wanted for he disagreed with House. Conscription accompanied by disturbances in Ireland might, he argued, create a bad impression in America, but it would depend very much on how the British handled their case. The announcement would have to be made with an eye on American opinion which Wiseman believed supported Redmond's moderate position on Ireland and wanted a home rule bill to be put into operation.[53] Lloyd George had this advice very much in mind when he presented the bill to extend conscription to Ireland on 9 April, and immediately coupled it with the statement, 'Meanwhile we intend to invite Parliament to pass a measure of self-government in Ireland.' Since it was proposed to conscript boys of eighteen and men of fifty, he explained, Ireland could not be exempted again. His argument was, on the face of it, reasonable. Large numbers of American troops were not due to arrive until the summer and the strain of German advances in March required that men be found quickly. But Irish members resisted the demand. Ireland had been through a revolution, Ireland had been deceived before, and Ireland would not be conscripted to fight for the rights of small nations unless the principle of self-determination was first extended to her![54]

Towards the end of the debate, on 16 April, Lloyd George spoke of America, having just received a letter from Lord Reading.[55] He made it quite clear that President Wilson's conduct of the war was being handicapped by the state of American public opinion towards Ireland. The Irish question had to be settled both for Ireland's sake and to convince America that justice was being done. It was an essential war measure. 'American opinion,' he said, ' . . . supports the justice of the Man-Power [conscription] Bill, provided self-government is offered to Ireland.' The coalition government was clearly split on the issue.

[53] Eric Drummond to Wiseman and reply, 5 April 1918, *ibid.*, File 69.
[54] *Parl. Debs.*, Commons, 5th Series, 9 April 1918, v. 104, cols. 1357 ff.; 16 April, v. 105, cols. 343 ff.
[55] War Cabinet meeting 392 (13), 16 April 1918, *CAB.* 23/6.

Lloyd George knew that recruits were desperately needed and that he could not extend conscription on the mainland without at least declaring that it would also be introduced in Ireland. The Unionists would not tolerate it and there were serious doubts about the response of the trade unions and workers. But Liberal and Labour members of his government threatened, in effect if not in so many words, to bring Lloyd George down if conscription was forced upon Ireland without home rule. American opinion was known to be hostile, and he himself told the Cabinet that he was prepared to resign if a home rule bill was rejected by Parliament.[56]

Irish opposition to conscription rested on a score of broken promises and the Prime Minister did concede during the debate that conscription could not, in practice, be enforced if nationalists, Sinn Fein, the Church in Ireland, and organized labour felt that justice, in the form of an acceptable home rule bill, was not being done to Ireland. This was precisely what happened when Irish conscription was approved by the House of Commons on 16 April before proposals for home rule had been presented to Parliament. Sinn Fein, moderate nationalists, labour and the Roman Catholic bishops continued to oppose conscription in Ireland as unjust. The government struck back on 17 and 18 May by arresting De Valera, Griffith, and about one hundred and fifty other Irishmen for the duration of the war on evidence of a Sinn Fein-German conspiracy which was too flimsy to sustain a prosecution against any of them.[57]

In America Wilson was told of a large meeting at Catholic University, Washington DC, attended by three cardinals, which expressed its fear for the consequences in America should conscription not be accompanied by home rule, and Wilson himself regretted that there was no way for him to influence

[56] War Cabinet meetings 377 (10), 29 March 1918, *CAB.* 23/5; 383 (17), 5 April; 389 (9), 11 April; 433 (2), 19 June, 1918, *CAB.* 23/6.

[57] The War Cabinet was told on 24 April 1918, meeting 398 (9), that there was no evidence that De Valera was in communication with the enemy. *CAB.* 23/6. When the Chief Secretary, Shortt, presented evidence of an Irish-German conspiracy to the Cabinet on 22 May 1918, meeting 414A, it was very thin. Most of it was over a year old and supplied by unnamed informants. He admitted that there was insufficient evidence for a court of law, but enough for detentions. Capt. Hall of Admiralty Intelligence attended but added nothing concrete. Lord Curzon and General Smuts were particularly dubious of the government's claim that a plot existed. *CAB.* 23/14.

the situation.[58] His Secretary, Tumulty, privately suggested to Lord Reading that it would be a mistake to introduce conscription before home rule and Reading replied that the Prime Miniser would keep his word – home rule was certain and would be immediate![59] Wilson refused to intervene any further in the matter. For example, late in April, Sir William Wiseman suggested that the President might make a statement that he was glad the Irish convention had recommended a form of home rule which the British government intended to legislate and that he now felt sure the Irish would do their part in the war. Wiseman argued that this might check Sinn Fein's opposition to the war.[60] Wilson would do nothing. He was certainly aware of the American opposition to conscription and a general cynicism regarding the latest home rule suggestion. A mass meeting organized by the 'Irish Progressive League' was attended by fifteen thousand people in Madison Square Gardens on 4 May 1918, where emotional resolutions were adopted which attacked conscription as an attempt to exterminate the Irish race and as a violation of Ireland's right to self-determination.[61] Wilson was also quite aware, for example from letters written by T.P.O'Connor, then in the USA, that Ireland was itself seething, that the Church, labour, the former Prime Minister, Asquith, and many others were opposed to Irish conscription.[62] Now was not the time to cast off his customary caution.

The Irish conscription question even affected American military organization. On 28 April, from London, General Pershing cabled to Newton D. Baker, US Secretary for War, that the British were able to ship whole American divisions to Europe, thereby avoiding the necessity for smaller American units to fight under British command, as had been feared. It had been desirable to form autonomous American units quickly, he added, because Britain had the Irish question on her hands and British

[58] M.F.Egan, US Ambassador to Denmark, to Wilson, 10 April 1918 and reply 12 April 1918, *Wilson MSS.*, Series VI, Box 558, File 3926.

[59] Tumulty and Lord Reading used Shane Leslie as their intermediary. See Leslie to Tumulty, 23 April 1918, *ibid.*, Box 520, File 3926.

[60] Wiseman to House, 25 April 1918, in House to Wilson, 26 April 1918, *ibid.*, Series IIB, Box 111.

[61] Peter Golden, Secretary, Irish Progressive League to Wilson, telegram, 4 May 1918, *ibid.*, Series VI, Box 520, File 3926.

[62] T.P.O'Connor to Wilson, 9 April 1918, *ibid.*, Box 558, File 3926, and to Tumulty, 26 April 1918, *ibid.*, Box 520, File 3926.

troops would probably be sent to Ireland to enforce conscription. He warned that the political repercussions from Irish-American soldiers having to fight under the British flag in these circumstances would be very bad.[63]

Through May and June the British government genuinely struggled to formulate an acceptable home rule formula, having rejected the Plunkett scheme, presented as the majority report of the Irish convention, which was based upon Dominion home rule for a united Ireland. However, they completely misjudged Sinn Fein's hold on nationalist Ireland. On 6 April, for example, Lloyd George believed that only the question of the control of Irish customs prevented Sinn Fein endorsing the Irish convention report.[64] This was quite wrong. Sinn Fein wanted an independent Irish republic. By late June the attempt to find a settlement had been set aside, although Irish conscription was still envisaged, and on 25 June the Prime Minister confessed that the government could not force such a contentious issue through Parliament during the war. He still regretted his failure to find a solution. 'Not to settle it,' he said, 'is not merely increasing our difficulties in conducting the war; it is increasing the difficulties of the United States of America in conducting the war.' This he knew from Reading's cables.[65]

Opposition to British policy continued to grow in Ireland. In July a resolution was introduced in the House of Commons by John Dillon, who had become leader of the Parliamentary Party when Redmond died in March. It demanded that Wilson's principle of self-determination should be applied to Ireland and it was heavily defeated.[66] In June, Irish nationalists organized an appeal to Wilson opposing the introduction of conscription into Ireland, a nation denied the right of self-determination, and attacking British control of the seas. It was not simply a Sinn Fein document, for a very wide range of Irishmen had signed it includ-

[63] General John J.Pershing to Newton D.Baker, telegram, 28 April 1918, *N.D. Baker MSS.*, Box 8. The British wanted some American troops in action as quickly as possible, under British or French command if necessary. The US government gave Pershing discretion in this matter but he was very wary of political repercussions in America. See War Cabinet meetings 304 (12) 21 December 1917, and 338 (1), 4 February 1918, *CAB.* 23/4.

[64] War Cabinet 385, 6 April; 433 (2) 19 June 1918, *CAB.* 23/6.

[65] *Parl. Debs.*, Commons, 5th Series, 25 June 1918, v. 107, cols 957 ff.; Murray to Reading, telegram, 26 June 1918, *Wiseman MSS.*, Drawer 91, File 107.

[66] *Parl. Debs.*, Commons, 5th Series, v. 109, 29 July 1918, cols. 85 ff.

ing the moderate nationalists Joseph Devlin, John Dillon, Tim Healy and William O'Brien. Therefore, when the Lord Mayor of Dublin, Laurence O'Neill, asked the British government to send the appeal to the United States, it was considered politically inexpedient not to do so. But first Balfour arranged with the United States' Embassy in London that no publicity would be given to the letter in America. It was handed to Lansing by the British Chargé d'Affaires in Washington and by 13 August was quietly in the White House. However, in Ireland it was known to have been sent and on 1 August Sir Edward Carson and other Unionists wrote to Wilson in reply. They insisted that the war was no time to discuss the follies of the past, that the Union had brought very real benefits to the Irish, that the most active nationalists had already been charged with conspiracy with the enemy and were in league with the Church in 'spiritual terrorism'.[67] There is no record of Wilson's reaction to these two letters or to a suggestion made by John Dillon in the House of Commons that the Irish question be submitted to the President for settlement.[68] He was, in the main, unsympathetic to the public pleas of the Irish at home and abroad. 'This is the most inopportune time for any delegation to visit me on the so-called Irish question', he had written in December 1917, and he refused to meet a delegation from the New York Irish Race Convention in May 1918 which represented, so Tumulty made quite clear, 'Sinn Fein elements'. To Wilson Sinn Fein and its American allies, Devoy, Cohalan, O'Leary, *et al.*, were anathema, but so divided were the rest of the Irish that Wilson's commitment to any one faction, be it British government approved or not, would have been foolish, even had he overcome his normal sense of diplomatic propriety to do so.[69]

Since US soldiers were now involved in the war, there was bound to be criticism of Ireland's resistance to conscription from both sides of the Atlantic. In fact *Freeman's Journal* threw this back by arguing that Irish volunteers had been in the war while America stayed out, and that proportionally to the Irish contribution, the USA would have to send six million men to France

[67] Ronald McNeil, *Ulster's Stand for Union*, London: John Murray, 1922, pp. 287–99; Colville Barclay, British Chargé d'Affaires to Lansing, 3 August, and Lansing to Tumulty, 13 August 1918. *State Department:* 841d. 22/–.

[68] *Parl. Debs.*, Commons, 5th Series, 29 July 1918, v. 109, Col. 106.

[69] Wilson to Tumulty, 11 December 1917, 24 May 1918, *Wilson MSS.*, Series VI, Box 558, File 3926.

before she had a case against Ireland.[70] Similar arguments were put by a former British army captain, invalided out of the war and by then resident in New York, William J.M.A.Maloney, in the *New York Globe* and the *New York Evening Post*, although his unsupported figures put the proportion of American casualties necessary to match the Irish at 5½ million dead![71] The situation in Ireland was by now so serious, and the war so nearly over, that this debate had little impact. In October, the United States Military Attaché in London reported to the State Department that 87,469 British soldiers, and 1,634 airmen were tied down in Ireland whilst the plan to evade the conscription problem by recruiting Irish volunteers had produced only 8,000 new recruits by October 2.[72] The period of that campaign was twice extended unsuccessfully, but meanwhile the US Army was proving decisive in France, and the war was being won, Ireland or no Ireland. The Irish were already preparing to carry their case to the Peace Conference.

[70] 'To Enlist the Irish under Old Glory', *Literary Digest*, 27 July 1918, v. 58, p. 14.
[71] McCarten, *op. cit.*, pp. 42–6.
[72] Report on the military situation in Ireland by Capt. Dennis, US Army, 7 October 1918, *State Department.*, 841d. 00/8.

8 The Irish and the Versailles Peace Conference, 1919

*'The great liberty loving President of America has braved
the deep that he may bring freedom to the oppressed
peoples of all nations. He has gone over to take poor
crucified Ireland down from the cross on which she has
been hanging for seven long centuries.'*

REV. JAMES FIELDING, CHICAGO,
22 DECEMBER 1918[1]

On 14 December 1918, the first British General Election since
December 1910 was held. The British Prime Minister, David
Lloyd George, insisted that his government required support
from the electorate on a wide range of issues, one of which was
Irish self-government. The mandate he received from the mass of
the Irish people was quite dramatic. Sinn Fein contested the
election with over a hundred of its leading members and forty-
seven of its candidates in jail, and with press censorship still in
force in Ireland. It stood unashamedly for the establishment of an
Irish Republic, the withdrawal of Ireland's representatives from
Westminster, the denial of Britain's right to legislate for Ireland,
the establishment of an Irish constituent assembly, and an appeal
to the Peace Conference for an independent Ireland. It contested
all but two constituencies and the final extraordinary tally held
Sinn Fein to have won seventy-three seats against twenty-six for
the Unionists. The Irish Parliamentary Party was reduced to an
ignominious five plus T.P.O'Connor representing the Scotland
Division of Liverpool. John Redmond had died in March and the
new leader of the party, John Dillon, was defeated in Mayo by the
imprisoned leader of Sinn Fein, Eamon De Valera.[2] The London

---

[1] James K.Fielding, *The Resurrection of a Nation*, Chicago: Mayer and Miller,
1934, p. 100.
[2] Macardle, *op. cit* , pp. 273–80.

166

Times on 9 January was prepared to concede that the result was as definitive as a plebiscite for Sinn Fein now represented more than two-thirds of the Irish people. In the United States the election confirmed the bulk of Irish-Americans in a sympathy for extreme policies which had been growing steadily since the Easter rising. and, without changing their major policy objectives at all, the leaders of the revolutionary Clan na Gael and Friends of Irish Freedom found that control of the great mass of organized Irish-Americans had passed to them by default.

The President of the United States had quite clearly accepted national self-determination as an American war aim. 'Self-determination is not a mere phrase,' he declared in February 1918. 'It is an imperative principle of action which statesmen will henceforth ignore at their peril.' The Irish in America seized upon this as the vehicle for their campaign and it was the theme of the Irish Race Convention in May 1918.[3] The universality of the principle and the moral tone of its enunciation precluded the admission that it applied solely to the territory of the enemy Central Powers.

In the closing days of the war and as Wilson prepared and journeyed to Paris, many appeals came to him for Irish self-determination. One, from the Irish College heads in Rome, had already been presented to the Pope.[4] In November, T. P. O'Connor introduced a resolution into the House of Commons demanding Irish self-determination in accordance with the principles laid down by President Wilson. He wrote to the President that the Irish were simply looking at the war 'from your own standard of "broad-visioned" justice'.[5] Petitions arrived from all over the USA and even from Argentina and Australia. The Irish also organized mass meetings – in New York, Boston, Philadelphia, Chicago, Los Angeles and elsewhere. A gathering of many thousands in and around Madison Square Gardens, New York, on 10 December, organized by the United Irish Societies, was addressed by Cardinal O'Connell of Boston, Daniel Cohalan, John Devoy, and Governor Whitman of New York. A resolution endorsing Irish-self determination was radioed from the meeting

[3] *New York Times*, 19 May 1918.
[4] Enclosed in George Creel to Joseph Tumulty, 14 November 1918, *Wilson MSS.*, Series VI, Box 558, File 3926.
[5] *Parl. Debs.*, Commons, 5th Series, 5 November 1918, v. 110, pp. 1962 ff.; Tansill, *op. cit.*, p. 290.

to the President who was by then *en route* for Europe and the Peace Conference in the USS *George Washington*.[6]

Before leaving the United States Wilson had appeared to commit himself, albeit very loosely, to the Irish cause, and his failure to present Ireland's case to the conference was to injure the Peace Treaty gravely in the following summer. Senator Thomas J.Walsh of Montana had asked him to work for an Irish settlement as a means for improving Anglo-American friendship, and on 2 December Wilson had replied, 'You may be sure that I shall keep this important interest in mind and shall use my influence at every opportunity to bring about a just and satisfactory solution.' The following day, 3 December, he answered a petition drawn up by the Rector of Catholic University, Thomas J.Shahan, and in his letter promised, 'It will be my endeavour in regard to every question which arises before the Peace Conference to do my utmost to bring about the realisation of the principles to which your letter refers.' Wilson made no reference to Ireland but, in the context of the petition, Shahan could be excused for his well publicized optimism.[7] Also on 3 December, at Union Station in Washington just before leaving for Europe, Wilson received a petition from the Rev. James Fielding of Chicago on behalf of 1,500 bishops and priests in Illinois. As Fielding tells the story, Wilson promised that the problem 'will have my most earnest attention to the fullest extent of my power', but as reported in the *Chicago Examiner* of 8 December, the story was headlined, WILSON AGREES TO HELP IRELAND.[8]

The Irish were not the only immigrants giving Wilson concern during the war and the Peace Conference. It was from hyphenated Americans that most pressure came for the recognition of new nations and governments in Europe. The American government was itself in large measure responsible for the problem. The United States deliberately cultivated the aspirations of national minorities in the territories of the Central Powers – Poles, Czechoslovaks, and so on – as an instrument of its own war policy and a campaign to win support for the war from immigrants from

[6] *New York Times*, 11 December 1918. Newspaper estimates on the number present varied from 15,000 to 25,000.

[7] Thomas J.Walsh to Wilson, 2 December 1918, *Wilson MSS.*, Series II, Box 158; Wilson to Thomas J.Shahan and Walsh 3 December 1918, *Wilson MSS.*, Series VII, Box 30, Nos 56–7; Tansill, *op. cit.*, pp. 290–1.

[8] Fielding, *op. cit.*, pp. 86–7.

these areas was handled by George Creel, Chairman of the Committee on Public Information, who maintained contacts with every conceivable immigrant community in America. His committee supplied 745 of their newspapers with a press service[9] and formed the organization 'Oppressed Nationalities of Austro-Hungary', in 1918, with Thomas Masaryk and Ignace Paderewski, of the future Czechoslovakia and Poland respectively, as leaders. In Creel's view it was one of the most effective of all US propaganda agencies.[10] In late October 1918, Masaryk presided at a meeting of 'Independent Mid-European Nations' in Independence Hall, Philadelphia, arranged by Creel's committee to establish a Mid-European Democratic Union. Eighteen 'nations' were represented, including Czechoslovaks, Poles, Yugoslavs, Ukrainians, Uhro-Russians, Lithuanians, Rumanians, Italian Irredentists, Unredeemed Greeks (!), Albanians, Zionists and Armenians. To this motley assemblage Wilson sent a message of encouragement, but before the end of the year the new organization had collapsed from disputes between rival contenders for governments and rival claims for territory, a sure sign of the chaos to come in Paris.[11]

The administration was not alone in its cultivation of ethnic identities. The Republican Chairman of the Senate Foreign Relations Committee, Henry Cabot Lodge, could be found at this time supporting the independence of Yugoslavia, Poland and Czechoslovakia, the return of Schleswig to Denmark, the partition of the Turkish Empire and a possible American mandate, protection of Armenians, Syrians and Greeks in Asia Minor, independence for the Letts, and Italian control of Trieste.[12] Whatever Lodge's motive, and there is clear evidence that it was in large measure party political, with an eye on the heterogeneous Massachusetts electorate,[13] this kind of activity

9 Park, *op. cit.*, pp. 444–7.

10 Undated memo by Creel, *Creel MSS.*, Box 3.

11 Masaryk to Wilson, 1 November 1918, and reply, 5 November *Wilson MSS.*, Series VI, Box 604, File 4813; Louis L. Gerson, *The Hyphenate in Recent American Politics and Diplomacy*, Lawrence, Kansas: University of Kansas Press, 1964, p. 97.

12 See the file, 'Peace Terms, Nationalities, etc.', 1918, in *Lodge MSS.*; Lodge to Bryce, 16 November, 14 December 1918, *Lodge MSS.*, 'General Correspondence 1918, A–G'; Lodge to Masaryk, 23 November 1918, *ibid.*, 'H–Q'.

13 George A. Bacon, Chairman, Massachusetts State Republican Committee, to Lodge, 17 December 1918, and reply, 19 December, *ibid.*, 'R–Z'; Gerson, *op. cit.*, pp. 98–9.

was to contribute to the problems and demands facing the Peace Conference.

There were, in fact, serious dangers for Wilson and the United States in the principle of self-determination which Robert Lansing appreciated rather better than the President. On 30 May 1918, Lansing wrote in his diary that he agreed that the promise of independence was not only just but should also be used to induce national minorities to revolt against the Austro-Hungarian Empire. By August, however, he had begun to counsel caution and Ireland figured very prominently in his argument. The following extracts from his diary illustrate his fears, although the extent to which he argued his case before Wilson at that time is unknown:

23 August 1918:

I feel ... that it is necessary to go very slowly before we take a step which commits this Government to the recognition of an independent state based upon the principle that a people who have been oppressed and their native land held in subjection by superior physical force are entitled to be free and to possess the land.

Immediately upon so broad a declaration by this Government the Central Powers would raise the question – at least I would if I had the conduct of their affairs – why, since we are so solicitous about oppressed nations, do we not take a definite stand for the independence of Ireland, Egypt, India, and South Africa.... From the viewpoint of domestic politics it would be a very unwise policy.

In addition ... we would be, I think, embarrassed in no small degree at the peace table by having admitted beforehand the claims of the subject races of the Central Powers and Turkey and by having ignored the claims of the Irish and others under the sovereignty of the Entente Powers.... Great Britain has already an unenviable reputation for having one rule for herself and another rule for other nations.

20 December 1918:

When the President talks of 'self-determination' what unit has he in mind? Does he mean a race, a territorial area or a community? Without a definite unit which is practical, application of this principle is dangerous to peace and stability.... These phrases will certainly come home to roost and cause much vexation.

30 December 1918:

The more I think about the President's declaration as to the right of 'self-determination' the more convinced I am of the danger of putting such ideas into the minds of certain races. It is bound to be the basis of impossible demands on the peace conference, and create trouble in many lands,

What effect will it have on the Irish, the Indians, the Egyptians, and the nationalists among the Boers? Will not the Mohammedans of Syria and Palestine and possibly of Morocco and Tripoli rely on it? How can it be harmonized with Zionism, to which the President is practically committed?
The phrase is simply loaded with dynamite. It will raise hopes which can never be realised.

This was no sudden realization on Lansing's part, but by the time he and Wilson arrived in Paris in mid-December there was only minimal contact between them and no intimate discussions. Lansing had counselled in vain in November against the President's going to Paris and had played only a minor role in formulating the provisional American peace terms.[14]
The Peace Conference formally opened on 12 January 1919, with an immense amount of business before it. Twenty states were represented but this unwieldy number yielded to the Council of Ten, and by March this in turn had yielded to the Council of Four – Wilson, Lloyd George, Clemenceau, and Orlando. Most of the period to 15 February, when Wilson returned briefly to the United States, was spent in writing the Covenant of the League of Nations which was presented to the conference by Wilson on 14 February. During these weeks pressure in support of Ireland was being applied from America in the form of resolutions from meetings, organizations and state legislatures. Wilson and the American Peace Commissioners were well aware of a growing clamour, both in the United States and Ireland. Copies of State Department correspondence on Ireland came to them regularly, and consuls in Ireland were alerted to provide more information.[15]
As early as December, Tumulty was pressing Wilson to discuss the future of Ireland with Lloyd George, and to publish his efforts in the USA.[16]
Mass meetings of Irish-Americans in December and January were simply preludes to the great Irish Race Convention held in Philadelphia on 22 and 23 February 1919. This marked the real emergence of the Friends of Irish Freedom as a powerful force

14 Lansing Diary, *passim.*, *Lansing MSS.*, Box 2, v. 1.
15 Acting Secretary of State Polk to US Consuls in Dublin and Belfast, 18 January 1919, *State Department*, 841d. 00/9.
16 Joseph Tumulty to Wilson, telegram, 29 December 1918, *Tumulty MSS.*, Box 2.

in American politics although it had been founded at the first Race Convention in 1916. The new convention was the sister in spirit of Dail Eireann, the parliament of the Irish Republic, which met for the first time on 21 January at the Mansion House in Dublin. Thirty-six of the Republicans elected in December were still in prison, but the Dail immediately set about defying the British government by adopting Ireland's declaration of independence and ratifying the establishment of the Irish Republic in 1916. Three delegates were appointed to present Ireland's case to the Peace Conference, Eamon De Valera and Arthur Griffith, who were still in prison, and Count Plunkett. Alderman Sean T. O'Kelly and George Gavan Duffy were sent to Paris to represent the Republic.[17]

The Philadelphia convention was planned with great skill. Thirty bishops and archbishops attended and Tansill describes how Cohalan induced the elderly and rather conservative supporter of Redmond's moderate home rule campaign, and later of Wilson's League of Nations, Cardinal Gibbons of Baltimore, then aged eighty-five, to be present at a convention which was called to support Ireland's right to full republican independence. Gibbons addressed the meeting of six thousand people and proposed a resolution, drafted by Cohalan and Devoy, which called upon the Peace Conference to apply the doctrine of national self-determination to Ireland. Other resolutions went much further than this by declaring that a state of war existed between England and Ireland, and that no League of Nations would be supported which did not guarantee Irish self-determination, freedom of the seas, and respect for the Monroe Doctrine. It was on these grounds, a mixture of support for Ireland and traditional American policies, that the Friends of Irish Freedom chose to campaign against the League a few months later. The campaign, of huge dimensions and great complexity, was made possible by the Irish Victory Fund which was launched at the convention. A sum of one million dollars was almost immediately pledged and in the months to follow the Friends of Irish Freedom were never short of money. When the fund closed on 31 August 1919, $1,005,080.83 had been collected.[18]

17 Macardle, *op. cit.*, pp. 283–9.
18 Tansill, *op. cit.*, pp. 298–301, 332; Splain in Fitz-Gerald, *op. cit.*, pp. 233–5; *Philadelphia Record*, 24 February 1919.

Commenting on the convention, the *Philadelphia Record* editorial of 24 February observed:

> The future of England depends very much on its relations with the US and we have done enough for England in the last two years to entitle us to consideration. The emancipation of Ireland would remove the only obstacle to the most perfectly fraternal relations between America and England, and would make the two great English-speaking nations supreme in the world for all good purposes. With the very great Irish population in this country it was not the easiest thing to go to the help of England, but we did it, and American feeling about the right of the self-determination of people ought to be allowed some weight in London.

The British government was in no mood, and probably in no position, to pay heed to this kind of appeal, although Lloyd George had conceded its validity during the conscription debate of 1918, a desperate period for the Allies, when he tried to couple Irish home rule with conscription to placate America and the Dominions.

Wilson returned to the USA for a short while in February 1919 and a committee was appointed to present the convention's resolutions to him. It was an eminent and wide-ranging sample of Irish-America and included Justice Daniel Cohalan. On 25 February the whole committee of twenty-four travelled to Washington where the President refused to meet them, or any other delegation, because, he said, he had an immense amount of public business to dispose of in less than two weeks. However, this delegation was from the massive Irish Race Convention and political considerations alone should have dictated a meeting.[19] Tumulty knew this and on 28 February he wrote a forceful letter to the President.

> I am sure that your refusal to see this delegation will give aid and comfort to the enemy. Further, from your letters to Senator Walsh and Bishop Shahan, you would, as you said in Senator Walsh's letter 'appreciate the importance of a proper solution of the Irish question' and that you would 'use your influence at every opportunity to bring about a just and satisfactory solution'.

[19] Tumulty to Wilson, 24 February 1919, and Wilson note, n.d., *Wilson MSS.*, Series VI, Box 559, File 3926; Tumulty to Senator T.J.Walsh, 26 February 1919, *Walsh MSS.*, Box 190.

Regardless of what we may think of Cohalan and his crowd, there is a deep desire on the part of the American people to see the Irish question settled in the only way it can be settled – by the establishment of a Home Rule Parliament in Dublin. It would help England as much as America to get this perplexing question out of the way.

Wilson did nothing and Tumulty renewed the attack on 1 March, stressing that Wilson's attitude was a danger to the Democratic Party, and that it would not only enable the Republicans to take advantage of the issue to embarrass him, but would strengthen the Sinn Fein element in the United States. That same day, in another note, he suggested a solution, that the delegation could be seen immediately after Wilson's scheduled address at the New York Metropolitan Opera House on 4 March. Wilson immediately agreed.[20]

The delegation sat on the stage during Wilson's address and followed him to a private room. At that point Wilson refused to meet them if Cohalan, whom he deemed to have been 'disloyal', was present. Cohalan withdrew, over the objections of the rest of the group, who then went in to present Wilson with the convention's resolutions.[21] A brief report to the American Peace Commissioners in Paris by the State Department Intelligence Division described the meeting:

The movement in America to have Ireland's position recognised is of sufficient strength to warrant this matter being brought to the attention of the Commissioners. . . . The President met the Irish delegation before he sailed – first, insisting on the exclusion of Judge Cohalan of New York – telling them that he could not present Irish claims at the Peace Conference, and that the question of Ireland's self-determination must come up in regular order after consideration of such states as Poland, Yugo-Slavokia [*sic*], and others in the war area.

Significantly, if this account was authentic, Wilson did not rule out consideration of the Irish case at Paris, but since he refused to present it himself there appeared to be little chance of it being raised at all. Later he confessed that the group's request that he should promise to ask the Peace Conference to make Ireland

---

[20] Tumulty to Wilson, 28 February, and twice on 1 March 1919, *Tumulty MSS.*, Box 3.

[21] Tansill, *op. cit.*, pp. 302–3. *New York Times*, 5 March 1919.

independent had made him very angry. His first impulse had been to tell them to go to hell![22]

This problem of the Irish Race Convention and its resolutions arose as Wilson was simultaneously faced with an embarrassing situation in Congress. Since the Casement agitation of 1916 no Irish resolution had passed into the committee stage or to a vote, although several had been introduced into the House. This changed immediately the war ended. On 12 and 13 December 1918, the House Committee on Foreign Affairs held hearings on a resolution presented by Rep. Thomas Gallagher, Democrat of Illinois, requesting the US Peace Commissioners to present Ireland's claim to freedom, independence and self-determination to the Peace Conference. The proceedings were demonstrations rather than hearings. Twenty delegates represented Chicago alone, and others came in force from fifteen states. Four hours of testimony were heard from interested Congressmen with a variety of Irish names and from representatives of Irish-American organizations. The only opposition came from George L. Fox of New Haven, a perennial opponent of Irish-American activities.[23]

Representative Flood, the chairman of the committee, wanted the passage of a resolution of some kind and believed the Gallagher resolution could pass in the House by a large majority if reported favourably by his committee. Flood wanted to avoid embarrassing the President and agreed to be guided by Wilson in the matter of re-drafting. In his view a simple resolution of support for Irish self-determination would have satisfied the House. Wilson tersely replied from Paris on 7 January, 'Sincerely hope passage of a resolution on Home Rule can be avoided'. Tumulty refused to let the matter rest and on 28 January cabled Wilson that opposition to the resolution would be interpreted as opposition to home rule, for which there was great support in America. Wilson replied more sensibly on 30 January:

I frankly dread the effect on British public opinion with which I am daily dealing here of a Home Rule resolution by the House of

[22] Memo from Current Intelligence Division, American Section, to Christian A. Herter, 6 March 1919, *White MSS.*, Box 6; David Hunter Miller, *The Drafting of the Covenant*, New York; G.P.Putnam's Sons, 1928, v. 1, p. 294.

[23] US Congress, House, Committee on Foreign Affairs, *The Irish Question: Hearings before the Committee on Foreign Affairs on H.J. Res. 357*, 12 and 13 December 1918, 65 Cong., 3 Session, House Doc. 1832, Washington DC, 1919.

Representatives and I am afraid that it would be impossible to explain such a resolution here, but I willingly trust your discretion in handling the matter at Washington. It is not a question of sympathy but of international tactics at a very critical period.[24]

The 'critical period', of course, covered the negotiations for the League of Nations, the major purpose of Wilson's visit to Paris, and he needed British co-operation. On 5 February Tumulty reported to Wilson Flood's view that only open and active opposition by the President could prevent an Irish resolution passing.[25] Ten days later, Assistant Secretary of State Polk cabled Lansing that both sides in the House were playing politics with the resolution for the Irish vote but Lansing replied, 'The President does not think that it would be wise for him to intervene in the matter discussed in your telegram but has instructed me to advise you to keep up the utmost pressure to see that the matter is not acted on at this Congress.'[26]

It was on 4 March, the day Wilson finally met the Irish Race Convention delegation in New York, that the House of Representatives voted on an amended Gallagher resolution. Tumulty and Flood had done their work well. The Foreign Affairs Committee had reported a concurrent resolution, apparently acceptable to Gallagher, which did not request the American Commissioners to represent Ireland's case for self-determination to the Peace Conference, but which read:

Resolved by the House of Representatives (the Senate concurring) That it is the earnest hope of the Congress of the United States of America that the peace conference, now sitting in Paris, in passing upon the rights of various peoples, will favorably consider the claims of Ireland to the right of self-determination.

After a debate which allowed full rein to orations on the deeds of Ireland and America's historic debt to that nation, the resolution passed by the massive majority of 216 to 45. As Congressmen saw it, this was a declaration of support, not a commitment to act, and in any case the Senate had adjourned on 3 March and could

[24] Tumulty to Wilson, telegram, 31 December 1918, 28 January 1919, and Wilson to Tumulty, telegram, 7, 30 January 1919, *Tumulty MSS.*, Box 2.

[25] Tumulty to Wilson, telegram, 5 February 1919, *ibid.*, Box 3; Tansill *op. cit.*, p. 307.

[26] Assistant Secretary of State Frank Polk to Lansing, telegram, 3 February 1919, *State Department*, 841d. 00/11a; Lansing to Polk, telegram, 15 February 1919, *ibid.*, 841d. 00/16; Tansill, *op. cit.*, pp 307–8.

therefore not vote its concurrence. Though formally reported to the House on 11 February, debate on the bill had been deliberately delayed until 4 March, the last day of the session.[27] Nevertheless, notice had been served that the Irish in America had forced a successful vote of support from the House of Representatives and Wilson could ignore it at his peril as he set out again for Europe late on the day of the vote. In fact an Irish-American delegation followed to lobby him in Paris.

Three members of the Irish-American delegation which met Wilson were authorized by the Race Convention to travel to Paris to secure a hearing for Irish delegates by the Peace Conference. Failing that, they were required to present the Irish case themselves. Before their names were announced Wilson had decided that should Cohalan be one, his passport application would be refused, but the delegates chosen were unimpeachable and no obstructions were placed in their way.[28] In fact, Lord Reading, the British Ambassador, advised Wilson that it would be unwise to deny them the right to travel to Paris.[29] Of the three, Frank P. Walsh, the leader, had been chairman of the Commission on Industrial Relations, joint president of the National War Labor Board, and had only recently become deeply involved in the Irish question, while Edward F. Dunne, a former mayor of Chicago and governor of Illinois, had cultivated the Irish as a politician but had never led them. Both were well known to Wilson. Michael J. Ryan, of Philadelphia, was the only delegate with a long record of activity in Irish-American organizations, notably Redmond's United Irish League, but even he had been a respected member of a public service commission in Philadelphia.[30] The three men arrived in Paris on 11 April and on 15 April Walsh called on Colonel House.[31] The following day the three

[27] US *Congressional Record*, 65 Cong. 3 Session, 1919, v. 57, pp. 3174, 5027–57.

[28] Polk to Lansing, telegram, 3 February 1919 *State Department*, 841d. 00/11a.; Polk to Wilson, 1 March 1919 and Gilbert F. Close, Confidential Secretary to the President, to Polk, 3 March 1919, *Polk MSS.*, Drawer 74, File 152.

[29] Polk to Ambassador Davis, 16 May 1919, *Polk MSS.*, Drawer 77, File 133.

[30] Tansill, *op. cit.*, pp. 312–13.

[31] Unless noted otherwise, data on the relations between the Irish-American delegates and the US Peace Commissioners is drawn from the House Diary, vols 15, 16, *House MSS.*, and US Congress, Senate, Committee on Foreign Relations, *Treaty of Peace with Germany: Hearings before the Committee on Foreign Relations*, 66 Cong., 1 Session, Senate Doc. 106, Washington DC, 1919, pp. 799 ff. See also US *Congressional Record*, 66 Cong., 1 Session, v. 58, 1919, part 5, pp. 4650 ff. for a slightly amended version of the hearings.

wrote to Wilson on behalf of the Irish Race Convention requesting that the United States use its good offices with the British government to secure safe-conduct passes for De Valera, Griffith, and Plunkett so that they might present Ireland's case to the Peace Conference. On 17 April Walsh met Wilson who, according to Walsh, referred him to Colonel House 'with instructions to say that he believed the request a proper one, and that it should be granted'. House was apparently deputed to intervene with the British but at no time did Wilson agree to any official action. The aid was to be strictly informal. House met the three men on 18 April and agreed to help, but he wrote in his diary, 'I did not encourage them to think that my efforts would be successful'. The delegates later reported that on 19 April House told them that he had communicated with the Prime Minister and that safe-conducts would probably be granted. House's diary entry for 19 April made it clear that he had not, in fact, yet contacted Lloyd George. He wrote:

One of the first things I took up today was getting the consent of the British to allow the delegates from the 'Irish Republic' to come to Paris. The Foreign Office is willing but it has not been put up to Lloyd George yet. I am promised a decision by tomorrow.

House was at that time dealing with Sir William Wiseman. He first discussed the matter with Lloyd George on 21 April over lunch when the Prime Minister agreed to meet the delegation the following week. By 29 April, however, Walsh, Ryan, and Dunne were complaining that the anticipated meeting had not materialized. House noted:

The Irish contingent, Dunne, Walsh and Ryan, came to tell me that Lloyd George had not only failed to make an appointment to see them this week as promised but in their opinion, he had no intention of seeing them at all.
Later Wiseman confirmed this. I am not surprised that George should try to wriggle out of this situation as he has so many others. Wiseman was so disgusted that he left nothing of denunciation for me to add. I shall get the Irish to write George a letter tomorrow which will put him on record one way or the other.

House was particularly angry now, for on the 25th he had written of his discussion on Ireland with Lloyd George, 'I believe he is earnestly trying to work out some solution. It has now become almost as much a political issue in America as in England'.[32]

Since there was no possibility of an interview for some time the three delegates accepted De Valera's invitation to visit Ireland. Through Wiseman, House was able to secure the co-operation of Lloyd George, who actually believed they were going at Wilson's suggestion.[33] Their passports were quickly amended and they were able to move around Ireland, then largely policed by the military, with far more freedom than was customary. Their tour, from 3 May to 12 May, provided a golden opportunity for Sinn Fein and was a source of great embarrassment to both the British and American governments. The Irish-Americans made it quite clear that they came as supporters of 'President De Valera', whom they met, and Dail Eireann. The British press, much of which had attacked both Lloyd George and Wilson for agreeing to the proposed visit, now gave detailed, and even lurid accounts of the Irish-Americans' progress through Ireland where they left the impression that the Peace Conference would consider Ireland's case.[34] Ian MacPherson, the new Chief Secretary, believed that their effect was disastrous and that the Irish rebellion grew worse following their trip.[35] Certainly republican Ireland received a great boost from the Irish-American visit, but as a result both Lloyd George and the Americans were able to use it as their excuse for dismissing Ireland's case at Versailles. They had never considered that the Irish question was a legitimate concern of the Peace Conference, but a formula had to be devised for evading it which might satisfy American public opinion, and this tour appeared to provide one. On 14 May, Bonar Law, who was Lloyd George's deputy, stated in the House of Commons that he had originally understood the purpose of the Irish-Americans' trip was to acquaint them with conditions in Ireland but that Lloyd George now had no intention of meeting them in Paris. 'He was willing to receive American citizens,' said Law, 'but he is not

[32] House to Sir Horace Plunkett, 25 April 1919, *House MSS.*, Drawer 19, File 47 and *Plunkett MSS.*

[33] War Cabinet meeting 567A, 14 May 1919, *CAB.* 23/15.

[34] Tansill, *op. cit.*, p. 314; Edward F.Dunne, *What Dunne Saw In Ireland*, New York; Friends of Irish Freedom, 1919; F.P.Walsh, 'Impressions of Ireland', *Nation*, 7 June 1919, v. 108, p. 907. For a long and critical account of the tour see Ambassador Davis to Lansing, 28 May 1919, *State Department*, 841d. 00/57.

[35] War Cabinet meeting 567A, 14 May 1919, *CAB.* 23/15.

willing to receive American citizens who go to Ireland and not only take part in politics, but in a rebellious movement.'[36]

The problem now had to be solved of the official American attitude to the Irish-American delegation. Its members clearly wanted the US Peace Commissioners to take up officially, and in a way endorse, the request for safe-conduct passes for De Valera and his colleagues. In an open letter to Wilson on 20 May the three members asked for a meeting with him, and Lansing's draft reply stated that the American Commissioners were in no position to approach the British officially on behalf of British citizens. House considered this too brusque and Lansing's final letter followed lines suggested by House and approved by Wilson[37] which paralleled the British policy. He wrote:

I am informed that when the question of approaching the British authorities with a view to procuring the safe conducts in question was first considered every effort was made, in an informal way, to bring you into friendly touch with the British representatives here, although owing to the nature of the case it was not possible to treat the matter officially. The British authorities having consented that you and your colleagues should visit England and Ireland, although your passports were only valid for France, every facility was given to you to make the journey. Before your return to Paris, however, reports were received of certain utterances made by you and your colleagues, during your visit to Ireland. These utterances, whatever they may have been, gave, as I am informed, the deepest offence to those persons with whom you were seeking to deal, and consequently it seemed useless to make any further effort in connection with the request which you desired to make. In view of the situation thus created, I regret to inform you that the American representatives feel that any further efforts on their part connected with this matter would be futile and therefore unwise.

Walsh replied that the Irish-Americans had made no request to meet the British representatives, that is, they expected the American Commissioners to act for them, and asked who exactly was offended by their remarks in Ireland since the Irish people and their elected representatives were not. Lansing made no reply.

Walsh sent copies of his letter to each of the Commissioners, but only one, Henry White, showed concern. As he explained in a

36 *Parl. Debs.*, Commons, 5th Series, v. 115, 14 May 1919, cols. 1581–2.

37 House Diary, v. 16, 20 May 1919, *House MSS.*, Lansing to Wilson and Wilson to Lansing, 22 May 1919, *Wilson MSS.*, Series VIIA, Box 51.

letter to Henry Cabot Lodge, Walsh had made no attempt to see him in Paris, and he felt it necessary, 'both for my own sake and also that of the Republican Party of which I am the only representative on our Delegation', to make it clear that he accepted no responsibility for the failure of the Irish-American mission.[38] His letter to Walsh disclaiming all responsibility was, in fact, included with other correspondence Walsh presented to the Senate Foreign Relations Committee in August.

Having failed to move the US Government to intervene in the matter of the safe-conduct passes, Walsh and Dunne (Ryan having returned to the United States dissatisfied with the extreme bias of the other two men) began a campaign to present Ireland's claim themselves, and to press for amendments to Article X of the proposed League of Nations so that mutual guarantees of the territorial integrity of members would only apply to territories where the populations had been allowed to exercise the right of self-determination. The five American Commissioners, Wilson, Lansing, House, White, and General Tasker Bliss, finally agreed on 31 May that they should each, individually and unofficially, meet Walsh and Dunne, but as these meetings were taking place there were two important new developments. First, on 6 June the two delegates supplied Wilson and Lloyd George with copies of their public *Report on Conditions in Ireland, with a Demand for Investigation by the Peace Conference*, which described Britain's military control of Ireland, the alleged zoo-like imprisonment of political offenders, and made detailed though undocumented attacks, under seventeen headings, of alleged British atrocities and violations of human rights. It concluded with a demand for an impartial investigation by a committee to be appointed by the Peace Conference. Eight days later the Chief Secretary for Ireland, MacPherson, presented a convincing point by point rebuttal of the atrocity charges to the Cabinet, which was published by the press in July.[39]

The report did not interfere with the meetings which individual

[38] Henry White to Henry Cabot Lodge, 29 May 1919, *Root MSS.*, Box 231.
[39] War Cabinet memo, G.T. 7485, *CAB.* 24/81; See cuttings from *Boston Sunday Advertiser* and *Boston Herald*, 20 July 1919 in *FO* 115/2514. MacPherson gave permission to US Consul Adams in Dublin to visit Mountjoy Prison which had been attacked by Walsh and Dunne in their report. Adams reported that conditions were no worse than was usual in prisons. Ambassador Davis to Lansing, 3 July 1919, *State Department*, 841d. 00/69.

American Commissioners were holding with Walsh and Dunne. On 6 June Lansing met Walsh who requested a formal interview with the entire American Commission because, he said, he and Dunne wished to present material concerning Ireland which had a bearing on the peace settlement with Germany and Austria. He added, as a threat, 'If you officially refuse to hear us it will give us a right to appeal to the law and to the electorate.' Lansing would not budge.[40] On 10 June Henry White met both Walsh and Dunne and was impressed by their report of conditions in Ireland which, he noted, 'according to their account certainly leaves a great deal to be desired'.[41] On 11 June they were due to meet Wilson himself, but by then the second new development had occurred.

Very early on the morning of 7 June, news arrived at the American headquarters in Paris that the Senate had approved a rather dramatic resolution in support of the Irish case which went further than the House of Representative's resolution on 4 March. The Senate requested the American Peace Commission to endeavour to secure a hearing for De Valera, Griffith, and Plunkett by the Peace Conference and further expressed its sympathy with Irish aspirations for self-government. The resolution passed by the incredible margin of sixty to one, although thirty-five Senators elected not to vote. Only Senator Williams, Democrat of Mississippi, dared to oppose. In the previous three months the League of Nations had become the burning issue in America and a working alliance had been forged between Senate opponents of the League and the leaders of the Friends of Irish Freedom. Senator Borah of Idaho was a leader of the Senate's anti-League 'irreconcilables' and it was he who introduced the Irish resolution on 29 May. By 6 June it had been massively endorsed.[42]

As if the simple fact of the resolution's passage was inadequate to communicate American feelings, Tumulty cabled Admiral Grayson, Wilson's physician, whom he constantly used as an avenue for important messages to the President, on 7 June:

[40] Memo on an interview between Lansing and Walsh, 6 June 1919, *Lansing MSS.*, Box 43.

[41] Memo on an interview between Henry White, Walsh, and Dunne, 10 June 1919, *Bliss MSS.*, Box 248, File 836a.

[42] Tansill, *op. cit.*, pp. 328–9, US *Congressional Record*, 66 Cong., 1 Session, 6 June 1919, v. 58. part 1, pp. 728 ff.

You cannot overestimate real intensity of feeling behind the Irish question here. It is growing every day and is not at all confined to Irishmen. The passage of resolution of sympathy with almost unanimous vote in Senate last night is but slight evidence of interest here. I wish the President could do just a little for I fear reaction here upon the League of Nations. If this situation could be straightened out it would help us a great deal.

Wilson replied on 9 June with an interesting message:

The American committee of Irishmen have made it exceedingly difficult, if not impossible, to render the assistance we were diligently trying to render in the matter of bringing the Irish aspirations to the attention of the Peace Conference. By our unofficial activity in the matter we had practically cleared the way for the coming of the Irish representatives to Paris when the [Irish] American commission went to Ireland and behaved in a way which so inflamed British opinion that the situation has got quite out of hand, and we are utterly at a loss how to act in the matter without involving the Government of the United States with the Government of Great Britain in a way which might create an actual breach between the two. I made an effort the day before yesterday in this matter which shows, I am afraid, the utter futility of further efforts. I am distressed that the American Commission should have acted with such extreme indiscretion and lack of sense, and can at the moment see nothing further to do.

There is no evidence to support Wilson's claim that the United States had 'practically cleared the way' for De Valera, Griffith and Plunkett to go to Paris. Tumulty was not dissuaded by Wilson and immediately replied, 'It is our political situation here and the fate of the treaty itself that concerns me'. He asked Wilson not to be influenced by the indiscretions of Walsh, Ryan, and Dunne, and described the propaganda being conducted by the Irish in every large city and town in the United States.[43]

The President had already agreed to meet Walsh and Dunne before he received their report or news of the Senate resolution. Walsh recalled the meeting, which took place on 11 June, when he testified before the Senate Foreign Relations Committee in August. He and Dunne put the Irish case to Wilson who replied that no small nation could be heard by the Council of Four without the approval of all four members and therefore, in effect,

[43] Tumulty to Grayson, telegram, 7, 9 June; Wilson to Tumulty, telegram, 9 June 1919, *Tumulty MSS.*, Box 3.

only 'nations' from the ex-enemy territories. The record shows that the Council of Four did not, indeed, discuss the Irish Question at all.[44] When questioned about the whole subject of self-determination Wilson replied, and here Walsh was quoting from the account he and Dunne composed immediately after leaving the President:

You have touched upon the great metaphysical tragedy of to-day. When I gave utterance to those words I said them without the knowledge that nationalites existed which are coming to us day after day. Of course Ireland's case, from the point of view of population, from the point of interest it has excited in the world and especially among our own people, whom I am anxious to serve, is the outstanding case of a small nationality. You do not know and cannot appreciate the anxieties I have experienced as the result of these many millions of peoples having their hopes raised by what I have said.

Lansing, standing in the wings at Versailles, would have felt vindicated had he heard this confession. When General Bliss met Walsh and Dunne on 13 June they told him, so he noted, that Wilson believed the Peace Conference would take up the question of Ireland and would act on it. However, Walsh and Dunne did not report this to the Senate Committee and if they said it to Bliss, they clearly mis-represented the President's position.[45]

Meanwhile, of course, the American Commissioners had to decide on their attitude to the important Senate resolution. The advice of Lansing, White, Bliss, and House, tendered in a letter because they were finding it very difficult to see Wilson for any purpose, was that the resolution should be forwarded to Clemenceau, the President of the Peace Conference, but without comment because the Irish question bore no relation to the German and Austrian peace treaties. This was done by Lansing on 16 June.[46] Clemenceau replied with a complete refusal to put the Irish question to the Peace Conference. He wrote to Lansing:

After due reflection, it appears to me absolutely impossible to grant the request of which you are the interpreter, without deliberately exposing myself to exceed the limits of our task. The Peace Conference,

44 Minutes of the Council of Four, *CAB.* 29/39.

45 Memo on an interview between Bliss, Walsh and Dunne, 13 June 1919, *Bliss MSS.*, Box 248, File 836a.

46 Lansing to Clemenceau, 16 June 1919, *Lansing MSS.*, v. 43.

instituted by the Allied and Associated Governments, has endeavoured in so far as possible, to institute better conditions of peace in parts of the territories which joined in the war against us. No one knows better than you how far from easy this task is, but it forced itself upon our deliberations and we have resolutely accepted it. Intervention in the affairs of Allied states seems to me a question which the present Peace Conference can in no way consider under any circumstance whatsoever. If such a thing were attempted, I cannot doubt that it would bring about very animated retorts, and the object of our work might be brought to nothing by endless dissensions.[47]

This was exactly the reply desired by Wilson, and was perhaps even arranged with American co-operation, for in his first sentence Clemenceau managed to convey that the American Commission had not officially presented the case for Ireland but had simply 'interpreted' it, had passed it on.

The American Commissioners had already evaded the Irish-American appeal by using the activities of Walsh, Ryan and Dunne in Ireland as a pretext and they now used Clemenceau to evade any responsibility to the Senate. J.C.Grew, the Secretary-General to the American Commission, explained to Walsh on 21 June, in a piece of pedantic legalism, that only Clemenceau, as President of the Conference, was competent to introduce the Irish question and, therefore, nothing more could be done. This was a far cry from July 1917, when Wilson had written to House:

England and France have not the same views with regard to peace that we have by any means. When the war is over we can force them to our way of thinking, because by that time they will, among other things, be financially in our hands. . . .[48]

In the United States, in the summer of 1919, the feeling was growing that, on the contrary, Lloyd George and Clemenceau had Wilson very firmly in their clutches. It was true, as a number of Democratic Senators had suggested to Wilson in a letter in March, that Britain stood to gain much more from the Peace Conference than the USA, but their corollary, that Wilson could demand Irish independence as the *quid pro quo*, was invalid.[49] Wilson had

---

[47] Undated copy of Clemenceau to Lansing, *State Department*, 841d. 00/52.
[48] Wilson to House, 21 July 1917, *R.S.Baker MSS.*, Series 1, Box 7.
[49] Senators P. G. Gerry, D.I.Walsh, R.Pittman, J.R.Kendrick, and T.J.Walsh to Wilson, 28 March 1919, *T.J.Walsh MSS.*, Box 190.

travelled to Paris to create the League of Nations and he needed British support. The issue was not one of American versus British bargaining power, but of Wilson's *personal* interest in the League versus British interests, and that was a far weaker hand for Wilson to play.

From Washington, Tumulty continued to plead for Ireland. A plaintive telegram on 18 June read, 'Just a word for Ireland would help a great deal', and on 25 June he endorsed extracts from the *New York Times* and *New York Post* which suggested that the President should play a part in securing an Irish settlement. Wilson would, or could, do nothing, and instead introduced another device for stalling Irish pressure. On 27 June, one day before signing the Peace Treaty, he replied to Tumulty:

I entirely agree with the general tenor of your cable ... and I firmly believe when the League of Nations is once organised it will afford a forum not now available for bringing the opinion of the world and of the United States in particular to bear on just such problems.[50]

In his book, *Woodrow Wilson as I Knew Him*, Tumulty wrote that when Wilson left America for the Peace Conference he already believed that the League would be a forum before which the case of Ireland and other oppressed people could be brought. In fact his draft Article III did provide that although members of the League would guarantee the territorial independence and integrity of each other, it should be possible to make territorial adjustments in accordance with the principle of self-determination. It provided that three-fourths of the delegates to the League could determine which adjustments should be made and unless these conditions were met the mutual guarantees would not apply. When the guarantee was finally written into the Covenant in Article X these provisions dealing with self-determination had been dropped at the insistence of Great Britain, France and Italy. Wilson did tell Lord Robert Cecil in March that the Irish question might get to such a state that its discussion in the League might be inevitable; the Irish would create so continuous a disturbance as to compel international attention. Cecil agreed that

50 Tumulty to Wilson, telegram, 18 and 25 June, Wilson to Tumulty telegram, 27 June 1919, *Tumulty MSS.*, Box 3.

this was so. However, although Article XI was mentioned in this context by Tumulty in his book and was extensively cited during the campaign for the treaty in America, neither it, nor any other section of the Covenant, made satisfactory provision for the demands of oppressed nations. No one reading the Covenant, or considering the membership of the League, could have believed that Ireland's aspirations were safeguarded by it.[51] Under Article XI any matter affecting 'international relations which threatens to disturb international peace or the good understanding between nations' could be brought before the League, but even if the Irish question could conceivably be introduced in this category there was no way to compel Britain to comply with a League recommendation.

Ireland was important in the American political scene but it was by no means the only problem created for the Peace Conference by the principle of national self-determination. Claims were advanced for a whole host of national groups – by the Jews, who were probably the most ably led at Paris, Armenians, Estonians, Lithuanians, Poles, Ruthenes, Georgians, Syrians, Lebanese, Egyptians, Aaland Islanders, Schleswigers, Indians, Indochinese, and by many others, including two Koreans from Siberia who set out on foot in February 1919, and arrived in December![52] Such was the power of an idea. Wilson, who was its major publicist, had to retreat. The new states of Czechoslovakia and Poland contained millions of Germans; the Italian price for entering the war had to be paid and many Austrians were destined to live in Italy by the Treaty of Saint-Germain; Wilson acceded to a British request to recognize their protectorate over Egypt and thereby killed the hopes of Egyptian nationalists who had, as he knew from diplomatic dispatches, been fired by the principle he had developed;[53] Armenia's right to self-government was effectively killed because no great power would act to safeguard the independence of a new Armenian state. Lansing was correct, the phrase 'national self-

---

[51] Joseph Tumulty, *Woodrow Wilson as I Knew Him*, New York: Doubleday, Page and Co., 1921, pp. 397, 403–4; Miller, *op. cit.*, p. 294; Robert Lansing, *The Peace Negotiations: A Personal Narrative*, Boston and New York: Houghton Mifflin, 1921, Ch. vii.

[52] H.W.V.Temperley, *A History of the Peace Conference of Paris*, London: Henry Frowde-Hodder and Stoughton, 1920, 6 vols, v. 1, p. 246.

[53] The Egyptian problem can be traced in *White MSS.*, Box 4; *Wilson MSS.*, Series viic, Box 176; and the House Diary, *House MSS.*

determination' was bound to raise hopes which could never be satisfied. It remained to be seen how it would return to plague Wilson when he returned to the United States to fight for the ratification of the Peace Treaty.

9 The Defeat of the League of Nations, 1919–20

*'During the first two years of the war we were told that
if Ireland got Home Rule it would bring the United
States in on the side of the Allies; and after she came in
it was said that unless Home Rule was conceded she
would not exert her full strength. Now we are warned
that without Home Rule there can be no Anglo-American
friendship and no League of Nations. The last assumption
is as false as the others.'*

BELFAST NEWS LETTER, 16 APRIL 1919

President Wilson need have paid little attention to the Irish
question had it not been very much an American question. Ireland
was part of the American political environment, and in the battle
for the League which Wilson faced in America it played a critical
role. The theme of William Maloney's influential articles in the
journal *America*, in October and November 1918, later released
as a book, was that the peace settlement would be judged by how
it treated Ireland. 'If out of the war a League of Nations be
formed,' he wrote, 'a league that lacks the nation of Ireland, may
not its first duty be to aid England against Ireland as the Holy
Alliance aided Turkey in Greece?' He also argued a point now
well understood by theorists of collective security though not
often discussed at the time, that the members of a collective
security system must have an absolute superiority over any potential aggressor. To him, British naval superiority defied this condition and a free Ireland was necessary to break British naval control over the Atlantic.[1] Maloney would have been satisfied with a
league if independent Ireland was a member and so too would
De Valera and Dail Eireann, which endorsed a message to the

1 William J.M.A.Maloney, *The Irish Issue*, New York: America Press, 1919,
pp. 29, 52–4.

American President to this effect on 11 April 1919. However, Irish-American opposition to the League was far more forceful than qualified Irish and Irish-American support for it, and powerful allies were to be found in the ranks of the Republicans, German, Italian and Jewish-Americans, and in the anglophobic Hearst press.[2]

The Irish-American campaign against the League was conducted by the Friends of Irish Freedom from the Irish National Bureau in Washington with Daniel O'Connell, a Massachusetts lawyer, as its director. Ample resources were provided by the Irish Victory Fund launched at the Irish Race Convention in February. Hundreds of branches of the organization and hundreds of thousands of Irish-Americans from coast to coast were supplied with a stream of information and propaganda. The Irish National Bureau issued press statements, a weekly news bulletin, pamphlets and articles, and advertised in the press, notably in towns visited by Wilson on his speaking tour later in September. The campaign had a double-pronged attack – the first in support of Irish freedom, the second directed against 'Britain's League' and in defence of 'American interests'. In December 1918 Viscount Grey, the former British Foreign Secretary, then retired in Northumberland, warned House of this second approach. He wrote:

It has happened before, that treaties have been opposed or even wrecked in the Senate, when it was supposed that they were inspired by England, or that England had a special interest in them; and we see already, according to the newspapers, that such opposition is gathering.[3]

When De Valera expressed support for Senator Walsh of Montana, a pro-League Democrat but a supporter of Ireland, he was told by Daniel O'Connell to mind his own business because Irish-Americans intended 'to save America against England and all those whom she could influence'.[4]

Such Americanism left very little room for sensible calculations

[2] Gerson, *Hyphenates*, pp. 98–106.

[3] Viscount Grey, formerly Sir Edward Grey, to House, 30 December 1918, *House MSS.*, Drawer 9, File 9; G.M.Trevelyan, *Grey of Fallodon*, Boston: Houghton, Mifflin Co., 1937, p. 396.

[4] Daniel T.O'Connell, 'Irish Influence on America's Foreign Policy', in Fitz-Gerald, *op. cit.*, p. 238.

of the American national interest. The sentiment was a nineteenth century one and it had changed its language very little in two generations. In 1864, for example, Brigadier General Kiernan, lecturing to the Fenian Brotherhood in America, had said:

The struggle between the United States and England is as inevitable, as unavoidable from their relative positions, the antagonisms of their institutions and the rivalry of their commerce, as that between Rome and Carthage.[5]

In his *Freedom of the Seas*, published by the Friends of Irish Freedom in 1919, Daniel Cohalan attacked Britain as a huge empire ruled by a hereditary few with the Cecil family in control. Britain controlled the seas and was determined on commercial superiority over the United States· 'There must come', he wrote, 'an inevitable contest between the United States and the British Empire for those markets.' In his contribution to the *Voice of Ireland*, published in 1924, Cohalan wrote, 'America and England can no more mix than oil and water. The nature of one must change before it can become like the other.'[6] A bizarre editorial in the *Chicago Tribune* of 15 July 1919 forecast a long and costly Anglo-American war for an Irish republic. But Kiernan, Cohalan, and the *Chicago Tribune* were wrong and a policy based upon their assumptions could have done nothing but harm to the United States. War with Britain was neither desirable nor inevitable and Britain was not a military threat. It was true, of course, that doubters could find evidence to the contrary in British statements. Lloyd George told House in 1918 that Britain was prepared to spend her last guinea to maintain a navy superior to any other, including the American,[7] and Winston Churchill publicly stated that though Britain would work to make the League of Nations a powerful reality the League would be no substitute for the supremacy of the British fleet.[8] The British also rejected American demands for freedom of the seas in peace and war, and the League Covenant contained no reference to this, the second of Wilson's Fourteen Points. However, Lloyd George

[5] Kiernan, *op. cit.*, p. 15.

[6] Daniel F. Cohalan, *The Freedom of the Seas*, New York: Friends of Irish Freedom, 1919, p. 6; Daniel F. Cohalan, 'America's Advice to Ireland', in Fitz-Gerald, *op. cit.*, p. 214.

[7] Seymour, *op. cit.*, v. 4, p. 186.

[8] *New York Times*, 27 November 1918. See also 6 December, 1918.

and Churchill were living in the past for the British navy could never again dominate the seas. If Cohalan believed that the United States had Britain to fear he too was out of date and his brand of Americanism was dangerous.

Anglophobic appeals like Cohalan's were really less important to the Irish than the practical alliance they forged with the Congressional opposition to the League. The mid-term elections in November 1918 had resulted in Republican majorities in both houses. The small Republican majority in the House was increased but the Republicans now gained control of the Senate. Since the Senate's approval was necessary for the passage of the Peace Treaty and the Covenant of the League of Nations which it contained, it was there that the battle for the League of Nations was to take place. British statesmen should have been well aware of the Senate's threat to Wilson's position at Versailles. The President had publicly staked his reputation on a Democratic victory in November and by his own measure he had been rejected by the American people. Yet after the election he declared that he would go to Paris.[9] The Chairman of the Senate Foreign Relations Committee, Henry Cabot Lodge, wrote to Arthur Balfour that the election was a Republican victory and particularly warned that it would be unfortunate to tie the League of Nations to the Peace Treaty.[10] This was done, however, and both were subsequently rejected in the USA.

The League Covenant was substantially complete when Wilson temporarily returned to America on 15 February and on 26 February he met with members of the Senate Foreign Relations and House Foreign Affairs Committees at the White House. The Democrats were pleased with what they heard of the League, but

[9]

	65th Congress		66th Congress elected 1918	
	Senate	*House*	*Senate*	*House*
Democrats	53	210	47	191
Republicans	42	216	48	237
Others	1	9	1	7

See Bailey, *op. cit.*, pp. 653–5.

[10] Henry Cabot Lodge to Arthur Balfour, 25 November 1918, *Lodge MSS.*, '1918, General Correspondence, A–G'.

Republicans were already prepared to argue that the United States would surrender vital portions of her sovereignty to it, would lose control over Chinese and Japanese immigration, and would leave Ireland to the tender mercies of England.[11]

Senator Borah of Idaho, who introduced the Irish resolution so overwhelmingly endorsed by the Senate on 6 June 1919, was one of a small group of Republican 'irreconcilables' who opposed a league at all costs and in any form. He was American to the core, but his America was the isolated land of Washington and Jefferson and his notion of foreign policy was cemented into a rigid early nineteenth-century mould of non-involvement in Europe and championship of US rights and authority in the western hemisphere. He had little experience of foreign affairs and his first deep involvement was the battle for the League, which he saw as a holy war in defence of the American constitution. He wrote of his campaign, 'What I have opposed from the beginning is any commitment of this nation to a firm line of procedure in a future exigency the facts as to which could not be known before the event.'[12] As he saw it, the Senate had been given the constitutional right to review foreign policy and it could not sign away its authority in the form of a blanket commitment to future international action under the direction of an international agency. This was very similar to the arguments used to defeat the arbitration treaties negotiated by McKinley, Roosevelt and Taft, and it was an attitude eagerly adopted by a group of influential Irish-Americans.

Borah's sympathy for the Irish was certainly not the reason for his crusade against the League, although he was very ready to cultivate them as allies. One author, analysing his oratorical style, wrote:

Appeals to patriotism, that is, praise of great moments, revered leaders, and noble traditions, served to stir his auditors. He stimulated hatred by associating the League with such terms as 'Prussianism', 'Bolshevism', 'militarism', 'repression', 'imperialism', 'secret diplomacy', all of which had repulsive emotionalized connotations. Irish-Americans were moved by his denunciations of the British Empire. . . .

11 Denna F. Fleming, *The United States and the League of Nations*, New York: C.P. Putnam's Sons, 1932, pp. 134–5.

12 John C. Vinson, *William E. Borah and the Outlawry of War;* Athens, Georgia: University of Georgia Press, 1957, p. 1. See Chapters 1 and 2.

In February 1920, when the fanatical hate for the 'enemy' commenced to wane, a similar appeal reinforced his contention that the Treaty condemned Continental Europe to 'perpetual hunger' and 'chronic revolution'.

In addition Borah warned of the danger of Trotskyism, higher taxes, intervention in American affairs by inferior people, the violation of the American constitution and the abandonment of a traditional foreign policy.[13]

These last two points, the American constitution and America's traditional foreign policy, were the real crux of the issue for Borah. He wanted America to follow Washington's advice to leave Europe to the Europeans, but, paradoxically, he could still write, as he did to the Friends of Irish Freedom in Portland, Oregon, suggesting American interference in Britain's affairs:

If America ever wants to do anything effective for little Ireland whose people fought so valiantly for us in the Revolutionary war she had better do so before this League of Nations is clapped down upon the world and fastened upon it by military power.[14]

And in a message to a New York meeting addressed by Cohalan he wrote of the League, 'Ireland, Egypt, Korea, India and all subject peoples alike can find no door of escape from this autocratic machine save that of war with all the great powers combined against this.'[15] However, these statements were part of his campaign to woo allies against the League, not promises of action.

On 4 March Borah began a tour ranging from Massachusetts to Oklahoma to counter the growing support for a League of Nations and, whenever he could, he addressed Irish-Americans.[16] In his speeches on the tour and in the Senate he was provided with information on Ireland by Daniel Cohalan who was himself campaigning widely in the east, in Boston, Detroit, New York and Washington, as part of a nation-wide Irish-American attack on the League. Cohalan advised Borah on his Irish resolution[17]

[13] Waldo W.Braden, *William E.Borah's Senate Speeches on the League of Nations, 1918–1920*, Reprint from 'Speech Monographs', v. IX, 1943, a digest of an Iowa State University Ph.D. dissertation, 1943, pp. 63, 66, 68.

[14] Borah to Thomas Mannix, 29 March 1919, *Borah MSS.*, Box 550.

[15] Borah to James McGurrin, 27 October 1919, *ibid.*

[16] Braden, *op. cit.*, pp. 60–1; *Borah MSS.*, Box 194.

[17] Braden, *op. cit.*, p. 61; Tansill, *op. cit.*, pp. 326–7, 330; Borah to Cohalan, 29 May 1919, *Borah MSS.*, Box 550.

and also helped when Borah became worried by a Senate speech made on 26 June by Senator Phelan, Democrat of California, urging Irish-Americans to support the League. 'Once established,' said Phelan, 'the principles of the League . . . become an accusing arraignment against England until she accords self-determination to the best qualified of her dependencies.' There was a suggestion that Phelan spoke with the authority of 'President' De Valera. 'I leave it to your judgment as to how the matter should be handled, but it is very important,' Borah wrote to Cohalan, who was about to leave New York for a protest meeting in Indianapolis. Cohalan replied that the Irish believed the League was a cloak for an alliance with England and France. He added that they opposed it on strong American grounds which included the Monroe and Washington doctrines, and because they believed an economic war with England had already begun. He followed this up by organizing a mass meeting in New York's Madison Square Gardens on 10 July to counter Phelan and to attack the whole League of Nations scheme.[18]

Another Senator who co-operated with the Irish, Henry Cabot Lodge, was far less of a natural ally for he was one of a breed of New England gentlemen, many of them like him, Harvard trained, who found friendship with Britain natural and easy. Like Theodore Roosevelt, he found the possibility of war with England unbelievable, not inevitable. During the war he had written of the Irish, 'It is strange that they cannot see the only thing for them to do is to go in and help the rest of us against the Germans, and then we should all be bound to help them'.[19] This was forgotten in his quest for allies to defeat the League and his attempt, as a Republican, to gain from Irish-American disaffection with the Democrats. This was a danger Tumulty anticipated in May 1919 when he cabled Wilson:

There is a decided reaction evident against the League, caused in my opinion, by dissatisfaction of Irish, Jews, Poles, Italians and Germans. Republicans taking full advantage and liable, in order to garner disaffected vote, to make absolute issue against League.[20]

18 Borah to Cohalan, 27 June, and Cohalan to Borah, 30 June 1919, *Borah MSS.*, Box 550; Tansill, *op. cit.*, p. 330.
19 Lodge to Moreton Frewen, 12 June 1918, *Lodge MSS.*, 'General Correspondence, 1918, A–G'.
20 Tumulty to Wilson, telegram, 26 May 1919, *Tumulty MSS.*, Box 3. On May 8 1919, Tumulty had reported that there would be *no* serious opposition.

Many people in Europe saw the Republican support for Ireland as a move to embarrass Wilson. Henry White, himself a Republican, put this view to Elihu Root in a letter from Paris early in August,[21] but in fact no American political party could afford to alienate the Irish, and since the Irish-American leaders opposed the League it was the Republican Party which gained most. Where Democrats received Irish backing, as the former Massachusetts Governor David I. Walsh had when successfully running for the Senate, they found it necessary to oppose Wilson's wishes regarding the League. Lodge explained the situation as he saw it in a letter to Henry White in July:

> Wilson's attitude has forced the Irish question to the front. The resolution of sympathy for Ireland, demanding a hearing – which I think their representatives were entitled to – was brought about by Wilson's attitude and it may assume a very much more serious aspect. You know what the Irish vote is in this country. As far as I can make out, they are bitterly opposed to the League, and the fate of the Democratic party in the Northern States is in their hands. They are having great meetings and all pronouncing against the League.[22]

In general, American opposition to the League was far from flippant, or necessarily directed by personal animosity to Wilson. For example, Ireland's problem was implicit in this perceptive statement by Senator Elihu Root:

> In this country the census of 1910 showed that 35% ... of our people were of foreign birth or the children of foreign parents. We can call upon these people to stand by America in all American quarrels, but how can we control their sympathies and their action if America interferes in foreign quarrels and takes sides in those quarrels against the countries to which they are attached by tradition and sentiment? ... Article X confronts us with consequences very similar to those which Washington had in mind when he advised us to keep out of the quarrels of Europe and to keep the quarrels of Europe out of America.

Root also argued that many of the agreements made at Versailles, particularly those involving national minorities – Germans in Czechoslovakia, Austrians in Italy, and so on – were unjust and not worth protecting under Article X's blanket guarantee.

[21] Henry White to Elihu Root, 5 August 1919, R*oot MSS.*, Box 231.
[22] Nevins, *Henry White*, p. 455.

Americans in ten or twenty years, he reasoned, would certainly not agree to fight to maintain these agreements and, having signed the League Covenant, the USA would not be able to honour it.[23] This position owed nothing to pro-Irish politicking or to anglophobia and very little to Washington and Jefferson but it revealed a great deal about the general weakness of Wilson's position, and the inherent weakness of collective security agreements.

The problem of the Monroe Doctrine particularly worried most Republicans. In Henry White's view, it was designed to protect Latin America from European imperialism and the League provided this same protection, but to Lodge and most others, the Monroe Doctrine meant American hegemony in the Americas in return for American abstinence from the affairs of Europe.[24] This latter view was utterly incompatible with the principle of collective security. It was true that, under the terms of Article XXI of the League Covenant, regional arrangements like the Monroe Doctrine were exempted from the provisions of the Covenant, but the difficulty of defining exactly what the Doctrine meant and the broad scope of Article X did not reassure many Americans that the League would not act in defiance of American interests in Latin America.

The Peace Treaty, which included the League Covenant as its first twenty-six articles, was signed at Versailles on 28 June 1919, and was submitted to the Senate on 10 July. Most of its provisions had been known for two months and an unofficial draft had been sent to the Senate on 9 June, so that the battle lines were drawn already. T.A.Bailey records that public opinion in the USA at that point appeared to favour the League – thirty-two state legislatures had endorsed it and thirty-three state governors had publicly supported it. However, Lodge was not prepared to yield to this kind of pressure and was prepared to stall until the tide turned. He began by reading the treaty aloud in the Foreign Relations Committee, a procedure which consumed two weeks. There then followed six weeks of hearings, some relevant and some far from relevant to the subject of the Peace Conference, with the Irish question falling into this latter category.[25]

[23] Root to Lodge, 19 June 1919, *Root MSS.*, Box 231.

[24] See, for example, White to Lodge, 7 March 1919, *Root MSS.*, Box 231; Lodge to L.A.Coolidge, 10 February 1919, *Lodge MSS.*, '1919, Peace, League, Political, A–H.'

[25] Bailey, *op. cit.*, p. 671.

The hearings were published and contained, besides the Irish testimony, representations on behalf of Albania, China, Czechoslovakia, Egypt, Estonia, Fiume, Greece, Hungary, India, Yugoslavia, Latvia, Lithuania, and the Ukraine. In August, Borah countered the President's claim that the whole world wanted the League by arguing that the Irish, Koreans, Chinese, Egyptians and Indians would not be heartbroken by its defeat,[26] and in the Senate hearings the Republicans believed they could prove this.

It was an Irish-American, Dudley F. Malone, who presented the Indian case to the committee, but the representative of the Egyptians was more interesting. He was Joseph W. Folk, a former governor of Missouri. His testimony paralleled the Irish, as well it might, for behind it was a fellow Missourian, Frank P. Walsh. While in Paris as a member of the Irish-American delegation, Walsh had been retained by Zaglul Pasha, the Egyptian nationalist, as Egyptian counsel in the United States. He secured the co-operation of Folk and founded the League of Oppressed Peoples with part of the money supplied by the Egyptians. Since Walsh was an important witness for the Irish in these hearings, Folk presented the Egyptian case.[27]

At 10 a.m. on Saturday, 30 August 1919, Cohalan, Walsh and the Irish descended in force on the Republican members of the Senate Foreign Relations Committee, the Democrats having refused to appear at this ritual sacrifice of the League. The list of Irish-American delegates, representing Friends of Irish Freedom groups from all over the USA, ran to one and a quarter pages of small type in the Congressional Record. Cohalan already knew the Senators well. He had regularly travelled to Washington on a Friday evening to lobby them and to organize the campaign with Daniel O'Connell.[28]

Cohalan, claiming to represent twenty million Irish-Americans, introduced the Irish case against the League and he followed the pattern already well established in the national campaign under-

26 Braden, *op. cit.*, p. 65.

27 US Congress, Senate, *Treaty of Peace with Germany, Hearings before the Committee on Foreign Relations*, 66 Cong., 1 Session, Senate Doc. 106, Washington, 1919, pp. 651–78, 750–6. The Egyptian representation was discussed by W.J.M.A. Maloney in a memo he prepared on a meeting with F.P.Walsh, 30 December 1921, *Maloney MSS.*, Box 22.

28 Tansill, *op. cit.*, p. 332.

taken by the FOIF.[29] He objected to the surrender of American sovereignty to a 'super state' and repeated his arguments on the freedom of the seas. Article X came under stronger attack than any other part of the Covenant. It read, in part:

> The members of the League undertake to respect and preserve as against external aggression the territorial integrity and existing political independence of all Members of the League.

The Irish, using revolutionary licence, consistently ignored the adjective 'external' in this article. Cohalan, for example, said:

> Under the proposed league of nations we should have to guarantee the territorial integrity of the Japanese Empire, the British Empire, the only two empires remaining, and guarantee to them the possession of all the spoils and the loot that they have gathered up in their existence in all parts of the world. No relief could be given Ireland as in the sixteenth century Spain went to the help of Ireland in her fight against England, for we would be compelled to make a fight, and would be compelled to send our men to Ireland, not for the purpose of helping them in their struggle but in order to help England to rivet the chains upon her.

That, Cohalan noted, would be 'utterly un-American', as if the United States had a particular tradition of intervening on the side of the oppressed in revolutionary wars in distant lands. True, the United States could not aid the Irish in a revolt without committing aggression against Great Britain, but how Cohalan could argue that the USA would be obliged to join Britain in suppressing the Irish was unclear. This ambiguous use of Article X was a feature in the Irish campaign, and J.C.Vinson, writing of Borah, also noted:

> Under Article X, said the Senator with more imagination than factual proof, the international army could be called out to quash the threat to peace which the British might see in the struggle for Irish independence.[30]

Cohalan completed his testimony by presenting a petition from a vast number of Irish-Americans and their political, social and religious organizations. This denounced the League and Article

---

[29] The Irish testimony is in US *Treaty of Peace with Germany*, pp. 757–933. See also US *Congressional Record*, 66 Cong., 1 Session, v. 58, pt. 5, pp. 4650 ff.

[30] Vinson, *op. cit.*, p. 24.

X in particular, but it also attacked Article XI. Advocates of the League argued that the case of Ireland could be brought before the League by a friendly member state on the ground, provided in Article XI, that the Irish question was one 'affecting international peace or the good understanding between nations'. This was flimsy reasoning for there was nothing in the Covenant to *compel* Britain to change its domestic policies, even if these did affect its 'good understanding' with other nations, and no hope for the Irish unless the British could be forced to yield to 'world opinion' mobilized through the League. There was no way of overcoming the fact that, as was noted in the previous chapter, Wilson had lost the chance to incorporate the principle of self-determination in the Covenant in January and February at Versailles.

What was most significant about this petition, attacking as it did the Wilsonian position, was the range of its signatories. They covered the whole Irish-American spectrum, from Wilson's arch-enemies in the Clan na Gael, through Bourke Cockran, essentially an Irish moderate before 1916, to M.F. Doyle of Philadelphia, a man absolutely loyal to Wilson throughout the war. The whole of organized Irish-America now supported policies which in 1914 would have been considered extreme and revolutionary, and even the most conservative of Irish-American nationalist organizations, the Irish Fellowship Club of Chicago, was, as Sir Horace Plunkett observed in 1919, pro-Sinn Fein.[31]

Frank Walsh next addressed the committee and presented his record of the Irish-American delegation's work in Paris. His testimony was long with frequent questions from the committee and it took on the character of a demonstration, with frequent applause. Walsh was followed by his fellow delegates in Paris, Ryan and Dunne, and the Irish verbal testimony ended with a very long masterpiece of a statement by W. Bourke Cockran, which was a far cry from the often bizarre onslaught by Cohalan. He conceded that British government was the best in Europe and that Britain's rule benefited her colonies, but she had shown a chronic inability to do justice to Ireland. The League, he argued, would do nothing to redress this wrong and would prevent foreign intervention to help the Irish. Cockran closed the case for Ireland and there were no witnesses to put the British case.

[31] Digby, *op. cit.*, p. 245.

This Irish testimony took most of one day and occupied a large part of the published hearings. The Friends of Irish Freedom distributed about 100,000 copies of that part containing the Irish testimony, and Borah in fact sent out 5,000 of these using his Senate franking privilege. Tansill cited further evidence of the scale of the FOIF campaign. They distributed, he noted, 700,000 copies of *The Irish Republic Can Pay its Way*, 500,000 coloured maps illustrating Irish Republican gains in the 1918 election, and 100,000 copies of *America First*.[32]

The testimony of the Secretary of State was particularly harmful to the President. He explained to the committee that he and the other American Commissioners in Paris were not consulted by Wilson on the Peace Conference decision to allow Japan to take control of the Shantung peninsular in China from Germany, which meant the denial of immediate self-determination to its Chinese inhabitants. The press seized upon this.[33] On 7 August the *New York Herald, Times, World, Sun, Tribune, American*, the *Philadelphia Ledger*, and many other papers stressed the President's personal responsibility for the treaty and for this violation of self-determination in Shantung. This became a recurrent theme in the Irish-American campaign. Japan, it should be remembered, was still Britain's ally and therefore a fit subject for Irish hostility.

The British House of Commons debated the Peace Treaty late in July, when it was simultaneously being considered by the Senate Foreign Relations Committee, and there too Ireland was a feature of the discussion. In fact two post-war House of Commons debates in which the American interest in Ireland was recognized illustrated the dilemma facing Lloyd George. These were in November 1918, and the Peace Treaty debate in July 1919.

On 5 November 1918, T.P.O'Connor moved that the Irish question should be settled in accordance with Wilson's principle of self-determination before the British government took part in the Peace Conference.[34] In O'Connor's view, the future security of the British Empire depended on a League of Nations. That League would be ineffective without the United States and there

---

[32] Daniel O'Connell to Borah, 13 November 1919, *Borah MSS.*, Box 551; Tansill, *op. cit.*, p. 332.

[33] US, *Treaty of Peace with Germany*, pp. 149 ff.

[34] *Parl. Debs.*, Commons, 5th Series, v. 110, 5 November 1918, cols 1962 ff.

were in America five million Irish-Americans who would resist such a League unless Ireland was first granted home rule. He had, he said, just spent thirteen months in America and knew two things: that good Anglo-American relations were essential to the security of the Empire and that good relations depended on satisfying the Irish race in America. The former Prime Minister, Asquith, supported O'Connor. 'A resolution such as this,' he said, 'would be passed with unanimity in every Parliament in every self-governing Dominion of this Empire. I am certain it would pass – of course it might be said it was outside their purview – in the Congress of the United States of America.'

By now, of course, no one could pretend that O'Connor and the Irish Parliamentary Party represented Ireland and the reply of the then Chief Secretary for Ireland, Shortt, became a series of taunts. He cited the German 'plots', which were used as the pretext for arresting De Valera and others in 1918, he asked if the House was prepared to coerce Ulster, and he argued that the Irish had already been offered self-determination by the Irish Convention but had failed to agree among themselves. When Richard Hazleton pointed out that Lloyd George, as recently as February 1918, had stated in the House that an Irish solution should be based on a single legislature for Ireland with adequate safeguards for the interests of Ulster and the British Empire, Bonar Law replied, 'What I should have liked to hear . . . is not pious aspirations, but a clear expression of the course which is possible to any British government'. He was correct. Just how could Wilson's principle of self-determination be applied to Ireland, including Ulster with its own claim to self-determination, at this late date? Irish-American resolutions and Irish Parliamentary Party motions did not answer the question. Most Irish-Americans seemed ignorant of Ulster, and the Irish in Parliament preferred to deny that an Ulster problem really existed. When the vote on O'Connor's motion was taken the Irish, with Labour and some Liberal support, lost again, by 115 votes to 196.

The British press was divided on the question of Ireland in 1919. The London *Times*, owned by Lord Northcliffe, time and again stressed the importance of an Irish settlement for Anglo-American relations. Ulster, it insisted, had to accept home rule for a united Ireland within the British Commonwealth; 'the Government is not pledged to order the affairs of the United

Kingdom to the sole convenience of one political party'.[35] But whereas the London *Times*, London *Daily News*, and the *Manchester Guardian* were prepared to recognize and emphasize the importance of an Irish settlement to Anglo-American relations, the hard core Tory press, the London *Morning Post*, *Daily Telegraph*, *Spectator*, and the *Belfast News*, for example, rejected this view. Ireland, they argued, was of no concern to America and at best the Senate resolution of June was simply a vote-catching device. Lloyd George, they insisted, was 'flunkeying' to Wilson who was playing upon the Irish-Americans for domestic political purposes. These newspapers stood by Ulster.[36]

On 21 July Ireland was debated again in the House of Commons during the discussion, as in America, of the Peace Treaty.[37] By now the once powerful Irish Party in Parliament had shrunk to an ineffective handful, a sorry decline from their great power in the years before 1914. When Joseph Devlin, one of the few, referred to the government's failure to provide self-determination for Ireland, Lloyd George replied:

> The real difficulty is that [Devlin] cannot... get his countrymen to face the facts. They are not satisfied with getting self-determination for themselves without depriving others of the right of self-determination.

He had, he insisted, offered self-determination to Ireland at the time of the Irish convention but two Irish parties had failed to attend. One was led by the late member for Cork, William O'Brien, and 'the other party was that one which not merely claimed a majority but at the last election demonstrated it by an overwhelming majority. They would not come near the place.' The nationalists who did come, he continued, split into three groups, and the Unionists into three or four. 'That was my attempt to apply the principles of President Wilson to Ireland.' To Lloyd George, then, it was the Irish themselves who had repudiated self-determination, and there was no more to be done.

---

[35] See, for example, Col. House's Diary, v. 15, 14 April 1919, for his discussion with Northcliffe on this theme. *House MSS.* The view of the London *Times* is discussed in *Current Opinion*, v. 67, September 1919, pp. 148–50 and J.G.S. MacNeill, 'An Irish Settlement and Public Opinion', *Contemporary Review*, v. 116, September 1919, pp. 264–73.

[36] See *Current Opinion*, v. 66, June 1919, pp. 350–2; v. 67, July 1919, pp. 11–13, August 1919, pp. 81–2, September 1919, pp. 148–50.

[37] *Parl. Debs.*, Commons, 5th Series, v. 118, 21 July 1919, cols 995 ff.

There were many in Ireland and America who were prepared to argue that the election of seventy-two Sinn Fein candidates in December 1918 constituted a pretty fair test of Irish self-determination, but no coalition government in Britain could afford to alienate Ulster and the Unionist Party by accepting Sinn Fein's mandate. When Irish members in the House of Commons argued that the Germans in the new Czechoslovakian state numbered proportionately more than the Ulstermen in Ireland, they were missing the point. Lloyd George was holding a coalition government together in Britain and, to maintain his Unionist support, Ulster had to be satisfied. At home he was no longer a member of the victorious alliance which had been able to redraw the map of Europe, he was a precariously poised Prime Minister courting sudden political death.

In June 1919 the British and American problems of Ireland were linked when Eamon De Valera dramatically appeared in New York. This visit will be examined in the next chaper, but for the moment it can be said that the Irish clearly believed that there was more to be gained by agitating in America than in Britain and that De Valera's presence was not without embarrassment for the leaders of the Irish-American campaign against the League. He had no interest in the problem of Senate constitutional prerogatives or the Republicans' personal attack on Wilson. He was not opposed in principle to the League of Nations, though he did join in the general attack on Article X and argued that it should be amended to provide that no member could hold any territory against the will of its inhabitants. In his appearances at meetings throughout the country for the next four or five months he often found himself joining with opponents of the League in supporting Ireland's claims. At a great meeting in Chicago on 13 July, addressed by De Valera, Frank Walsh, and Edward Dunne, a resolution was adopted advocating the recognition of an Irish republic, but another forcefully opposed the Covenant of the League of Nations because 'it impairs American sovereignty, imperils the constitution of the United States, destroys the Monroe Doctrine and guarantees the world supremacy of the two remaining despotic empires in the world, Great Britain and Japan.'[38] Another meeting in July at Butte, Montana, at which

38 Enclosed in Judge Kirkham Scanlon to Borah, 25 July 1919, *Borah MSS.*, Box 552.

De Valera spoke, was more restrained, however, and simply opposed the League unless it embodied the principle of self-determination and recognized the Irish nation.[39]

The campaign against the League made good ground. On 26 July 1919, for example, after a bitter debate, the Massachusetts Democratic State Committee resolved to oppose the 'League of Nations which attempts to commit this Republic to recognize, and to hold for ever, the title of England, to own and to rule Ireland against the expressed will of an overwhelming majority of the Irish people'. The state Democratic Convention followed suit in October.[40] In Wilson's own state of New Jersey, in October, the State Democratic Party Convention opposed the League unless it was amended to ensure Irish freedom.[41] The Friends of Irish Freedom maintained the pressure with meetings, pamphlets, posters, newspaper advertisements, and cables and letters to Senators and Congressmen. Their recurrent themes were self-determination, recognition of the Irish republic, condemnation of British atrocities in Ireland, and Americanism.[42]

Wilson avoided the Irish issue if he possibly could, though Tumulty was alert for opportunities to improve the President's image. On 25 July he warned Wilson that Cardinals O'Connell of Boston and Hayes of New York were making great efforts to organize Catholics against the League of Nations. Cardinal Gibbons of Baltimore, however, appeared to be opposed to this. Tumulty's advice, which Wilson followed the same day, was a solicitous letter to Gibbons thanking him for his support of the League and stressing the continued urgency for the adoption of the League. Tumulty hoped that Gibbons' attitude might lessen the Irish influence on the Senate.[43]

On 3 September Wilson set out to take his sagging case to the people. He passed through Ohio and Indiana and made for the

[39] Enclosed in James E.Murray to Senator T.J.Walsh, 30 July 1919, *Walsh MSS.*, Box 190.

[40] Michael A.O'Leary, Chairman, Massachusetts Democratic State Committee, to Wilson and Tumulty, 26 July 1919, *Wilson MSS.*, Series VI, Box 559, File 3926; *Springfield Republican*, 5 October 1919.

[41] *New York Herald*, 3 October 1919.

[42] See, for example, *Scrap Book, 1918–1922*, compiled by a member of the national executive of the Friends of Irish Freedom, in the New York Public Library.

[43] Tumulty to Wilson and Wilson to Cardinal Gibbons, 25 July 1919, *Wilson MSS.*, Series II, Box 160.

west. His reception in Montana, Washington, Oregon and California was enthusiastic, but in Pueblo, Colorado, on 25 September he collapsed and was quickly taken back to Washington where he lay gravely ill during the critical months of debate and amendment of the Peace Treaty.[44]

Wilson must have known that he would have to face up to Irish-American charges on this tour. The White House was consistently passing messages addressed to Wilson by Irish-American organizations on to the State Department and evading responsibility for the replies. When Lansing asked Wilson quite directly on 22 August how the Department should answer them and what US policy regarding Ireland actually was, Wilson gave no guidance at all.[45] A few days before he left on his tour he received a letter from Senator Phelan of California, a state on his itinerary, who complained, 'The Irish are in a fair way to leave the Democratic Party'. Phelan urged Wilson to show sympathy for Ireland and to illustrate how the League could serve Irish freedom. On 1 September the President promised him, 'I shall try to do my best'.[46] However, on the tour Wilson was absolutely firm in his commitment to Article X of the League Covenant as it stood and his references to the Irish were hardly conciliatory. In a press statement in San Francisco, for example, he argued that Ireland's case would be covered by Article XI and he explained that Ireland was not considered at Paris because she was not a defeated territory.[47] In his speeches he attacked the Irish euphemistically through 'Germanism' and 'the hyphen'. In South Dakota, for example, he spoke of the pro-German element lifting its head to keep the USA out of the League and in Denver he charged that the only opposition to the Peace Treaty outside Congress was from those who opposed the government in the war; 'The hyphen is the knife that is being stuck into this document.'[48]

Irish-Americans had already prepared the ground over which Wilson travelled. In mid-August large advertisements were placed

[44] Bailey, *op. cit.*, pp. 672–4.

[45] Lansing to Wilson, 22 August 1919, *Lansing MSS.*, vol. 45. I can find no reply from Wilson in either the Lansing or Wilson MSS.

[46] Senator James Phelan to Wilson, 31 August 1919, *Wilson MSS.*, Series II, Box 163; Wilson to Phelan, 1 September 1919. *Wilson MSS.*, Letterbooks, Box 31.

[47] *New York Times*, 18 September 1919; *Wilson MSS.*, Series VI, Box 602, File 4767.

[48] *Boston Post*, 9 September 1919; *New York Times*, 26 September 1919.

in newspapers throughout the country attacking the League, and this was repeated in each city visited by Wilson, both on the day of his appearance and for several days thereafter. Costs were met by the Irish Victory Fund.[49] In a further attempt to deny the President popular support several 'irreconcilable' Republicans followed the President with speaking tours of their own, notably Borah and Hiram Johnson, of California, who was already tipped by Borah and the Friends of Irish Freedom as their choice for President in 1920.[50] In addition, the Hearst press had attacked the League for some time and had stressed the Irish case from coast to coast. The Hearst *Los Angeles Examiner*, for example, observed on 31 July:

> May we not suggest – modestly of course – that Mr Wilson include China, Ireland, India, Persia, Egypt, South Africa and several minor seaports in his itinerary? He will undoubtedly be greeted by large, if somewhat unconvinced, audiences – particularly in Ireland.

Wilson gave little help to his own supporters. Senator T.J. Walsh of Montana, an Irish-American with a considerable number of Irish-Americans in his electorate, offered to present a resolution of his own asking the Senate to declare that as soon as the United States became a member it should use Article XI to present Ireland's case for self-government to the League of Nations. He hoped this might break down the formidable Irish-American opposition to the Peace Treaty, but Wilson's reply was as austere and discouraging as ever. He wrote:

> I value your letter of July 17th. I am not sure that it would be wise at the present time to act upon its suggestion, but you may be confident that I shall do anything that seems possible for me to do in the great matter we are both so deeply interested in.[51]

Because of this opposition Walsh did not present his resolution until September but on 28 July he did speak in the Senate of Article XI as an avenue for Irish freedom, apparently with the President's approval.[52]

[49] Tansill, *op. cit.*, p. 335.

[50] Braden, *op. cit.*, p. 61; Bailey, *op. cit.*, p. 637; Borah to *San Francisco Bulletin*, telegram, 16 June 1919, *Borah MSS.*, Box 552.

[51] T.J.Walsh to Wilson, 17 July 1919, and Wilson to Walsh, 19 July 1919, *Wilson MSS.*, Series II, Box 159, *Walsh MSS.*, Box 190.

[52] Fleming, *US and the League*, p. 280. Walsh claimed that Wilson urged him to speak on this subject in Walsh to Hon. A.E.Spriggs, Montana, 4 August 1919, *Walsh MSS.*, Box 190.

Walsh was very conscious of the rising tide of Irish opposition, including in his own state of Montana. He wrote to a friend:

> I have reached the conclusion that those of our Irish friends who are opposing the League are in no frame of mind to listen to a calm consideration of the conditions confronting us. They want to see England 'licked'; they want to beat the League of Nations so that some day or other, however remote in the future it may be England may get what is coming to her, and they do not want wars, even world wars, to be made impossible or only remotely possible, because in some great war the British Empire may go to smash.... I am under the gravest suspicion. Not I alone but every man of Irish blood in the Senate is equally disappointing to the men led by Dan Cohalan and Frank Walsh.... When Cohalan came here with De Valera they came to see none of us, but confided their purpose and aspirations to Borah.

Walsh finally introduced his resolution on 17 October, just three days after his friend had written that other friends and fellow Irish-American Democrats were turning against him because of his attitude towards the League.[53] Wilson was too ill to object, the League was failing fast, and Walsh had to look to his own interests. He destroyed his own case, however, by conceding in his speech that if Britain insisted that Ireland was a purely domestic matter the League could do nothing. His resolution went no further. It was never brought before a committee or to a vote. Lodge, the Chairman of the Foreign Relations Committee, was certainly not going to consider it and instead he read into the *Congressional Record* a statement by Daniel O'Connell, Director of the Irish National Bureau, that in the 'court' to try Britain, the British would control six votes, those of herself, her Dominions and India, to America's one.[54]

The Foreign Relations Committee reported the Peace Treaty to the Senate on 10 September 1919, with forty-five amendments and four reservations, but the amendments were dropped on the ground that the Peace Conference would have had to be reconvened to consider them, and instead the fourteen interpretive 'Lodge Reservations' were added for debate. In total the fourteen

53 Walsh to Hon. William Scanlon, Montana, 2 September, and Scanlon to Walsh, 14 October 1919, *Walsh MSS.*, Box 190.
54 US *Congressional Record*, 66 Cong., 1 Session, v. 58, pt. 7, 17 October 1919, p. 7048; 18 October 1919, pp. 7109 ff.; 20 October 1919, p. 7156.

reservations did strike hard at Wilson's conception of the League.[55] The second, for example, attacked the automatic mutual guarantee in Article X and was reminiscent of amendments to the arbitration treaties discussed earlier. It was not simply that the Senate reserved the right to approve action which the USA might take to fulfil a League obligation but that no obligation to act could exist in any particular contingency without the Senate's consent. Reservation five provided that the Monroe Doctrine would not be the subject of the measures for arbitration or enquiry which were provided in the Covenant for all disputes. Wilson would not yield to these or the other reservations and on 18 November he wrote to Senator Hitchcock that the Peace Treaty would be nullified, not ratified, in the form proposed by Lodge. When the vote on the Treaty *with* reservations was taken on 19 November, thirty-nine voted in favour and fifty-five against. The minority included thirty-five Republicans and four Democrats – Gore, Shields, Smith and David Walsh of Massachusetts. Those opposed included the large bulk of the Democrats, who remained loyal to Wilson to this point and refused to accept the treaty with reservations, and thirteen Republicans who were opposed to any League. When the treaty was then voted upon *without* reservations these Republican 'irreconcilables' joined the 'reservationists' to defeat it.[56]

The Irish had gained nothing from this controversy. Perhaps they were sufficiently unbalanced to believe that the defeat of the League would facilitate American intervention on their behalf, but this was as unthinkable to traditional isolationists like Borah and Johnson, and to Lodge, who respected the British, as it was to Wilson. Cohalan nevertheless interpreted the vote as a victory and cabled to Borah that this, the 'greatest victory for country and liberty since the revolution', was largely due to him. Borah replied in equally glowing terms:

You have rendered in this fight a service which no other man has rendered or could have rendered. Your country will always be under a debt of gratitude to you. In addition to that too much cannot be said in honor of the Irish people who have helped to make this great

[55] Fleming, *US and the League*, Ch. xvii, 'The Reservations'.
[56] Senator Gilbert M.Hitchcock, 'Events Leading to the World War, Entry of the United States and the Fight for World Peace'. Address to the Nebraska Historical Society, 1925, *Hitchcock MSS*. See also Bailey, *op. cit.*, p. 675.

fight. Of course some people will say that they did it because of their dislike for England but I know from my experience during the last six months that they did it first because of their love of America. Second, because of their profound sympathy for the country of their birth or their ancestors, and third because of their belief that this whole scheme was a scheme of oppression.[57]

Despite this setback, the Peace Treaty was not yet dead. The American people appeared to want a settlement and an overwhelming majority in the Senate approved of some kind of treaty, whether with or without reservations. On 16 February the Senate reopened the debate with House, Tumulty and many others urging Wilson to compromise and accept the reservations. By not doing so, Tumulty argued, Wilson would aggravate the world situation and would be responsible for the perils and consequences of the failure to secure a peace settlement. The President was as intransigent as before.[58]

On 18 March an interesting new reservation was added to the fourteen. Introduced by Senator Gerry (Democrat, Rhode Island), it read:

In consenting to the ratification of the treaty with Germany the United States adheres to the principle of self-determination and to the resolution of sympathy with the aspirations of the Irish people for a government of their own choice adopted by the Senate, on June 6, 1919, and declares that when self-government is attained by Ireland, a consummation it is hoped is at hand, it should promptly be admitted as a member of the League of Nations.[59]

Senator Thomas (Democrat, Colorado) immediately moved an amendment of sympathy with Korean aspirations for self-government, one of his favourite subjects, in an attempt to force the Senate to accept the full consequences of the general principle of self-determination. This failed by thirty-four to forty-six, with sixteen not voting. Lodge then tried to strike out the words, 'the principle of self-determination', but failed and announced that he

---

[57] Cohalan to Borah, 19 November 1919, and Borah to Cohalan, 22 November 1919, *Borah MSS.*, Box 550.

[58] House to Wilson, 27 November 1919, enclosed in House to US Attorney General T.W.Gregory, 27 November 1919, *Gregory MSS.*, Box 1; Tumulty to Wilson 27 February 1920, *Tumulty MSS.*, Box 4.

[59] US *Congressional Record*, 66 Cong., 2 Session, vol. 59, pt. 5, 18 March 1920, pp. 4499 ff.

could not vote for the reservation as it stood. He explained to the Senate:

I am not myself ready to vote for a reservation in which the United States gives its adherence to the principle of self-determination which is not in the treaty in any form. Moreover, self-determination put in as a general principle involves the United States in every possible claim for self-determination all over the world, whether a good claim or a bad one.

When Lodge next tried to add the words 'for the people of Ireland', after the reference to self-determination, he again failed, although he received the support of his fellow Senator from Massachusetts, David Walsh. In fact, the only alteration in wording accepted by the Senate was the substitution of the words 'such government' for 'self-government'. The final vote on the reservation was forty-five to thirty-one with thirteen not voting. In favour, for a variety of reasons, were Borah, Johnson and other 'irreconcilables', who saw the reservation both as another nail in the coffin and as a means of appeasing their Irish supporters, the Democrats Phelan, T.J.Walsh, and Hitchcock, who needed to demonstrate clearly their sympathy for Ireland, and D.I. Walsh of Massachusetts, a Democrat but a Lodge 'reservationist', now catering to his Irish-American constituents. Lodge's position was a difficult one to explain to Irish-Americans. He had been on very close terms with their leaders, particularly Daniel O'Connell, during the Senate debate thus far. Their relations were still good and O'Connell took steps to put the record straight. He sent letters to a number of Irish supporters explaining that Lodge's vote against the Gerry reservation had not implied opposition to Ireland, and the *Gaelic American* published this for its wide audience to see.[60]

Of course one must remember that this reservation involved simply a declaration of intent and in no way affected the substance of the treaty. It required no approval by the British. On the question of reservations Lloyd George had already made it clear to Wilson in February that, so long as other powers were not expressly called upon to agree to them, they were a matter for the American

[60] Enclosed in Daniel O'Connell to Lodge, 31 March 1920, *Lodge MSS.*, '1920, General Correspondence, M–O'.

government alone.[61] The British would probably have accepted all fifteen reservations had Wilson accepted them, but the President believed that they would alter the character of the League by establishing precedents for the wholesale evasion of obligations under the Covenant.

On 19 March the Senate voted on the treaty *with* reservations for the last time, and the result was a reversal of the November decision, forty-nine in favour and thirty-five against. Opposed were twelve Republican 'irreconcilables' and twenty-three Democrats, but twenty-one other Democrats now deserted Wilson to vote with Lodge. The President did not have to veto or accept this decision because the vote fell short of the two-thirds majority required for the ratification of a treaty, and the Peace Treaty died. In May Wilson did veto a joint resolution of Congress declaring an end to hostilities and he determined to fight the 1920 election on the issue of the Peace Treaty.[62]

The Irish once again claimed credit for the victory, arguing that presidential policy thought detrimental to Ireland had been defeated. In the few days prior to the vote the Friends of Irish Freedom had climaxed their campaign with a flood of telegrams to the White House and the Senate, insisting on Irish self-determination and recognition of the Irish Republic.[63] Daniel O'Connell, who directed the Irish campaign from Washington, later claimed that the Irish prevented the United States from being swept into the League, but this was a not untypical Irish overstatement.[64] By publicizing the issue and working very closely with a number of key senators, the Friends of Irish Freedom had played a vital role, but they could have done nothing without the conjunction of Senatorial interests, Irish-American interests, and Americanism which had been such a potent combination in the past. As one writer astutely commented:

[Irish-Americans] considered the defeat of the League their greatest victory. Perhaps they overestimated their contribution to the eventual

---

[61] The former British Foreign Secretary, Grey, had put the British position, unofficially and without authority, in a letter to the London *Times* on 1 February 1920. Lloyd George then put the same view to US Ambassador Davis who sent it to Washington. See Davis to Lansing, telegram, 6 February 1920, *Wilson MSS.*, Series VI, Box 45, File 40.

[62] Bailey, *op. cit.*, pp. 676–8.

[63] *Wilson MSS.*, Series VI, Box 559, File 3926.

[64] O'Connell in Fitz-Gerald, *op. cit.*, p. 236.

outcome of the struggle but certainly they were the first in the trenches and remained in the front line until the last shot was fired.[65]

No one should dispute this judgement and when Senator Hitchcock later spoke of political partisanship, personal animosities and an unyielding President as factors in the defeat of the League, he also stressed the importance of 'the race prejudice of the Germans and the Irish'.[66]

In 1920 George Creel, Wilson's wartime Director of Public Information, attributed the introduction of 'nationalities' into the campaign on the League to the Republican Party. 'The forces of hyphenism,' he wrote, 'were boldly called into being and no effort was spared to revive and exaggerate the divisive prejudices of American Life.'[67] In fact, however, the course of the Irish campaign in particular was set by a small group of Irish-Americans who shared an antipathy to the League with the Republican 'irreconcilables'. They knew that, as it stood, the League could never help Ireland. It was designed to legitimize and protect a *status quo* which favoured British rule not only in Ireland but throughout the Empire. This could never be tolerated by the revolutionary Irish. In addition, generations of inbred Irish-American anglophobia placed Cohalan and the leaders of the Clan na Gael in the very centre of the campaign for 'Americanism' with its peculiar combination of traditional American isolation and bellicosity towards the British. Cohalan and his colleagues needed no organizing by the Republican Party. Rather, the Republicans and the Irish-Americans were prepared to use each other for their own ends, and they were mutually content with the result.

[65] Nelson M.Blake, *The United States and the Irish Revolution, 1914–22*, unpublished Ph.D. dissertation, Clark University, Mass., 1935, p. 318.

[66] Hitchcock, *op. cit.*, p. 21.

[67] George Creel, *The War, the World, and Wilson*. New York: Harper, 1920, p. 330.

10 De Valera's Visit to America, 1919–20

'Our first duty as the elected Government of the Irish people will be to make clear to the world the position in which Ireland now stands. There is in Ireland at this moment only one lawful authority, and that authority is the elected Government of the Irish Republic.'

EAMON DE VALERA, NEW YORK
New York Times, 25 JUNE 1919

Eamon De Valera escaped from Lincoln Prison, England, on 3 February 1919 and secretly made his way to Ireland. A month later the British released all their Irish political prisoners and on 1 April De Valera was elected *Priomh-Aire*, First Minister or President, by Dail Eireann. As the senior surviving combatant from the Easter rising, leadership had been thrust upon him, and it was a sign of the times when in the middle of June he secretly travelled to America to continue his fight for Irish freedom. On 23 June he met Cohalan and Devoy for the first time and on 24 June he issued his first American press statement. It declared the Irish republican government to be the only lawful government of Ireland.[1] In fact, however, this assertion was in dispute in America, even amongst Irish-Americans themselves.

Patrick McCartan, who had represented the Irish republican movement in America since July 1917, argued that the Irish had exercised self-determination in the British General Election of December 1918 by a two-thirds majority and had severed all political links with Britain.[2] Cohalan, on the other hand, believed that the best way of bringing Ireland's case into the open was to use the President's principle of self-determination by arguing not

[1] *New York Times*, 25 June 1919.
[2] For a detailed account of Patrick McCartan's long visit to America see his *With De Valera in America*, Dublin: Fitzpatrick, 1932.

214

that Ireland had already exercised it, but that she should be allowed to exercise it. In 1919 rival meetings were organized in New York by McCartan and those supporting Cohalan's view and at the Irish Race Convention in February a backstage tussle developed over resolutions, with Cohalan winning. On 24 February, while the convention was in progress, he wrote to McCartan that there was no Irish republic, it controlled no territory, had no army or police force, and that for the United States to recognize it was tantamount to declaring war on Britain. However, when Cohalan publicly stated on 23 March that the Irish republic had already come into existence it became clear that the dispute was more complex. There were, in fact, other problems involved: one was McCartan's resentment of the fact that although in the USA as the representative of the Irish people he could exercise no influence over the Irish-American movement directed by Cohalan and Devoy. Another problem was the political use already being made of the Irish question in the campaign against the League of Nations early in 1919. McCartan cabled Sean O'Kelly, an Irish representative in Paris, that President Wilson was Ireland's friend and that he opposed the anti-League bias of Cohalan and other Irish-Americans which was apparent at the Irish Race Convention.[3] In March he warned W.J.M.A.Maloney against the anti-League movement and added, 'God save Ireland – from her friends'.[4]

There was a split, then. On the one hand were Cohalan, Devoy, the Clan na Gael, the Friends of Irish Freedom, and the powerful newspapers, the *Gaelic American* and the *Irish World*. On the other hand were McCartan, Maloney, and Joseph McGarrity with the *Irish Press* which he founded in Philadelphia in 1918. It must be admitted, however, that the Irish-American movement was still overwhelmingly dominated by the Cohalan-Devoy faction and that until De Valera came personally into a dispute with Cohalan over its leadership and direction the split was of minor significance.

De Valera's visit to America was his first sustained exercise in statesmanship and the politics of leadership, but his apprentice-

---

[3] Tansill, *op. cit.*, pp. 293–5, 305; McCartan, *op. cit.*, pp. 82, 93; John J.Splain, 'The Irish Movement in the United States since 1911', in Fitz-Gerald, *op. cit.*, p. 234.
[4] McCartan to Maloney, 10 March 1919, *Maloney MSS.*, Box 21.

ship in the Gaelic League, the Irish Volunteers and British prisons, and his rapid promotion were only a very partial training for the tasks he had set himself. He had a great deal to learn. Almost at once he began a hectic round of speaking engagements, addressing public meetings and a number of state legislatures from coast to coast. In August 1919, *Current Opinion*, a survey of journals and newspapers in America, reported that the Irish republic was no longer a joke; De Valera had quickly become a world figure and a serious topic of conversation.[5] The newspaper coverage he received was excellent throughout the country. There were complaints that he was illegally using American territory to attack a friendly state, but the US Attorney General reported to Secretary of State Lansing in November, 'The Bureau of Investigation has been carefully observing the activities of M. De Valera [*sic*], and to this date he has not ... made any speeches which bring him within the purview of any Federal statute.'[6] De Valera could have been charged with entering the country illegally but, for both the British and American governments, the truth was spoken when a Member of Parliament asked that representations be made to the Americans to curb his activities and Bonar Law replied, 'I think there is no doubt that from the diplomatic point of view we would have a right to take the course suggested ... but it is not a question of right; it is a question of what is expedient'.[7] De Valera had been given a splendid welcome in America and could not be curbed without sparking off an explosion of protest.

De Valera was 'President of Ireland' to audiences throughout America but this enthusiastic reception told him very little about the nature of the leadership which Cohalan and the Friends of Irish Freedom were exercising in the Irish-American movement. As he was busy travelling and speaking a dispute was growing with Cohalan and those whose views he represented. De Valera's most important task in America, and the primary purpose for his visit, was to raise money both for the expensive *de facto* administration of government and justice in Ireland and for the conduct of the growing war, but there had already been acrimony over

[5] *Current Opinion*, August 1919, v. 67, pp. 83–5.
[6] Attorney General Gregory to Lansing, n.d. (1919), *State Department*, 841d. 00/97.
[7] *Parl. Debs.*, Commons, 5th Series, 8 December 1920, v. 135, col. 2081.

the disposal of Irish-American funds. The Irish Victory Fund was being used more to defeat the League of Nations than to achieve Irish independence. McGarrity, for one, tried to divert this money to Ireland but was unsuccessful. By the end of 1920 only $115,000 had been sent out of total disbursements of more than $887,000. A further sum of almost $27,000 was provided for De Valera's expenses and $25,000 was subscribed, as we shall see, for Irish bond-certificates, but the remainder was spent on organization, propaganda and publications by the Friends of Irish Freedom, a sum of over half a million dollars.[8] De Valera set out to change this. After Cohalan and other Irish-American lawyers made it clear that it would be illegal for an unrecognized republic to float an official loan in America, he adopted a plan to sell Irish bond-certificates which were to be exchanged for bonds after international recognition of the Irish republic and the withdrawal of British troops. Frank P. Walsh became head of an organization, the American Commission on Irish Independence, to promote and organize the bond-certificate campaign, while James O'Mara, a trustee of the Dail Eireann National Loan, travelled to America to handle the financial details. The Dail 'Loan for Home Subscription' was fixed at £250,000 ($1,250,000) but the American target was a huge $20,000,000.[9]

The Friends of Irish Freedom advanced $100,000 to begin the campaign early in October 1919 although Liam Mellowes, who was working with De Valera in America, wrote to Ireland in September, 'Gang [Cohalan and Devoy] not pulling with De Valera. Want to run him. He won't be run. He has seen through them. . . . Never saw a sicker man. Disillusionment isn't the word.'[10] De Valera himself wrote to Arthur Griffith that he refused to act as Cohalan's rubber stamp.[11] He had already realized what McCartan knew many months before, that the movement in Ireland could exercise very little control over Cohalan and the Friends of Irish Freedom. In Cohalan he was facing a man with a great deal of experience in organizing or manipulating anglophobia, who possessed a set of guiding

[8] Tansill, *op. cit.*, pp. 344–7.

[9] *Ibid.*, pp. 347–53; Eamon De Valera, 'Ireland Can Stand Alone', *Independent*, 19 July 1919, v. 99, p. 89; John J.Splain, 'Under Which King?' in Fitz-Gerald, *op. cit.*, pp. 242–3.

[10] Desmond Ryan, *The Phoenix Flame*, London: Arthur Baker, 1937, p. 312.

[11] Tansill, *op. cit.*, p. 343.

principles for the conduct of American foreign policy. The object of the organization Cohalan and Devoy had moulded was not simply Irish freedom but the promotion of particular foreign policies for the United States which were of little interest to Ireland. De Valera seems not to have understood that although these men were Irish-Americans they were also simply Americans. A public mask of harmony was maintained through January 1920 as De Valera, Cohalan, Devoy and others met regularly to plan the bond-certificate drive, but there were fierce battles between them in private.

The whole country was soon organized with state and local committees and the US Treasury raised no objections to the campaign save to insist that there should be no attempt to induce Americans to exchange their US Liberty Bonds for Irish bond-certificates. Frank Walsh agreed to this condition.[12] The drive opened on 17 January 1920, and in the next year and a half Irish-Americans and their supporters managed to contribute more than $5,500,000 to the Irish republican cause by buying bond-certificates. This effectively ended the control exercised by the Friends of Irish Freedom over Irish-Americans as a source of funds. The Irish Victory Fund was closed in August before the bond-certificate drive began and De Valera secured the American Commission for Irish Independence as a base from which to challenge Cohalan. Meanwhile the FOIF continued to co-operate with the commission because they had no choice. For example, they purchased certificates to the value of $25,000. Refusal to aid the 'President' would have cost them popular support because, as John Redmond had shown before, the chosen leader of Ireland could claim the loyalty of the mass of the Irish in America. Only World War I had broken Redmond's control and now De Valera, representing very different principles, inherited his mantle.

Relations between the leaders rapidly worsened from February 1920. On 6 February the London journal, *Westminster Gazette*, published an interview with De Valera in which he declared that Ireland would accept a form of 'Monroe Doctrine' from Britain. Britain could, he believed, declare that it would not allow Ireland to enter into alliances designed to restrict the freedom of Great Britain or allow Ireland to be used for military or naval purposes

---

[12] Frank Walsh to State Chairmen, 17 February 1920, *Cockran MSS.*, Box 17. W. Bourke Cockran was the New York State Chairman.

by any third power. The interview was granted to a London journal and in the context of British politics might have been wisely pragmatic, but to the Irish-American leaders compromise with Britain represented surrender. The *Gaelic American* condemned the interview and this prompted De Valera to write to Cohalan on 20 February attacking what he called, 'the general attitude of mind [the articles] reveal'. His tone was challenging, authoritarian, and showed signs of strain. He wrote:

I am answerable to the Irish people for the proper execution of the trust with which I have been charged. I am definitely responsible to them, and I *alone* am responsible. It is my obvious duty to select such instruments as may be available for the task set me. . . .

I see added force being applied day by day, to the power end of the great lever of American public opinion, with which I hope to accomplish my purpose. I must satisfy myself as to the temper of the other end of the lever.

The articles of the *Gaelic American*, and certain incidents that have resulted from them, give me grounds for the fear that, in a moment of stress, the point of the lever would fail me. I am led to understand that these articles in the *Gaelic American* have your consent and approval. Is this so?

De Valera was wide open to an expert counter-attack. In his reply Cohalan denied any responsibility for the *Gaelic American* and defended Devoy's right to publish what he pleased. He accepted that De Valera was responsible to the Irish people but insisted that he himself was an American citizen with American interests at heart. It was ultimately as an American that he supported Ireland's demand for complete independence. He stated his position in this way:

If Ireland were to change her position, and to seek a measure of self-government that would align her in the future with England as an ally, in what I regard as the inevitable struggle for the freedom of the seas that must shortly come between America and England, every loyal American will, without hesitation, take a position unreservedly upon the side of America.

Referring to De Valera's use of 'levers' and 'instruments' he asked, 'Do you really think for a moment that American public opinion will permit any citizen of another country to interfere, as you suggest, in American affairs?' In conclusion he warned De

219

Valera of the dangers involved for both Ireland and America in imperilling the unity of American sympathy for Ireland. Cohalan had side-stepped the challenge and thrown it back. He had no intention of relinquishing control of the American movement to De Valera.[13]

A truce was arranged on 19 March at a New York meeting of a hundred or so leading Irish-Americans where De Valera claimed that for six months his opponents had been conspiring to oust him. The meeting was a chaotic one with his forces heavily outnumbered. However, after many hours the opposing sides agreed that Ireland should insist on unqualified independence, that De Valera should be supported as President, but that American opinions and judgement should be consulted on the course of the Irish movement in America.[14] The truce was short-lived for on 10 April James O'Mara demanded that Diarmuid Lynch, National Secretary of the Friends of Irish Freedom, should supply an account of the Irish Victory Fund. 'Such money morally belongs to Ireland', he wrote. In reply the FOIF National Council decided to restate, as it saw them, the purposes of the Irish Victory Fund. These were four: the education of American opinion to demand that the objects for which America entered the war be fully attained, the recognition of a republican government in Ireland, opposition to any League of Nations which did not safeguard American rights, and the preservation of American ideals of government against false British propaganda. Since the treasury of the Irish republic was now in a sound condition, the council argued, the fund would be used in America for these purposes.[15]

The Irish in America were, therefore, disastrously divided for the presidential election campaign which began in the summer of 1920.[16] Against the advice of Frank Walsh and others, De Valera decided to go to Chicago for the Republican convention in June and he was already established in banner-draped headquarters as the 'President of Ireland' when Cohalan arrived to represent the

[13] D.Gwynn, *De Valera*, pp. 96–101; Tansill, *op. cit.*, pp. 446–9.

[14] *Ibid.*, pp. 365–8; McCartan, *op. cit.*, pp. 168–9.

[15] Blake, *op. cit.*, pp. 346–7. See also resolutions of the National Council of the FOIF in *Maloney MSS.*, Box 10.

[16] For discussions of both party conversations see Tansill, *op. cit.*, pp. 373–83; D.Gwynn, *De Valera*, pp. 106–7; McCartan, *op. cit.*, pp. 198–9; Splain, 'Under Which King?' in Fitz-Gerald, *op. cit.*, pp. 248–9.

Friends of Irish Freedom. Before a sub-committee of the resolutions committee they presented separate testimony and resolutions. Walsh spoke for De Valera and demanded a plank calling for the recognition of the Irish republic. It was soundly defeated by eleven to one. Cohalan's resolution was more moderate in tone and expressed sympathy for all oppressed people. It simply recognized Ireland's right to self-determination. This was in accord with the only resolutions which had thus far found their way through Congress, but it was only narrowly adopted by seven to six on the casting vote of the chairman. It was when this new resolution was found to be unacceptable to De Valera that Chairman Watson withdrew it. The Republican Party platform therefore contained no reference to Ireland and both parties were on notice that the split in the Irish ranks would enable them to evade specific commitments at this stage.

De Valera then went to San Francisco for the Democratic convention in July. The Friends of Irish Freedom chose not to contest the issue again, and indeed it would have been difficult because Cohalan, Devoy, the *Irish World* and the *Gaelic American* had already backed the 'irreconcilable' Republican Senator, Hiram Johnson, for the presidency.[17] The Democratic Party was still Wilson's party and the convention adopted a strong plank supporting ratification of the Peace Treaty and the League of Nations. The Democrats were also in the welcome position of needing only a token effort to outbid the Republicans on Ireland. De Valera's resolution on recognition of the Irish republic was therefore defeated by thirty-one to seventeen in the resolutions committee and a plank was accepted by a two-thirds majority of the full convention which recalled that self-determination had been an American war aim and reiterated the sympathy of the Democratic Party for Irish aspirations to self-government.

Despite the fiasco at Chicago, the disappointment at San Francisco and the continuing division of the Irish leaders, the Irish question was bound to be a factor in the 1920 presidential election and preparatory election strategy had certainly not been ignored by politicians during the Senate battle on the Peace Treaty. In January 1920 Sir Horace Plunkett, on a visit to Michigan, wrote to Colonel House, 'The way in which the Republican party are fighting for the Irish vote is one of the most

17 Tansill, *op. cit.*, p. 373.

unedifying spectacles I have ever witnessed in the arena of party politics.'[18] Lord Reading, the British Ambassador, told Henry White of a visit from two unnamed Republican Senators who explained that to defeat the Democrats they were going to have to use the Irish question and to attack England mercilessly. They wished to inform the British government that there was no real animosity![19] An article in the American journal, *Fortnightly Review*, in June 1920, asked rhetorically, 'Is not the dominant Republican party practically mortgaged to the Irish vote?'

In fact the national conventions had shown the parties to be very wary of the Irish question and had exposed the division in the ranks of the Irish in America at that time. Lord Bryce was able to write in July, 'My American informants doubt whether Ireland will count for very much in [the] presidential campaign. Both parties [are] a little shy of it.'[20] However, this could not be said in October when the campaign was on in earnest. Cox, the Demcratic candidate, increasingly discussed the Irish question at his meetings, and his Republican opponent, Harding, played into his hands with an inept interview for the London *Morning Post* on 23 September. He clearly believed the Irish question was a domestic British one and suggested that America had already meddled abroad excessively without invitation. This was widely reported in the American press and on 8 October he was reported as saying to an Irish-American questioner, 'My dear man, do not pursue me to the point of discussing in detail the internal affairs of a foreign power. I would not undertake to say to Great Britain what she must do any more than I would permit her to tell us what we must do with the Philippines.' However, he went on to claim, 'I have a sympathetic feeling myself . . . for Irish freedom. I voted that way in the United States Senate.' The Democratic National Committee immediately issued to the press details of Harding's voting record in the Senate. He voted against the Pittman resolution urging clemency for Irish political prisoners in 1916; he did not vote on the Borah resolution in June 1919; he voted that the Gerry reservation of 18 March 1920 be laid on the table, that is killed, and he voted against the reservation when it finally came to a vote. Lodge, Borah and others might be

18 Plunkett to House, 13 January 1920, *House MSS.*, Drawer 12, File 2.
19 Nevins, *Henry White*, p. 456.
20 Lord Bryce to Plunkett, 11 July 1920, *Plunkett MSS.*

campaigning for the Irish vote but clearly Harding was not nominated because of his appeal to Irish-Americans![21]

For the Democrats Cox tried to answer Irish-American doubts about the Peace Treaty by insisting that nothing in the League Covenant could require the USA to join England in suppressing Ireland, and in Kansas City on 2 October he even promised to invoke Article XI if the Irish question remained unsolved by the date of his inauguration.[22] But when a questioner in the House of Commons asked if the war in Ireland could be referred to the League of Nations in this way the British Prime Minister answered simply, but firmly, in the negative.[23] When Cox repeated his offer before a mass audience in Madison Square Gardens on 23 October, he added that he did not believe that Ireland was a domestic British question. 'I know it is not,' he declared, '. . . whenever a war becomes a war of extermination it becomes a world tragedy.'[24] Two hundred thousand copies of a pamphlet containing his statement were distributed after Sunday mass a few days later by New York Democrat Irish-Americans[25] but Cox was hampered because few really prominent Irish-Americans took part in his campaign. Bourke Cockran tried to help in New York and Casement's lawyer, M.F.Doyle, at the request of the chairman of the Democratic National Committee, published an open letter of support, but little more was done.[26]

To what extent the Irish question really influenced the result of the presidential election is almost impossible to determine. T.A. Bailey writes, 'There were dozens of issues, ranging from prohibition of alcoholic beverages to self-determination for Ireland, and it would be absurd to say that the results were a mandate on any one of them.'[27] The fact that women received their first presidential vote confuses any attempt to study the voting records. The USA was weary of the Peace Treaty issue, of Democrats, of Wilson, of the war, and turned to the 'normalcy' promised by Harding. This utterly unimpressive man scored a percentage of

[21] *Washington Post*, 8, 9 October 1920.
[22] 'What President Cox will do for Ireland,' *Weekly Review*, 13 October 1920, v. 3, p. 304.
[23] *Parl Debs.*, Commons, 5th Series, 11 November 1920, v. 134, col. 1385.
[24] *New York Times*, 24 October 1920.
[25] J.J.Noonan to Tumulty, n.d., *Wilson MSS.*, Series VI, Box 559, File 3926.
[26] Doyle to Tumulty, 1 November 1920, *ibid.*; Wittke, *op. cit.*, p. 291.
[27] Bailey, *op. cit.*, p. 679.

the total vote that was not exceeded until Johnson defeated Goldwater in 1964. Even F.D. Roosevelt could never manage as much. Harding scored 404 to 127 in the electoral college and led by seven million in the popular vote. Consul Dumont reported from Dublin that the Sinn Fein press was full of statements that Harding owed his election to the votes of Irish-Americans, but this was certainly an exaggeration.[28] Wilson had beaten Hughes by only 591,385 votes while Harding had won by seven million, and no Irish-American swing could account for that.

There were states with large Irish populations where the Democratic vote dropped markedly, for example in California, Wisconsin, and particularly Illinois, but Massachusetts, New Jersey, Connecticut, New York and Pennsylvania, all with large numbers of Irish voters, followed the national trend of a relatively unchanged Democratic total and dramatic Republican gains. When one considers the pattern of voting around the country it seems likely that many of the Irish moved with the population in general.[29] This itself involved a break with the traditional loyalties of previous elections but it was certainly not decisive and there was no dramatic breakdown of Irish-Democratic control in traditional Irish districts. It would have been truly remarkable had this happened for it would have taken more than Warren Harding to break the habit with the patronage and power it represented.

The election had been closely followed in Ireland where, from the date of the European armistice in 1918, another war had been growing.[30] It was a classic guerilla confrontation. A republican force of perhaps 15,000 men at its prime, acting under the command of Michael Collins, with shelter and co-operation from hundreds of thousands of willing Irishmen, transformed orderly British administration into unsuccessful and brutal military rule. The British were prepared to yield only on terms favourable to themselves and attributed the conflict to the terrorism of an

28 US Consul Dumont to Secretary of State, 28 January 1921, *State Department*, 841d. 00/314.

29 Edgar Robinson, *The Presidential Vote, 1896–1932*, London: Oxford University Press, 1934.

30 Unless stated to the contrary, data on the development of the war in Ireland and the *de facto* Republican Government is taken from Macardle, *op. cit.*, which discusses the war at great length in pp. 283–639. See also Edgar Holt, *Protest in Arms; The Irish Troubles, 1916–1923*, London: Putnam, 1960.

unrepresentative extremist minority. They insisted on a return to order before a settlement so that the majority could accept a solution free from terror and coercion. The problem for an observer was to decide whether the terrorist minority actually represented the wishes of the Irish majority and to what extent the British case represented a genuine concern for the well-being of the whole Irish population. It was certainly clear that a settlement could not long be delayed. One was absolutely necessary for Ireland's sake, for Anglo-American and Imperial relations, and because Britain's commitments around the world, in Egypt, India, the newly mandated territories and in Russia, were straining her resources to the limit.

De Valera had been campaigning in the USA for six months when Lloyd George introduced his new plan for Ireland on 22 December 1919. Two Irish parliaments were proposed, one for Dublin and one for Belfast with equal, though limited powers. External relations, trade, defence, war, the police and the post office were to be reserved to the Parliament at Westminster where Irish representation was to be cut to forty-two, a reform long overdue in view of the declining population of Ireland. Fewer powers were to be granted the Irish in these proposals than in the 1914 home rule act which was still suspended pending formal conclusion of the war. Six north-eastern counties with large pockets of nationalists, and including two counties, Fermanagh and Tyrone, with nationalist majorities, were to be represented in the Belfast parliament. The unification of all Ireland was the declared future aim and to this end a Council of Ireland, drawn in equal parts from the North and the South, was proposed to prepare the way.[31] Sinn Fein would have no part in these proposals but the Ulster Unionist Council accepted them. Ulster stood to gain only six of the nine counties it had traditionally claimed, but it was guaranteed union with Great Britain and a veto against unification in the Council of Ireland. The US Consul in Dublin, Dumont, immediately discussed the proposals with Arthur Griffith who insisted that they provided nothing for Ireland and were made to mislead American opinion. After another discussion with Griffith, Dumont wrote:

[Griffith] thinks a settlement satisfactory to any point of view of De

[31] D.Gwynn, *Partition*, pp. 185–7.

Valera a vital factor in the American political situation; that the Irish-American vote is the backbone of the Democratic Party; and that the Catholic Church in America, dominated as it is by Irish, can force America through politics into a position where she would be willing, even if she is not at present, to help Ireland obtain her freedom if that is to be the only solution.

Dumont added his own assessment of America's importance to Sinn Fein:

In my opinion, were it possible to stop all communication with the United States, Sinn Fein as an organization would slowly die out. The movement is kept very much alive by reports of the great progress the cause of Irish freedom is making in the United States. Every expression favourable to the Sinn Fein cause is given the greatest publicity in its own press. Frequent messages from De Valera giving exaggerated accounts of his receptions are published. It is taken for granted that no one listens to him in America from curiosity but from deep conviction. The slightest thing that could be interpreted as an official recognition on the part of the American government would give a tremendous impetus to his cause in Ireland. Most Irishmen take it for granted that the American people are all greatly interested in seeing Ireland obtain its freedom and cannot realize what a large percentage of them have no interest in or thought of Ireland.[32]

It was not until a full year later, in December 1920, that the Irish proposals received the Royal Assent after a great deal of debate and controversy. On 10 May Lord Hugh Cecil insisted in the House of Lords, 'We are here face to face with an attempt to satisfy foreign opinion, American opinion, opinion of the Dominions; we are not faced with any real attempt to govern Ireland.'[33] Of course no Prime Minister could ignore the Empire's major problem and a proposal of some kind was inevitable, but once this has been said it must be conceded to Cecil and Arthur Griffith that the state of Anglo-American relations was indeed crucial to the nature of the British government's proposals. When Viscount Grey, the former Foreign Secretary, agreed to go to Washington as temporary Ambassador in 1919, he thought the Irish question so important to his job that he extracted a pledge

[32] Dumont to Secretary of State, 23 December 1919, Tansill, *op. cit.*, pp. 399–400, and 2 January 1920, *State Department*, 841d. 00/119.
[33] Macardle, *op. cit.*, p. 353.

from the government that it would try to settle the problem.[34] The Cabinet admitted its obligation to Grey when it discussed the Irish proposals in November 1919. A Cabinet committee on the Irish question outlined other reasons for its recommendations, which were substantially those presented to Parliament in December 1919, in a report to the Cabinet which included the following statement:

The Committee are agreed that in view of the situation in Ireland itself, of public opinion in Great Britain, and still more of public opinion in the Dominions and the United States of America, they cannot recommend the policy either of repealing or postponing the Home Rule Act of 1914. In their judgement it is essential, now that the war is over, and that the Peace Conference has dealt with so many analogous questions in Europe, that the Government should make a sincere attempt to deal with the Irish question once and for all.

Their proposal to establish the two parliaments in Ireland was designed to convince opinion in America and the Dominions that the British were offering autonomy to the whole of Ireland, or rather to both Irelands, with self-determination to both Ulster and the rest of the country. As Arthur Balfour pointed out in a Cabinet meeting, if Ulster was offered self-determination it would choose to maintain the existing union, but Britain's foreign relations required that it be offered home rule and a parliament it did not want.[35] In his House of Commons speeches on 22 December 1919 and 31 March 1920, Lloyd George further solicited the support of 'our American friends' by arguing that De Valera's demand for complete secession was precisely that made by the American South and resisted by Lincoln. The reply from Ireland, of course, was that the American analogy was the War of Independence, not the Civil War. Ireland was a nation struggling to be free, not a seceding state of the Union.

During 1920 the liberal press in Britain continuously urged the granting of self-determination to Ireland in part, at least, to

[34] Cabinet meeting 5 (19), minute 2, 11 November 1919, *CAB.* 23/18. Grey worked very closely with Colonel House in assessing the importance of the Irish question and framing his request to the Cabinet. See memo by Grey, 11 August 1919, in *House MSS.*, Drawer 34, File 52.

[35] First report of the Cabinet Committee on the Irish Question, 4 November 1919, C.P.Paper 56, *CAB.* 24/92.

improve Anglo-American relations, but the Tory press consistently argued that the American agitation was simply a vote-catching device. The hard-core Unionist opposition was inflexible and Carson spoke for it in May when he declared:

> The proposal [to establish two Irish parliaments] is one which . . . I think we can discuss without dragging in, as we frequently do during these debates, the influence of America upon our politics. I think it is high time that America – or those who pretend to speak for America, but are not real Americans – should learn to understand that we are still a great power, and that we are not subordinate to America or to any other Power.

Carson's resentment was shared by a very large section of the British public, Ambassador Davis reported.[36] But in January and June of 1920 Ireland replied to the government's proposals of the previous December by returning Republican majorities in nearly all the local government elections outside Ulster, and indeed in many which were in Ulster. In June Dail Eireann established *de facto* courts of equity and justice to augment its existing courts of arbitration. Sooner or later the British had to come to terms with these facts. Affairs in Ireland in 1920 were in a very bad state. For a while the government confidently anticipated another Easter Monday rising and almost 250 IRA and Irish Volunteer leaders were deported in the first four months of the year.[37] In March the Black and Tans began the operations which were to make them so notorious. All these developments occurred before the new and inadequate Irish proposals were enacted into law in December 1920.

The US government was very well informed on these events by Ambassador Davis and Consuls Dumont (Dublin), Kent (Belfast), and Mitchel (Cork). These men supplied often massively documented reports which were all highly critical of Sinn Fein but were often also critical of the British. Arthur Griffith confided to Dumont that he still expected some kind of decisive American move. In September 1920 he confessed that the future looked dark for Sinn Fein but, looking overseas to the American

36 *Parl. Debs.*, Commons, 5th Series, 18 May 1920, v. 129, col. 1272; Davis to Secretary of State, 31 May 1920, *State Department*, 841d. 00/204.

37 Wright to State Department, telegram, 17 March 1920 and Davis to Secretary of State, 3 April 1920, *State Department*, 841d. 00/151, 178; Sir Nevil Macready, *Annals of an Active Life*, London: Hutchinson, 1924, p. 439.

election campaign, he argued that in a couple of weeks the USA would be forced to show its hand in support of Ireland.[38] However, there was no sign of appeasement by the British to clip Irish-American wings and to prevent the Irish question from becoming an election issue. Instead the Restoration of Order in Ireland Act, approved in August, granted extraordinary powers and immunities to the military, *habeas corpus* was suspended and secret courts martial were introduced.[39]

The greatest opportunity to appease the Irish, and perhaps help a settlement, came with the case of Terence MacSwiney, the Lord Mayor of Cork and a veteran of the IRA, who was arrested in August 1920 and court-martialled on a charge of possessing revolutionary documents. He chose to protest with a hunger strike which caused his death in Brixton Prison, London, on 25 October. Two others who were arrested at the same time died after hunger strikes in Cork Prison but an international agitation focused on MacSwiney. From America A.G.Gardiner, former editor of the liberal London *Daily News*, reported to this paper that the MacSwiney case was bigger news in the American press than the presidential election. He gave this description of Irish-Americans:

They form the most solid and formidable political mass in the country. They are formidable, not so much because of their number, as because they are the one political body moving with a single idea in a compact mass through the life of the nation. They have come across the Atlantic with bitterness in their hearts, and they are revenging themselves upon their oppressor in the New World. They are not socially negligible. They are in the seats of the mighty. . . . The most brilliant writers on the Press are Irish. Nearly every political caucus is under Irish control. Most of the great cities have Irish mayors. The police are almost invariably Irish. One of the most virulent supporters of Mr Hearst's ant-British crusade is an Irish judge [Cohalan] of the Supreme Court of New York State. The Irish vote is the crucial element of every election. No candidate, whether for a mayoralty, a state governorship, the Senate, or the Presidency, can ignore it. . . . The Atlantic bridge that Anglo-American good will must erect, must have Ireland as the keystone of its central arch. Without a reconciled Ireland there can be no enduring reconciliation

[38] Dumont to Secretary of State, 28 September 1920, *State Department*, 841d. 00/243.
[39] Macardle, *op. cit.*, pp. 394–6.

with America. That is why the tragedy at Brixton Jail has such momentous reverberations across the Atlantic.[40]

The MacSwiney agitation quickly came to the attention of the American government in August – from Arthur Griffith via Consul Dumont, from MacSwiney's brother, living in New York, and his sister, teaching in a Catholic college in North Carolina, from Cardinal O'Connell, Frank Walsh, and many others.[41] On 2 September Tumulty passed on to Wilson a telegram from 'a good Irish friend of ours' which, rather extravagantly, advised him that he could ensure ratification of the Peace Treaty if he spoke up for MacSwiney and thereby rehabilitated himself with the Irish. Wilson snapped a reply, 'This is more than futile: it is grossly impertinent. I wish I knew some way to rebuke it. It is a piece of confounded impudence.'[42] However, that same day Wilson's new Secretary of State, Bainbridge Colby, also wrote to him:

There has been a crescendo pressure on the State Department for the last few days, in the shape of letters, telegrams (nearly a hundred), personal calls from 'picketers', and Mr Frank P.Walsh – all asking some intercession on behalf of the Mayor of Cork, now in Brixton jail, and who seems to have brought himself to death's door by voluntary starvation. It is needless for me to even mention to you the entire absence of legal justification for any representations or actions on our part. MacSwiney is a British subject, in jail as the result of the infraction of a British law, and the judgement of a presumably competent tribunal. Even on 'humanitarian grounds' – the basis of most of the appeals to which I have referred – there seems to be a lack of support for any intervention, as the man is the victim of himself and no one else.

And yet – his death would be deplorable, and its effect not easy to estimate in advance.

The thought occurred to me that I might take advantage of my acquaintance with the officials of the British Embassy to express, in the most informal and friendly way, our concern for the effect on public opinion of a successful martyrdom, and the hope that the British government might find a way to avert the man's death, without too great a sacrifice of consistency.

---

[40] 'Ireland an American Question', *Literary Digest*, 6 November, v. 67, pp. 20–1.
[41] See *State Department*, 841d. 00/217–232 and *Wilson MSS.*, Series VI, Box 642, File 5315, 'Terence MacSwiney'.
[42] Tumulty to Wilson, 2 September 1920, and Wilson to Tumulty, n.d., *ibid.*

Or – is the subject one which I had best let alone?[43]

There is no evidence that Wilson would allow Colby to do anything. His resistence to Irish-American demands was by now well established and no amount of pressure could have forced him to intercede.

What effect MacSwiney's hunger strike had on the American elections of 2 November 1920, cannot be known, although his death on 25 October, and the huge memorial meeting at the New York Polo Grounds addressed by Governor Al Smith and De Valera on 30 October certainly focused attention on the Irish question at a critical time.[44] It was attention which Cohalan and Devoy might have preferred to see focused on the defeat of Wilson, his League of Nations, and his party. MacSwiney's death and the execution of a young Irishman, Kevin Barry, aged eighteen on 1 November, were dramatic developments just days before the American elections which could have been averted, equally dramatically, by British clemency had Lloyd George been primarily concerned for American opinion. Sir Henry Wilson recorded in his diary that the British Prime Minister was restricting reprisals in Ireland until after the election, but this must be seriously questioned in view of the timing of the MacSwiney and Barry tragedies.[45]

During the whole of 1920 the battle for control of the Irish in America continued. In August De Valera stated his terms for a settlement of the dispute with the Friends of Irish Freedom. These included the decentralization of the organization to provide for greater power at the state council level and consequently less power in Cohalan's hands.[46] The dispute finally came to a head at the 17 September meeting of the National Council of the FOIF in New York where De Valera arranged for the Massachusetts State Council to propose amendments to the constitution to bring about the changes he desired. The attempt failed and De Valera left the meeting with his supporters.[47] By way of reprisal, on 22 October De Valera's colleague, Harry Boland, announced

---

[43] Colby to Wilson, 2 September 1920, *Colby MSS.*, Box 3.

[44] *New York Times*, 1 November 1920.

[45] C.E.Calwell, *Field Marshal Sir Henry Wilson: His Life and Diaries*, London: Cassell, 1927, v. 2, p. 265.

[46] Tansill, *op. cit.*, p. 387.

[47] *Ibid.*, pp. 391–9; McCartan, *op. cit.*, p. 213.

to the press in the name of the Supreme Council of the IRB, that the Clan na Gael was no longer affiliated with the IRB. He and McGarrity organized a second Clan, the 'Clan na Gael Reorganized', which held meetings until 1921 but was never more than a token organization.[48] The more important innovation was De Valera's Association for the Recognition of the Irish Republic (AARIR), founded in November 1920 and designed to displace the Friends of Irish Freedom. Its growth was rapid for De Valera impressed the average Irish-American to whom he was still 'President'. State committees appeared in every state, often with prominent members of the FOIF as state chairmen. In Montana, for example, there were a reported twenty branches and four thousand members by February 1921.[49] Robert Monteith, Casement's colleague in 1916 and an organizer for the AARIR in Ohio, claimed that membership there reached 30,000.[50] Macardle claimed that the national membership total rose to 800,000 in a year but this seems an extravagant estimate. At the peak of their strength in 1919 the Friends of Irish Freedom numbered only 100,749 'regular' and about 175,000 'associate' members, and it seems unlikely that the AARIR could have surpassed this by so much. However, the new organization bit deeply into the FOIF whose 'regular' membership fell to 20,000 in 1921.[51] This was a great tribute to De Valera's effect on the Irish-American movement which had never been better organized than under Cohalan.

On 13 December 1920, De Valera was smuggled out of the United States as secretly as he had been smuggled in eighteen months before. He arrived home in a deeply troubled Ireland in time for.Christmas 1920, to find his American visit hailed as a triumph.[52] Count Plunkett, his Minister for Foreign Affairs, claimed that De Valera had welded the Irish at home and in America into one body and had rescued the Irish movement from the control of American party politicians.[53] Liam Mellowes claimed that De Valera had 'changed an ignorant and either

[48] Tansill, *op. cit.*, p. 392.

[49] *Ibid.*, pp. 393–4; Splain, 'Under Which King?' in Fitz-Gerald, *op. cit.*, p. 252; James Murray to Senator T.J.Walsh, 9 May 1921 and circular dated September 1921 in *Walsh MSS.*, Box 190.

[50] Monteith, *op. cit.*, p. 240.

[51] Macardle, *op. cit.*, p. 426; Tansill, *op. cit.*, p. 395n.

[52] Gwynn, *De Valera*, p. 119.

[53] *Philadelphia Public Ledger*, 26 February 1921.

apathetic or hostile people into genuine sympathizers in two years'.[54] In fact, however, De Valera had rescued the movement from Irish-American leaders, not party politicians, and Mellowes underestimated the support for Ireland which already existed in America. Furthermore, De Valera had charged into the strange world of Irish-American politics rather like the proverbial bull in a china shop. He was never able to take control of the Friends of Irish Freedom or win the loyalty and affection of the bulk of their officers. He rejected the sensible advice of seasoned campaigners during the presidential election campaign in demanding a degree of commitment to the Irish cause from the two major political parties, in fact to the recognition of a non-existent republic, which had never been accepted before. Unwilling to compromise, he had received almost nothing from them. Yet he admitted to the Dail when he returned to Ireland, 'If I were President of the United States myself, I could not, and would not recognize Ireland as a Republic.'[55] He wrote to Michael Collins in January 1921:

> Though I was working directly for recognition in America, I kept in mind as our main political objective the securing of America's influence, in case she was to join a League of Nations, to securing us also a place within the League.... Recognition we will only get in case of a war with England, though, of course, we should never cease our demand for it.[56]

If this really was his aim in America his tactics demonstrated his inexperience for one could not have deduced it from his behaviour. In 1922 Patrick McCartan, whose book severely attacked De Valera's conduct in the United States, gave the advice to Gavan Duffy, the Irish Free State Foreign Secretary, that Ireland's representatives in America should try to influence Irish-Americans, not dictate to them.[57] This was one lesson of De Valera's mission, that no matter how right or wrong in their attitudes towards Ireland, the leaders of the Irish in America were independent Americans with their own American view of the world.

Even in Ireland De Valera continued to influence the American

[54] Cited in Macardle, *op. cit.*, p. 426.
[55] McCartan, *op. cit.*, p. 232.
[56] Piaras Beaslai, *Michael Collins and the Making of a New Ireland*, London: Harraps, 1926, v. 2, p. 145.
[57] McCartan to G.Gavan Duffy, 23 January 1922, *Maloney MSS.*, Box 21.

movement. He substantially contributed to factionalizing the Irish in America while he was there and then split his own faction after he had left. He appealed to the AARIR National Convention in April 1921 for a guarantee of $1,000,000 a year for Ireland. James O'Mara, who was still working on the bond-certificate campaign, reacted very strongly. With 'loans' and 'guarantees', plus relief funds then being collected, he argued, De Valera was simply making unreasonable demands on Irish-American generosity and damaging future loan projects at a time when nearly three million dollars lay in America, as unexpended proceeds of the bond-certificate drive, at the disposal of the Irish republican government. He resigned in protest.[58] In August 1921 De Valera claimed that the whole amount subscribed, five million dollars, was in the Irish treasury and Frank Walsh attended a Dail session to receive the thanks of the Irish people.[59] But in fact less than four million dollars had been sent to Ireland (of which only $400,000 finally found its way into the Irish Free State treasury). In 1928 over two and a half million dollars, the bulk of the sum mentioned by O'Mara plus interest, was still in New York banks. After extended litigation in New York, involving the Irish Free State and representatives of the bond-certificate holders backed by the AARIR, the remaining funds were redistributed in 1930 to only half of the original subscribers, those who had responded to letters from court-appointed receivers.[60]

Nevertheless De Valera achieved a great deal in America. He limited the power of Cohalan and the Friends of Irish Freedom and by setting up the American Commission on Irish Independence and the AARIR he brought the majority of organized Irish-Americans back into a movement controlled from Ireland. Their energies could thus be used very positively to build a new Ireland rather than being used to attack the British Empire and President Wilson and to influence the general course of American foreign policy. He also re-established the massive financial support for Ireland which had existed under Parnell and Redmond

[58] Enclosed in Dumont to Secretary of State, 22 July 1921, *State Department*, 841d. 00/402.

[59] *Freeman's Journal*, 18 August 1921.

[60] Detailed correspondence on the issue as in *State Department*, 841d. 51/— and *Maloney MSS.*, Boxes 19, 22. See also Macardle, *op. cit.*, pp. 1024–5 and Katherine O'Doherty, *Assignment America: De Valera's Mission to the United States*, New York: De Tanko, 1957, pp. 64–9.

but which had virtually lapsed during the reign of the Friends of Irish Freedom. He had, on balance, done well for Ireland, and that was his only concern.

De Valera had been a magnificent publicist for Ireland. For eighteen months he had gone his way unmolested by the American government while the British formulated proposals for Ireland which he and his colleagues in Dail Eireann were rendering irrelevant to the demands of the Irish majority. Both governments agreed that his tour could not be stopped because his martyrdom would have benefited neither of them. On 19 December 1920, however, Norman Davis, the US Under-Secretary of State, recorded this interesting conversation with the British Ambassador, Geddes:

[Geddes] said that while the British Government understands that the Federal Government has no control over the municipalities in the United States, and hence their official receptions to De Valera, it was impossible to get the British public to understand this. That his Government fully realised that the Irish question was also very difficult for this Government to deal with, at least as long as the Irish agitators keep within reasonable bounds; that they had, however, been considerably concerned about De Valera's recent statement, published in the *New York Times*, November 23, 1920, advocating assassination, and so forth; that this had had a very disconcerting effect, and he desired to know if this Government had taken notice of this statement, if they were contemplating doing something about it, or felt that it could, or that it would be expedient to do something. That it had occurred to him that the raising of funds in the United States and permitting them to Ireland in furtherance of a revolution, and statements inciting assassination, would at least justify, if not make it incumbent on this Government, to deport at least any alien connected with such activities. He realised that it might be more difficult for us to deal with such actions on the part of the Americans, but that we might feel justified in deporting British subjects who were guilty of such practices. I jokingly told the Ambassador that the Irish question was almost as great a source of embarrassment to this Government as to his own Government, and that as we have many or more Irish than they have we might be justified, in looking at it from one standpoint, to complain to the British Government for the reflex action in the United States caused by the trouble in Ireland. I told him, however, that while it was not clear to me that it would be expedient for this Government to take any such action as that indicated by him, if we were able to do so I would think the matter over and let him know later if anything could or would be done. He told me that his Government might decide to file a complaint, but that he had desired to discuss the matter with me informally.[61]

This conversation took place just a few days after De Valera had secretly departed from the United States. It was no longer relevant to him, but the Anglo-American problem of Ireland was far from over. In fact it was just entering its climatic year.

[61] Memo on conversation between Norman Davis and Ambassador Geddes, 19 December 1920, *Davis MSS.*, Box 9.

11 The Settlement, 1920–1

The De Valera-Cohalan split was disturbing but it by no means stopped Irish-American pressure on the US government or the flow of direct aid to Ireland. The Irish question still played its important role in Anglo-American relations and the range and complexity of Irish activities was considerable. The proceeds of the bond-certificate drive began to arrive in Ireland in 1920, and even before then limited sums of money were sent by the Clan na Gael to the Irish republicans.[1] Serious Anglo-American problems were created by Irish-Americans who returned to Ireland to fight for the republicans, believing that their American citizenship gave them immunity from arrest. 'Some of the most dangerous gunmen in Ireland can produce American passports', reported Consul Kent in a slightly melodramatic despatch from Belfast in February 1921. The British released several Irish-American terrorists at the request of the American government, which was constantly being badgered by Congressmen whose constituents had been 'unjustly' imprisoned in Ireland.[2] Close liaison was maintained between British and American security services and consignments of arms suspected of being *en route* to Ireland were seized in America,[3] but the Irish Republican Army was always short of weapons and supplies. Irish-Americans could supply only very limited quantities and then only by the most devious channels.

On the propaganda front in America the Friends of Irish Freedom maintained a torrent of propaganda against the British government. Rossa Downing of Washington, DC, gave an account of the activities of the Washington branch which included: publishing; lobbying the President and Congress;

[1] Eoin MacNeill to Devoy, 16 April 1919, acknowledged receipt of £1,000, *Devoy MSS.*, 10,611.

[2] Consul Kent, Belfast, to Secretary of State, 15 February 1921, *State Department*, 341d. 1121 B44/3. Some cases of released Irish-Americans are recorded in *State Department*, 341d. 1121. See also Beaslai, *op. cit.*, v. 2, p. 215.

[3] For example see *State Department*, 841d. 00/- .and memos of conversations between Secretary of State Hughes and Ambassador Geddes, 21 June and 28 July 1921, *Hughes MSS.*, Box 175; *FO* 115/2061,2671.

parading round the White House for seventy-four nights during Terence MacSwiney's hunger strike; picketing the British Embassy and bailing out women pickets who were arrested; the adoption of the Irish town of Mallow to which they sent $10,000 in aid; a donation of $1,000 to a committee investigating conditions in Ireland; a subscription of $10,000 to the Irish Victory Fund; subscriptions totalling $50,000 to the bond-certificate drive; a boycott of British goods, and pressure to cancel British insurance in Washington.[4] Until the formation of the AARIR in November 1920 activities by both pro- and anti-De Valera factions were sponsored throughout America by the FOIF, and even in 1921 and 1922 the Friends continued their own active programme. They published pamphlets, *News Bulletins* in 1919 and 1920, and *Newsletters* from August 1919 to the end of 1922. It was certainly clear from the pages of the *Gaelic American* that the movement was split, but it was generally not possible to detect it from these other publications. They were widely distributed in America and some found their way overseas.[5] In addition, the Irish case was presented through the editorial and news columns of sympathetic journals and newspapers such as the *Boston Globe*, the nation-wide Hearst press, and the journal *Nation*.

Several months before the American elections in 1920, William Maloney, a supporter of De Valera, moved to establish a commission for Ireland to emulate the 1915 investigation of alleged German atrocities in Belgium conducted by Lord Bryce. *Nation*, edited by Oswald Garrison Villard, formally sponsored it.[6] On 25 September 1920, *Nation* announced the establishment of the Committee of One Hundred on Conditions in Ireland. This committee grew to 150, including governors, US Senators and Congressmen, numerous mayors, Episcopal, Methodist and Roman Catholic bishops, and, before his death, Cardinal

[4] Rossa F.Downing, 'Men, Women and Memories', in Fitz-Gerald, *op. cit.*, pp. 216–17.

[5] Between them, the New York Public Library and the American-Irish Historical Society probably have the best collection of these publications.

[6] McCartan, *op. cit.*, pp. 210–11. Maloney spent almost $10,000 of his own money to start the campaign and had to be reimbursed. *Maloney MSS.*, Box 19. Unless stated otherwise, data on the American Commission on Conditions in Ireland are from *Evidence on the Conditions in Ireland* and *Interim Report*, both published in 1921 by the Commission.

Gibbons. The range was very impressive – from the Democratic Senators Phelan and David Walsh to the conservative Republican Hiram Johnson and the radical Republican Robert La Follette. Only one of the five governors, Edwards of Rhode Island, represented a traditional, high density Irish area, the others were from the west. Responsible to the committee was a commission of eight members who were non-Irish public and professional figures with L. Hollingsworth Wood, lawyer, humanitarian and Quaker, as chairman. There was a clear absence from the commission of 'professional Irish-Americans' from the FOIF and the Clan na Gael and even Maloney played no public role, but the *Gaelic American* saw it as his work, nevertheless, and forecast its failure. The *Irish World*, still supporting the Clan against De Valera, attacked the commission for declaring its intention to promote Anglo-American friendship by removing the Irish barrier to better relations.

The composition of the commission was designed to disarm critics in America and Great Britain and although the British believed its investigation could be harmful unless Ireland had first experienced a period of calm and stability, they could do little actually to stop it. In December they refused to allow members of the commission to visit Ireland and the State Department refused to intercede, arguing in reply to protesting Senators, 'The government of the United States has never acquiesced in the right of any other nation to question its action in such matters.'[7] The British did allow Irish witnesses to travel to America to testify, although the behaviour of Donal O'Callaghan, Lord Mayor of Cork, was designed to incriminate them on this count. O'Callaghan arrived in Newport News, Virginia, without a passport on 4 January 1921, and immediately set off a jurisdictional dispute between American government departments. The Acting Secretary of State, Norman Davis, refused him admission as a stowaway but the Secretary of Labor, Wilson, approved his temporary admission as a seaman, pending his reshipment abroad. During the dispute O'Callaghan was free to move around the United States on parole. He testified before the American Commission on Conditions in Ireland, addressed the National Press Club and received wide publicity in the press. The *New*

[7] Norman Davis to Senator Norris and others, 11 January 1921, *State Department*, 841d. 00/265.

York Times, for example, bitterly attacked Secretary Wilson and his 'law breaking department'.[8]

O'Callaghan was quickly represented as a political refugee and a persecuted Irishman who dared not return to his home. This was the message which a delegation from the AARIR brought to Norman Davis late in January. Davis expressed his sympathy for Ireland but insisted, 'I really don't believe I am helping the Irish if I don't enforce the law which I am sworn to enforce and if I do something which would cause international friction.' O'Callaghan was not a political refugee, Davis concluded. He had been able to testify to the commission and that should be enough for him.[9]

Davis was sufficiently worried by all this to warn the Secretary of the British Embassy, Craigie, on 31 January, that if the British did arrest O'Callaghan on his return it would look suspiciously like reprisal. On 9 February Craigie called on Davis with the news that O'Callaghan had never applied for a passport, although he had requested information about one. If he went back to Britain the British government had no intention of prosecuting him either for testifying in Washington or for leaving Britain illegally.[10] The Americans accepted this assurance and O'Callaghan's appeal to the State Department to be allowed to remain as a political refugee was rejected. He left as a seaman.

The whole O'Callaghan affair seems to have been a device to attract attention. Since the British would not oblige by barring witnesses the Irish may well have decided to act as if they had. O'Callaghan was, in fact, the only witness from Ireland to arouse much public interest. Others who came quite legally included Mrs Muriel MacSwiney, the widow of Terence MacSwiney, and Lawrence Ginnell of the Irish Republican Cabinet and Dail Eireann.

Public hearings by the commission, amounting to two thousand

[8] The case is discussed in Secretary of Labor W.B.Wilson to Tumulty, 17 January 1921, with enclosures, *Wilson MSS.*, Series VI, Box 559, File 3926. See also Senator T.J.Walsh to Secretary Wilson, 1 February 1921, Wilson to Walsh, 5 February 1921, and Secretary of State Colby to Walsh, 8 February 1921, *Walsh MSS.*, Box 190. For newspaper comments see *Davis MSS.*, Box 77, 'Scrapbook, 1921'.

[9] Memo by Davis on meeting with an Irish-American committee headed by Major Kinkead, n.d., *Davis MSS.*, Box 11.

[10] Memos on conversations with Craigie 31 January and 9 February 1921, *Davis MSS.*, Box 9.

typewritten pages of testimony, were held in Washington in November and December 1920, and January 1921, and published material was also considered.[11] The British case was not presented and the report published in March 1921 constituted a predictable indictment of British rule. British forces had, the commission reported, killed the innocent and tortured the suspected, farms were destroyed, individuals held hostage, and villages punished in reprisal. British forces were undisciplined and drunken. The Irish, it concluded, were overwhelmingly republican. This report had, in fact, been written by the originator of the scheme, William Maloney.[12]

In December 1920, just before leaving for America, O'Callaghan had urgently cabled the American Red Cross for aid to relieve distress caused by the burning and sacking of Cork as a reprisal by British forces. The American Red Cross sought the advice of the State Department on the political implications of such aid. The question was passed on to President Wilson who replied, 'I think it would be extremely unwise for the Red Cross to respond to the appeal. . . . It would be an international act of the most questionable sort, and I hope that you will express, in my name if you choose, our sense of its unwisdom at this time.'[13] Early in 1921, however, the American Committee for Relief in Ireland was organized as the American collection agency for Irish relief and once again the initiative went to William Maloney who prepared the pamphlet, *A Summons to Service*, with which the campaign began.[14] The American Red Cross finally made a contribution of $100,000 following great Irish-American pressure on its branches throughout the country and after the British Red Cross had assured them that British authorities would not object.[15] The new committee was also able to secure the greetings of the new President, Harding, and Vice-President Coolidge for a benefit

[11] *Norris MSS.*, Tray 28, Boxes 5, 6, 7, 8. Senator George Norris was a member of the eight-member commission.

[12] McCartan, *op. cit.*, pp. 235–6.

[13] O'Callaghan to American Red Cross, 12 and 20 December 1920, *State Department*, 841d. 48/5; Wilson to Davis, 16 December 1920, *Davis MSS.*, Box 67.

[14] McCartan, *op. cit.*, pp. 223–6. See also *Maloney MSS.*, Box 19. Unless otherwise stated, data on the relief committee are drawn from *Report of the American Committee for Relief in Ireland*, published by the committee in 1922.

[15] Memo by Third Assistant Secretary of State 'R.W.B.' on meeting with Mr Persons and Dr Bicknell of the American Red Cross, 28 March 1921, *State Department*, 841d. 48/19.

concert at the Metropolitan Opera House, New York, on 3 April.[16]

Meanwhile an impressive organization had been built. Morgan O'Brien, a man long recognized as a moderate in the Irish-American movement, became chairman of the executive committee which also included the Rev. M.J.Gallagher of Detroit, the National President and figurehead of the Friends of Irish Freedom, Cardinal Gibbons, L.Hollingsworth Wood, and Senators David Walsh, Thomas Walsh and James Phelan. Honorary vice-chairmen included nineteen state governors, Samuel Gompers of the American Federation of Labor, Cardinal O'Connell, William McAdoo, and William Randolph Hearst. This was the most eminent collection of patrons ever assembled by an Irish-American organization and by August its fifty state committees had raised five and a quarter million dollars. Senator T.J.Walsh, a member of the executive, wrote to a constituent:

It was our purpose to enlist in the cause as directors American citizens of Irish blood who have become eminent in the industrial and business world and who have not, to any large extent, been identified with movements intended to bring about political changes in Ireland. It was believed that through such an organization the end would be most surely attained, and the chances of an interdict by the British government upon its operation be minimized.[17]

He wrote to another constituent that 'general starvation . . . seemed imminent' in Ireland.[18] There the Irish White Cross was formed under Sinn Fein's control to distribute relief funds and again it operated under the most auspicious of patrons with Cardinal Logue as President.

Advertisements sponsored by the Committee for Relief in Ireland appeared in American newspapers in April declaring that Ireland was suffering from famine, pestilence and death, and that children trudged daily to relief stations set up in schools for their only meal of the day, a hot drink and bread. To combat these distortions a press statement was released from Dublin Castle. It reported that Ireland's prosperity was unequalled in its history,

---

[16] Harding and Coolidge clearly had not understood the political implications of the relief organization. British Ambassador Geddes protested at their endorsements. Geddes to Foreign Secretary, 31 March 1921, *FO* 115/2673.

[17] Walsh to John McBarron, 10 January 1921, *Walsh MSS.*, Box 190.

[18] Walsh to Rt Rev. McLenihan, n.d., *ibid.*

poverty and destitution were below pre-war levels, the mortality rate was falling, there was greater unemployment in England, and there was no general shortage of money. Any distress which existed, it stated, was produced by the IRA campaign of destruction involving roads and bridges, and it explicitly denied the story of children's relief stations.[19] The British had contributed their share to the destruction of property, which was not acknowledged by the press release, but most of the information they presented was true.

In February a group nominated by the Committee for Relief, comprising six members of the American Society of Friends, arrived in Ireland to arrange for the distribution of American aid. The American Friends Service Committee had itself refused to co-operate with the mission because it would not have had full control of the aid programme. The Executive Secretary of the Society of Friends, Wilbur K. Thomas, wrote to the Secretary of State, 'The evident purpose of the committee was to trade upon the name of the Friends. . . . We feel that our English and Irish Friends can do this work without complicating the international situation.'[20] At the suggestion of Herbert Hoover, then Harding's Secretary of Commerce, Capt. John E. Lucey, who had earned a fine record in European relief programmes since 1914, agreed to administer the Irish relief programme although both he and Hoover really preferred that the American Friends Service Committee should do this work as it had in other European countries. In the middle of April Lucey resigned because of the anti-British tone of the operation. He had also been surprised to find that Ireland was in fact quite prosperous compared with other parts of Europe. Hoover then withdrew his support.[21]

The members of the visiting American committee proved to be very gullible. They spent most of their time in the company of Sinn Fein supporters and agreed that the Irish White Cross should dispense the relief funds. They evaded luncheon invitations from General Macready, the British Commander-in-Chief in Ireland, and Consul Dumont had to arrange for a secret meeting

[19] Discussed by the Irish Attorney General, Henry, in *Parl. Debs.*, Commons, 5th Series, 21 April 1921, v. 140, cols 2051–4.

[20] Thomas to Secretary of State, 8 February 1921, *State Department*, 841d. 48/3.

[21] Hoover to Secretary of State, 11 March 1921, *State Department*, 841d. 48/7; G. Howland Shaw, State Department, to Secretary of State, 15 April 1921, *ibid.*, 841d. 00/339.

with Macready at which they explained that had they lunched with him they would have destroyed their usefulness in Ireland. In reality they would have lost the confidence of the republicans yet they seemed unaware of the political implications of their co-operation with people deemed to be rebels by the British.[22] They published a report which stated that damage amounting to $20 million had been caused by British military or police forces in the twelve months to 31 March and that 100,000 people were in need of instant assistance. The need, they argued, was for funds to rebuild houses and industries and to relieve distress caused by the economic stagnation allegedly resulting from the conflict. In Belfast Consul Kent commented on 30 April that Ireland had always had 'poverty, idleness and squalor', that the shortage of houses was no worse than in America, and that unemployment, arising from a general business depression, was greater in England, Wales and Scotland than in Ireland. Kent noted that the report was inspired by Sinn Fein but on the strength of it Senator T.J.Walsh, for one, was prepared to write to a number of people, 'It is perfectly evident that there is a set purpose to destroy the productive capacity of the people that they may be starved into submission.'[23]

Although the American public at large was treated to a uniform diet of Irish distress, made convincing by virtue of sheer repetition, and although there did exist the misery, hunger, poverty, and terror in parts of Ireland that any civil war begets, Ireland as a whole was not suffering the acute social and economic crisis that the propagandists in Ireland and America sought to convey. Furthermore, despite their doubts about the motives of the American relief organization, General Macready and the Under-Secretary for Ireland, Sir John Anderson, treated the visiting Americans with courtesy and they supplied passes which enabled the visitors to move with relative freedom around the country. It was clear that rebuilding, particularly of co-operative creameries which had been extensively damaged in reprisal and other attacks by the British, was the most useful task the Americans could perform since there was no general shortage of food. Shipments of food which arrived from America in January and

22 Dumont to Secretary of State, 22 March 1921, *ibid.*
23 W.P. Kent to Secretary of State, 20, 30 April 1921, *State Department,* 841d. 00/348 and 841d. 48/22B; T.J.Walsh to J.D.Sullivan, 25 May 1921, *Walsh MSS.,* Box 190.

February had already been sold for cash to finance buildings.[24] The American target for relief funds was finally set at $10 million and a sum of $5,250,000 was actually collected from meetings, dinners and donations. After expenses almost $5 million was available for the Irish White Cross.[25]

Several times in May, and as late as 6 June, the British Ambassador, Geddes, who personally wanted his government to co-operate, told the Secretary of State, Charles Evans Hughes, that the British could not accept the plans of the American Committee for Relief in Ireland. The committee was not impartial, he said, and was co-operating with the rebel-dominated Irish White Cross. Furthermore, aid to Ireland was absolutely unnecessary. Hughes forced the British to retreat by warning that sooner or later the committee would appeal to the President to intercede and there would be intense hostility aroused among the many Americans who had contributed solely from humanitarian motives. Given the hostile state of opinion in America, he added, it was dangerous to aggravate it further. Congress might even resolve that the Irish Republic should be recognized. Geddes agreed and passed Hughes' views on to London. There they prevailed and the distribution of American relief funds began in the summer of 1921.[26]

The Irish-Americans had succeeded in embarrassing the British government with the American Commission on Conditions in Ireland and the American Committee for Relief in Ireland, but while they were winning, as it were, a diplomatic victory with the aid of a new US administration which was unencumbered by any long-standing hostility to their leaders, 1921 was proving to be a barren year for their activities in Congress. The Friends of Irish Freedom were less powerful now, the elections were over, the Republican Party was in control and had no interest in embarrassing President Harding, and resolutions introduced on Irish self-determination failed to gain recognition. The language and oratory were as flowery as of old but no one appeared to be listening in Congress. Despite this, the

[24] Dumont to Secretary of State, 22 March 1921, *State Department*, 841d. 00/339.
[25] J.J.Pulleyn, Treasurer, to T.J.Walsh, 23 July 1922, *Walsh MSS.*, Box 190.
[26] Chargé H.G.Chilton to Foreign Secretary, 5 May and Curzon to Geddes 11 May, 6 June 1921, *FO* 115/2673; Cabinet 'C.P.' paper No. 2921, 9 May 1921, *CAB*. 24/123; Cabinet meeting 36/21 (4) 10 May 1921, *CAB*. 23/25; memo of meeting between Hughes and Geddes, 23 May 1921, *Hughes MSS.*, Box 175.

Irish republicans stepped up their campaign for international recognition. Frank Walsh and Harry Boland acted for them in the United States while Patrick McCartan travelled to Russia, with a draft treaty in his pocket, to secure the recognition which Litvinoff, of the Russian Foreign Minister, had ostensibly promised in 1918. McCartan found the Russians so eager for a trade agreement with the British that, notwithstanding dramatic British government allegations concerning a 'Bolshevik-Sinn Fein conspiracy', Russian recognition of Ireland was inconceivable.[27] In June 1921 the Dail Department of Foreign Affairs reported that in addition to the activities in Russia and the United States, there were Irishmen accredited by the Dail in France, England, Germany, Argentina, Italy and Chile. Press bureaux were operating in Paris, Rome, Berlin, Madrid, Fribourg and the USA, and an active propaganda was also being carried on in Denmark, Canada, South Africa, Australia, and various parts of South America. As Consul Dumont observed, the republicans were trying to win by propaganda as well as by war.[28]

There was almost no organized counter-propaganda for the British in the United States. The Loyal Coalition organization of Boston petitioned Congress and arranged meetings supporting the British government, and some of the churches, the Methodist, Episcopal, Baptist and Presbyterian, opposed American interference in British affairs. There was also a delegation of seven members from the Ulster Unionist Council, six of them clergymen, which visited America in late 1919 and early 1920 but these efforts had little impact.[29] The great bulk of the Irish material in circulation was devoted to atrocities and hardships caused by the British campaign in Ireland and very little of the distress there was attributed to Sinn Fein's own campaign of destruction and terror.

Occasionally something would happen to indicate a reservoir of support, or at least sympathy, for the British government's problem. For example, in London in June 1921 Admiral Sims, an outspoken anglophile who was head of the Navy War College

---

[27] There is a copy of McCartan's confidential report on his Russian mission in *Maloney MSS.*, Box 21. See also Great Britain, *Intercourse between Bolshevism and Sinn Fein*, 1921, Cmd. 1326, xxix, 489.

[28] Dail report dated 21 June 1921, enclosed in Dumont to Secretary of State, 22 July 1921, *State Department*, 841d. 00/402.

[29] Blake, *op. cit.*, pp. 326, 359–60.

in Rhode Island, recklessly sallied forth against the Irish. He declared:

There are many in our country who technically are Americans, naturalized and born there, but none of them American at all. They are American when they want money but Sinn Feiners on the platform. They are making war on America today. The simple truth of it is that they have the blood of English and American boys on their hands. They are like zebras, either black horses with white stripes, or white horses with black stripes. But we know they are not horses, they are asses. But each of these asses has a vote, and there are lots of them.

Senators fumed, Sims was called back to the USA by the Navy Department and officially reprimanded, and there was a flood of hostile criticism, but the *New York Tribune* reported, 'Admiral Sims cleared the air, and in so doing did a public service.' He had attacked the prevailing British notion 'that the behaviour of Sinn Fein mobs and of our pussyfooting politicians furnishes an accurate index of American opinion'. The *New York Evening Mail*, *New York Herald*, and the *New York Times* agreed. The *Boston Transcript* reported, 'A good, sound, natural indiscretion is needed now and then to clear the air of the miasma of diplomatic shift and shuffle.'[30]

Many who cast a wry smile at Sims and quietly applauded him valued Anglo-American co-operation, but there was little they could do to help bring about the Irish settlement they knew was a precondition for friendly relations. In 1920 Colonel House agreed to mediate at the suggestion of Sir Horace Plunkett, but all the parties were hardening their positions and nothing came of Plunkett's manipulations.[31] The US government made no formal

[30] In 1910, as Commander Sims, he was reprimanded by the US Navy Department for promising, in a London Guildhall speech, that 'every man, every dollar, and every drop of blood of your kindred across the sea' would be available to help the British Empire should it be menaced by a European coalition. He continued to antagonize anglophobes. See his 'When Germany Nearly Won', *Pearson's Magazine*, December 1919, and Burton J.Hendrick's description of Sim's career in *The World's Work* August 1919, v. 38, pp. 376–95. The Congressional discussion on the 1921 incident is in *Congressional Record*, 67 Cong., 1 Session, 1921, v. 61, *passim*. For a press summary see, 'Sinn Fein and the Admiral', *Literary Digest*, 25 June 1921, v. 69, pp. 7–9.

[31] Plunkett to House, 25 June, and reply 27 June 1920, *Plunkett MSS;* Plunkett to House, 1 July 1920, *House MSS.*, Drawer 12, File 2; Viscount Grey to House, 30 July, and reply 1 August 1920, *House MSS.*, Drawer 9, File 9.

overtures to Britain, under Wilson or Harding, but Consul Dumont was trusted by both the British and the rebels and was approached by the IRA in December 1920. At their request he arranged meetings with British authorities in Dublin. The IRA suspected that their partner in the war, Sinn Fein, was negotiating a settlement with the British and they took steps, through the good offices of Dumont and without opposition from Ambassador Davis, to open negotiations of their own.[32] Nothing came of these moves because the British were convinced that the Irish republican movement was weakening. This belief, rather than the completion of the US elections, primarily explains the stepped up military campaign waged by the British from December 1920. Cork, for example, was burnt that month as a reprisal against Sinn Fein raids.[33] Lloyd George knew from Ambassador Geddes' reports that American opinion was hostile to this campaign of reprisals but since he felt he had Sinn Fein and the IRA on the run, he went ahead. Indeed, the British Prime Minister believed that De Valera returned to Ireland because the militant Sinn Feiners were being beaten and he wanted to assume control of the proposed Parliament of Southern Ireland.[34] Lloyd George always believed that the Irish people would accept a 'reasonable' settlement if the small minority of extremists could be controlled, but British commitments around the world made even this task difficult. General Macready's forces had only a three to one advantage over the rebels, much too small a ratio as recent guerilla wars in Cyprus, Algeria, Malaya and Indochina have shown, but he thought he could hold them in check until their funds were exhausted.[35] When, in late April 1921, the British intercepted an appeal from De Valera to McGarrity for one million dollars to support Dail Eireann, probably his appeal to the AARIR which led to the resignation of James O'Mara, they believed the end was in sight.[36]

[32] Dumont to Davis, 6 December, enclosed in Davis to Secretary of State, 8 December 1920, *State Department*, 841d. 00/262.

[33] Macardle, *op. cit.*, pp. 429–31.

[34] George A. Riddell, Baron Riddell, *Lord Riddell's Intimate Diary of the Peace Conference and After, 1918–1923*, London: Gollancz, 1933, pp. 260, 271–2.

[35] Dumont to Secretary of State, 22 March 1921, *State Department*, 841d. 00/339. Macready commanded 32,000 men with another 15,000 in the police. He believed he needed at least 100,000 men.

[36] R. Wright, US Embassy, London, to Secretary of State, 29 April 1921, *State Department*, 841d. 00/345.

In the then context of Irish politics, De Valera was seen by the British as a moderate leading Sinn Fein in a battle for control with the extremist IRA led by Michael Collins. Basil Thompson, the Home Office Director of Intelligence, argued that it would be a tragedy if De Valera lost this contest for any compromise would then become impossible.[37] If De Valera was more willing to negotiate it was probably because the Irish nationalists had serious financial problems,[38] although why money was left in the bond-certificate account in America remains unclear. In June, De Valera did indeed accept Lloyd George's offer to open talks, an offer which was made just a few days after King George V opened the new Parliament of Northern Ireland in Belfast on 22 June.[39]

Americans were as much in the dark about these developments as the British people but they received the news of a truce enthusiastically. During the negotiations which followed liaison between the Irish negotiators and Irish-American leaders was very poor. Devoy and Cohalan temporarily suppressed their conflict with De Valera and cabled their support when he rejected the early British terms for a settlement in August but there was no way for Irish-Americans to influence directly the sequence of discussions which resulted in a treaty signed in London on 6 December 1921. Southern Ireland was granted virtual independence with Dominion status under the Crown but the republicans had to make major concessions on naval defence, on the status of Ulster which retained its autonomy and its own parliament, and on the question of the Irish Republic itself. They were to have a governor general and members of the Dail were to be required to swear an oath of allegiance to the King. Nevertheless, although the Irish republicans were offered less territory than in the 1914 home rule settlement which covered the whole of Ireland, they gained a degree of independence far in excess of that offered to Redmond. Proposals for home rule, federalism, or devolution were abandoned, and in their place came independence in almost every respect for all but six Irish counties.[40]

---

[37] *Ibid.*, 4 May 1921, *State Department*, 841d. 00/358.
[38] See Dumont to Secretary of State, 9 June 1921, *State Department*, 841d. 00/381.
[39] D. Gwynn, *Partition*, pp. 193–5.
[40] *Ibid.*, pp. 179–201.

De Valera had elected not to go to London for the final negotiations and the treaty was signed for the republicans by Arthur Griffith, Michael Collins, Eamon Duggan, George Gavan Duffy, R.C.Barton and Erskine Childers. In the opinion of Collins, the brilliant IRA Commander, 'Britain offered and agreed with us on a peace which the world considered a fair peace. ... World opinion is no longer against Britain in her dealings with Ireland. And Britain knows this: she knows well besides that she can keep world opinion with her without conceding a Republic at all.'[41] But De Valera, who had been considered the moderate and Collins the extremist in April and May, turned against the settlement and insisted on Britain's recognizing a united Irish republic. He argued that the delegates had exceeded their authority by signing the treaty and on 7 January 1922, fifty-four members of the Dail joined him in voting not to ratify it. Sixty-four members voted for peace but De Valera and the minority chose to fight on against the advice of Collins who had engineered the military situation which brought Britain to the bargaining table.[42] A savage and tragic Irish civil war developed and by the time a truce was declared in March 1923 Griffith was dead, Collins had been assassinated, and Ireland had been torn apart by hatreds which still survive.

Americans were confused. Their elation at the truce, the treaty and the prospect of peace turned to disillusion as the Irish began to attack each other. John Devoy, who might have been expected to support the continued struggle for an Irish republic, supported Griffith and Collins against his bitter enemy De Valera, and when he returned to Ireland in 1924 it was to a state welcome presided over by a British Governor General, Tim Healy. The *Gaelic American* attacked De Valera but the *Irish World* supported him. Diarmuid Lynch, the Secretary of the Friends of Irish Freedom, attacked the treaty as an insult to the dead but Cohalan argued, again because of enmity towards De Valera, that although Ireland had been out-generalled by Lloyd George the British had finally recognized the right to self-determination. The FOIF resolved that they still advocated a republican form of government and the withdrawal of all British restraints, but they refused to do anything to interfere with the treaty or the new Irish

[41] Fitz-Gerald, *op. cit.*, pp. 32–43.
[42] D.Gwynn, *Partition*, pp. 197–201, and *De Valera*, pp. 147–73.

Free State.[43] To overcome the dilemma posed by their inability to oppose the settlement because of De Valera's position, and their desire to continue to attack Britain, the leaders of the FOIF organized the All-America National Council in 1922 to co-ordinate Irish and other nationality groups with, as one of its founders recorded, 'a view to forestalling British interference in American concerns and safeguarding American sovereignty'.[44] Joseph McGarrity, with his newspaper the *Irish Press*, remained one of De Valera's few supporters in America and a republican until his death in 1940, although he at first welcomed the treaty. His colleague William Maloney refused to take sides and went to Ireland in August 1922 in an unsuccessful attempt to mediate.[45] The AARIR initially supported the treaty but reversed its position in February 1922 to support De Valera and in so doing split itself apart.[46] The new Irish government was supported by the funds of the American Committee for Relief in Ireland which were still used for reconstruction and redevelopment, a stabilizing influence in a time of mounting chaos. The divisions and the disintegration in Ireland were clearly reflected in the Irish-American movement.

How important had the problem of Anglo-American relations been in the British decision to deal directly with Sinn Fein in 1921? The London *News* reported that Ambassador Geddes' accounts of Irish strength in the United States and the ability of Irish-Americans to thwart every attempt to improve Anglo-American relations had shocked the British government into action, but the *Irish Times* argued that Sinn Fein had agreed to seek a peaceful settlement to an increasingly one-sided struggle because it realized that America was not going to intervene on its behalf.[47] Both views were in fact correct when taken together; the British had indeed had enough of Irish-American interference in Anglo-American relations and the American government was not going to intervene in the Irish question. But what was much more important in 1921 was the fact that an Irish agreement was by

[43] Wittke, *op. cit.*, p. 292; Blake, *op. cit.*, pp. 441–4. Resolutions of the National Council of the FOIF, 13 January 1922, are in *Maloney MSS.*, Box 22.
[44] Splain, 'Under Which King?', in Fitz-Gerald, *op. cit.*, pp. 253–4.
[45] Maloney note, n.d., *Maloney MSS.*, Box 20.
[46] Tansill, *op. cit.*, p. 436; Downing in Fitz-Gerald, *op. cit.*, pp. 221–2.
[47] 'America as the Decisive Factor in the Irish Truce', *Current Opinion*, August 21, v. 71, pp. 155–8.

then possible. With the opening of their own parliament in June the northern Irish achieved a degree of autonomy and security from southern dominance which it would have been impossible to change. Ulster therefore felt secure and the Unionists could consequently be persuaded to settle. This gave Lloyd George the chance to make the very great concessions to the rest of Ireland which many considerations, not least of which was the state of Anglo-American relations, had demanded for many years. He coupled his offer with a promise to wage all-out war to defeat the republicans if they refused his terms.

Tansill offers the view, however, that Britain, in view of America's post-war military and naval power, required an agreement on ship construction to maintain naval parity and that the Irish settlement was an attempt to conciliate American opinion and subsequently to ease the way for an agreement.[48] It is clear that the British wanted a naval agreement, a treaty or an alliance perhaps, to preserve the *status quo* in the light of the undoubted capacity of the USA to supersede Britain's sea power. Secretary of State Hughes was not very sympathetic to such an agreement but there was a strong Congressional campaign for naval disarmament or arms control, there was a great deal of public sympathy for a disarmament conference, and the British indicated in July that they were prepared to initiate one. The Americans were therefore forced to make a move and issued invitations to a Washington conference to begin in November 1921. However, there is no evidence that the Irish settlement was deliberately designed to pave the way for the agreements which followed.[49] The announcement of the Irish truce in July and the treaty in December were certainly welcomed in the United States where anglophobia markedly declined, but the Irish settlement, no matter how desirable for Anglo-American relations, was negotiated at that particular time because the circumstances in Britain and Ireland were appropriate. The Washington agreements were accepted in the United States not because the Irish question was settled but because the Senate felt that they posed no threat to its authority. The foremost proponent in the Senate

[48] Tansill, *op. cit.*, pp. 423–6.
[49] Cabinet meetings 43/21 (2), 30 May 1921, *CAB*. 23/25 and 56/21 (22), 30 June 1921, *CAB*. 23/26. See also *Hughes MSS.*, Box 169, particularly memo of conversation between Hughes and Balfour, 11 November 1921.

of the Five Power Naval Agreement, the Four Power Treaty on the Pacific, and the Nine Power Treaty on the 'Open Door' in China, all negotiated between November 1921 and February 1922, was Henry Cabot Lodge. Indeed he was one of the negotiators and he believed they involved no surrender of US sovereignty, national interest or Senate prerogatives. They were concerned with ending the naval arms race and the stabilization of the *status quo* in the Far East, but they were based upon goodwill and mutual trust. The deepest commitment was the provision in the Four Power Treaty for the parties to consult with each other concerning measures to be taken in case of aggression against the Pacific island possessions of the signatories – Britain, France, Japan and the USA.[50] A continuation of the Anglo-Irish conflict in Ireland would probably not have prevented the agreements, notwithstanding the attractions of the reverse hypothesis.

The *Irish World* of 3 December attacked Harding's internationalism, and the Friends of Irish Freedom, at their December convention, attacked the as yet unannounced agreements, whatever they might be.[51] In a pamphlet published by the new All-America Council, Daniel Cohalan attacked Senator Lodge's betrayal of George Washington's principles. The agreements, he argued, embroiled the United States in Europe, in the balance of power and the fate of dynasties. 'The British diplomats at the Washington Conference,' he wrote, 'evidently "dazzled the vision" of America's chosen spokesmen who "slept and disarmed" while Balfour wove the net into which America was to be delivered – a colony once again!'[52] Nevertheless the agreements were ratified and these protests were ineffective for a number of reasons. The party with which Cohalan was aligned in 1919 in the campaign against the League of Nations was now in power. His sometime ally Lodge had helped negotiate the agreements and even Senator Borah was a firm advocate of a disarmament treaty. These men no longer needed Irish-American help and, furthermore, although Lodge and the Republicans were probably little influenced by the Irish settlement, it did make Cohalan's task more difficult. At the precise time of the Washington conference

[50] Bailey, *op. cit.*, Ch. XLI, 'Harding and the Washington Conference'.
[51] Blake, *op. cit.*, pp. 442–3.
[52] Daniel F.Cohalan, *Senator Lodge, Past and Present*, Washington, DC: All America National Council, 1922, p. 7.

*I   253

in November and December 1921, Lloyd George was engaged in negotiations with the Irish which prevented him from travelling to Washington to lead the British delegation.[53] This concurrence of events made it impossible for Irish-Americans to organize their customary anti-British agitation to defeat the Washington agreements. In addition, De Valera's control of the AARIR and the damage he had inflicted on the Friends of Irish Freedom, had weakened the Irish movement as a factor in American politics without destroying its effectiveness as a factor in Irish politics. The movement could never have been as effective in its dealings with Congress, for example, with the guiding genius of Cohalan and his colleagues divorced from the popular, mass movement. Cohalan and the Clan na Gael were no longer a force to be reckoned with in the determination of the particular American foreign policies which they had pursued for twenty years. On the other hand, the highly successful activities of the American Commission on Irish Independence, the Commission on Conditions in Ireland, and the AARIR were devoted almost exclusively to doing something *for* Ireland rather than *against* Britain. They were very embarrassing to the British and there was certainly going to be an Irish problem for as long as American aid flowed into Ireland, and for as long as propaganda campaigns organized in America attracted world attention to the plight of the Irish. But the burden of this embarrassment was felt in Britain's dealings with Ireland rather than with America and the problem promised to be permanent unless the British could solve the Irish problem to the satisfaction of a very large number of people in the United States. This they did in December 1921.

It would be naïve to suggest, as Irish-Americans often did, that the British engineered an Irish settlement solely to secure a naval agreement with the United States, but it would be rash, at the very least, to suggest that the improvement in the Irish situation had no influence on opinion in the United States. It must be remembered that the British were holding their preliminary talks on the Washington conference with the United States in May and June when the campaign of the Committee for Relief in Ireland was at its height and Secretary Hughes was warning the British that they had to agree to the arrangements being made for the distribution

[53] Memo of telephone conversation between Hughes and Ambassador Geddes, 4 November 1921, *Hughes MSS.*, Box 176.

of relief funds. Furthermore, Hughes made it clear that he was reluctant to talk of a 'treaty' in view of the traditional American, and, as we have seen, implicitly Irish-American hostility to such agreements.[54] There was still an 'anti-British party' in America but by late 1921 it had lost the bulk of its crucial hard core Irish membership. The Irish were no longer the powerful force they had once been in America. Divided amongst themselves, and undermined by the Irish settlement, they had little *raison d'être* in foreign policy.

[54] See *Hughes MSS.*, Box 169, particularly memo of conversation between Hughes and Balfour, 11 November 1921.

12 Conclusion

*'I have heard several notes of depression about the
volume and violence of Anglophobia in the US. I told one
member of the [British] Government that I was surprised
that he should remark this, since they had unsuccessfully
dealt with the Irish for three centuries, was it graceful
to hold us responsible for so much of their failure as
went over the sea?'*

US AMBASSADOR WALTER HINES PAGE
TO WOODROW WILSON, MAY 1914.[1]

Today it requires sophisticated techniques of voting analysis to
demonstrate that Irish-Americans still exist as a group in
American political life for they have long since ceased their mass
meetings in support of Irish freedom. One might wish that these
statistical and polling techniques had been available to students of
politics during the period covered in this study but we have,
nevertheless, other more traditional ways of knowing that the
Irish were a force to be reckoned with in Anglo-American
relations at the beginning of the century. We have the private
papers, biographies and memoirs of British, American, Irish and
Irish-American politicians and leaders. We have the diplomatic
correspondence of the United States and Great Britain, parliamentary and congressional papers and press reports from
Britain, Ireland, and America. These all testify to the existence of
a most impressive campaign to influence the international relations of two of the major world powers of their day. There have
been similar campaigns in American history. One might cite the
examples of Polish-Americans seeking Polish independence,
Russian-Jewish immigrants opposing Russian anti-semitism,
Jewish support of Zionism, and so on. This present study was
designed to illustrate, using wherever possible new and original
sources, just one example of what must be regarded, therefore, as

[1] Page to Wilson, 1 May 1914, *Wilson MSS.*, Series II, Box 52.

256

a common phenomenon in American politics and foreign relations.

There is no intention of suggesting here that difficulties in Anglo-American relations were due entirely to the Irish problem. The Irish in America were not all-powerful, though they were certainly important. One must not accept the behaviour, speeches or writings of Irish-Americans as presumptive evidence that they were influential. What has been described so far is, first, the relationship between the Irish in America and the native Irish; secondly, the degree to which the Irish question was not only a British problem but also an American one because of the huge Irish population in the United States; thirdly, the occasions from 1899 to 1921 when these first two considerations affected Anglo-American relations. It remains the task of this chapter to draw what conclusions one can from the data and arguments presented.

The first conclusion must be that the Irish did play an important role in Anglo-American relations and in the formulation of American, and to a lesser extent British, foreign policy. It may not be easy to isolate the Irish as the single most important variable in the analysis of any particular foreign policy problem, but, if the impressions of those who were actually involved in making decisions are any guide, we can say that the Irish were thought to be important. We have the words of Roosevelt, Hay, Balfour, Asquith, Grey, Taft, Wilson, House, Tumulty, Lansing, Lloyd George, Northcliffe, Colby and many others to testify to this fact. For example, John Hay confessed to Theodore Roosevelt in 1903 that, in his view, the combined opposition of Irish-Americans and German-Americans was sufficient to prevent Anglo-American co-operation in the Far East. The 1905 arbitration treaties were going through the Senate, said Hay on another occasion, when they were destroyed by attacks made from two quarters, one of which was the Clan na Gael. It is true that he underestimated the independence of the Senate and the import-ance of its constitutional prerogatives to that body, but we must nevertheless accept his word that he believed the Irish in America to be a powerful interest group which, as Secretary of State, he could not discount. In fact, between 1897 and 1911, four Anglo-American arbitration treaties were negotiated by Republican adminstrations and both the British and American governments believed that Irish-Americans were an important factor in the defeat of the three which were rejected by the Senate. The release of Luke Dillon by the Canadian government, President Taft argued, would have done much to improve the chances of Irish-Americans accepting his arbitration treaty. He was probably wrong but he was sufficiently impressed with the point to make several requests to the Canadian government for Dillon's release.[2]

The Irish had lent 'their unequalled power of political organization' to the enemies of Britain, Ambassador Spring Rice reported in 1916, and for three months he pleaded with the British government not to make Sir Roger Casement a martyr to the Irish movement in America.[3] His German counterpart, Count Bernstorff, advised his own government to help Ireland because of the effect this would have on American public opinion and consequently on American foreign policy during the war.[4] In fact Wilson himself wrote in April 1917, shortly after the USA entered the war, 'The only circumstance which seems now to stand in the way of absolutely cordial co-operation with Great Britain is the failure so far to find a satisfactory method of self-government for Ireland.'[5] Arthur Balfour accepted this view when he was in the United States in May 1917, and in the House of Commons in April 1918, during the conscription debate, Prime Minister Lloyd George confessed that the Irish question was hampering the President's conduct of the war. He tried unsuccessfully to find some way to overcome this.[6] When the British came to formulate proposals for the partition of Ireland in 1919 they recognized that American opinion had to be satisfied and their proposals were, in fact, part of Britain's foreign policy in that they were designed to appeal to the United States and the British Dominions.[7] In addition, we know that the Irish in America were at the very heart of the American campaign to defeat the Peace Treaty and had the Irish Parliamentary Party not been eclipsed by Sinn Fein in November 1918 it might well have demanded, with Liberal and Labour support, immediate home rule as its condition for agree-

[2] See above, Chapter 3, 'Anglo-American Relations, 1899–1912', *passim*.
[3] See above, Chapter 5, 'Sir Roger Casement and the Easter Rising, 1916', *passim*.
[4] Bernstorff to German Foreign Office, 27 September 1914, Great Britain, *Documents re. Sinn Fein*, p. 3.
[5] Wilson to Lansing, 10 April 1917, *R.S.Baker MSS.*, Series I, Box 2.
[6] See above, Chapter 7, 'The United States enters the War', *passim*.
[7] First Report of the Cabinet Committee on the Irish Question, 4 November 1919, 'C.P.' Paper 56, *CAB.* 24/92.

ing to this treaty which granted self-determination to so many but not to the Irish.

Not everyone in Britain believed, or was prepared to accept, that the Irish question had to be solved for the sake of Anglo-American relations. Sir Edward Carson, for example, denied that Americans had any right to interfere in British affairs and some Americans, Admiral Sims, for one, agreed. The Americans had no right to interfere perhaps, but they had a very good reason, given the extent to which Britain's problem of Ireland was interfering with the American political process. As Balfour reminded the Cabinet during the war, every British Ambassador to the USA had become convinced of the importance of the Irish question in his work.[8] Pauncefote, Durand, Bryce, Spring Rice, Reading, Grey, Geddes, and an assortment of British consuls throughout the country – in New York, Boston, Philadelphia, Baltimore, New Orleans, San Francisco, Chicago, Portland, and elsewhere – repeatedly reminded the government of the difficulties created for their work by the Irish in America.

There was no question of Irish-Americans actually formulating particular foreign policy proposals which the American government was forced to adopt against its will. The only example referred to in this study of the United States yielding to such pressure was the case of the abrogation of the Russo-American Treaty of 1832, the result of a succesful Jewish-American agitation.[9] The American government often made *informal* representations to the British on behalf of Ireland. President Wilson did so, for example, in 1917. He made it known in the United States that he was discussing Ireland's case with the British but he never released details or offered proof. Although Ireland was debated frequently in the House of Representatives and the Senate, both of these bodies were in fact very cautious in their support of the Irish. They would not endorse the recognition of the Irish republic and they would do no more than pass resolutions of sympathy and tender general advice, but they did insist that they had a right to discuss the Irish question and to make

[8] War Cabinet meeting 379A, minute 2, 1 April 1918, *CAB*. 23/14.

[9] Naomi W.Cohen, 'The Abrogation of the Russo-American Treaty of 1832', *Jewish Social Studies*, v. xxv, January 1963, pp. 3–41; Alan J.Ward, 'Immigrant Minority "Diplomacy": American Jews and Russia, 1901–1912,' *Bulletin of the British Association for American Studies*, New Series, No. 9, December 1964, pp. 7–23.

general recommendations to the British government concerning Irish policy.

Far more important than the formulation of particular foreign policies for the United States was the role which Irish-Americans played in setting limits beyond which American foreign policy dared not stray. American governments cannot deviate too far from what public opinion, or rather from what the elector who has his say at regular intervals, will tolerate. The Irish were an extremely vociferous and influential element in American public opinion and a large number of them were voters. Their slogans were simple: they wanted freedom for Ireland as the American colonies had wanted their freedom, they opposed 'alliances' with Britain, they opposed any involvement in European affairs, they opposed imperialism. These were familiar tenets of traditional American foreign policy and, using them as cues, Irish-Americans were able to influence a large number of Americans by consistently leading the way with mass meetings and propaganda campaigns whenever Britain might be harmed. The coalitions thus formed were very powerful. Roosevelt and Taft both strayed beyond tolerable limits with far-reaching arbitration treaties which were destroyed as 'alliances'. Anglo-American co-operation in the Far East was ruled out of Roosevelt's foreign policy and not until 1921, at the Washington conference, was it possible for the United States and Britain to combine in an attempt to secure their joint interests in China. The multiple loyalties of the American people and the campaigns launched by German and Irish-Americans made the conduct of its neutrality policy by the American government a very harassing affair in World War I. 'We are not yet ready to meet the submarine issue squarely', wrote Lansing in January 1916, because 'we are still too young a nation to have assimilated and amalgamated the various nationalities which compose our population.'[10] Later that year both Wilson and Bernstorff were prepared to argue that it was not only the British 'blacklist' of American traders but also Britain's treatment of the Irish rebels which had contributed to the hostile state of American opinion towards Britain.[11]

[10] Private memo 9 January, *Lansing MSS.*, Box 2, v. 1, p. 37.

[11] Link, *Wilson: Progressivism and Peace*, pp. 20–1; Bernstorff to German Foreign Office, 8 August 1916, enclosed in Page to Wilson, 3 December 1917, *Wilson MSS.*, Series II, Box 131.

The Irish were not, of course, the whole of American public opinion and they could not control American foreign policy single-handed but their importance lay in the strength which they could bring to coalitions. They were courted by a number of groups who recognized that they would be very much stronger with the organized Irish-Americans on their side, and Irish leaders often offered reciprocal services. It happened that during the period under review the Irish found a considerable number of allies to enhance their own power. During the Boer War there were the Democratic Party and German-Americans; in a number of battles against arbitration treaties which were quite popular in the country at large, it was the United States Senate; in World War I the Irish were joined by German-Americans and traditionalists who believed that the United States should be bound by the advice of the Founding Fathers to stay out of European quarrels. At all times the Irish found allies among anglophobes, who were very often these same traditionalists, to whom the Britain of 1812 and the American Civil War was still the Britain of 1900 or 1914. This combination of forces was crucial in setting the boundaries within which the government of the United States could act.

Successive British governments understood that American foreign policy was circumscribed by the Irish question. For example, when Arthur Balfour was Leader of the House of Commons in 1900 he wrote that there existed between the United States and Britain a 'fundamental harmony' based upon a common culture but that closer co-operation was impossible. 'Of course I recognize', he wrote, 'that large numbers of the most loyal citizens of America are either not of British descent, or, if of British descent, come from that part of Ireland which has never loved England.'[12] In 1916 Lloyd George believed that there was a terrible possibility that Irish-Americans might be decisive in forcing the United States over to the German side or in forcing the United States to break the British blockade on Germany.[13] As Prime Minister in 1917 he assured the American Ambassador that he had the American situation constantly in mind when trying to settle the Irish problem and in 1918, during the conscription debate, he quite openly told the House of Commons

---

[12] Balfour to Henry White, 12 December 1900, *Balfour MSS*, 49739.
[13] MacDonagh, *op. cit.*, p. 225.

that the Irish question was hindering Wilson's conduct of the war and had to be settled.[14]

British governments were aware that the American Irish had a great influence on American foreign policy, but they also realized that Irish-Americans were largely responsible for keeping the Irish nationalist movement in Ireland alive with money and words of encouragement when many at home might have given up the struggle or might have settled for the cultural, substantially non-political nationalism of the Scots and the Welsh. Both the constitutional and revolutionary nationalist movements in Ireland were maintained and encouraged by Irish-Americans. The scale of the financial contributions to the Parliamentary Party, to the Dail Eireann National Loan, and to the American Committee for Relief in Ireland, were simply enormous. The rising of 1916 might not have taken place and Germany would probably not have been involved had it not been for Irish-American help, and five years later the great attention drawn to Ireland by the American Commission on Conditions in Ireland was a serious embarrassment to the British. Thus the Irish question remained such a serious problem in British politics in large part because of the support Ireland received from abroad. So long as the Irish problem in Ireland was sustained in this way it was inevitable that the overseas Irish would also seek to use foreign policy as an instrument to support Ireland's struggle for independence. Prime Minister Billy Hughes of Australia knew this well enough in 1917 because it was the reason for the defeat of his conscription proposals in the Australian referenda of 1916 and 1917,[15] and every American politician knew it too.

On a number of occasions American governments believed, justifiably or not, that Irish-Americans were advocating foreign policies which were not in the interest of the United States but were influenced by Irish or anglophobic considerations. This is the kind of risk which any society with great numbers of immigrants must take. A government cannot erase the memories of immigrants at a naturalization ceremony and it cannot quickly erase hyphenism and its concomitant mental, if not legal, dual nationality. In the first place memories of the homeland and the emotions they arouse may be too strong to be erased and,

14 See above, Chapter 7, pp. 157–63.
15 War Cabinet meeting 24, minute 11, 1 January 1917, *CAB*. 23/1.

secondly, hyphenism is itself a way by which immigrants come to terms with an alien and often hostile environment. Hyphenism is an identity and 'hyphenated America' is one of the many Americas – urban, rural, northern, southern, and so on – in which Americans find themselves comfortable and which differentiate the population. The fact that hyphenism creates problems for foreign policy may be unfortunate, but it would be difficult to eradicate it and finding a replacement identity for a great number of people would not be easy. Hyphenism does not exist because someone invented it but because it fulfils a need for immigrants.

It is true that hyphenism is a natural phenomenon in an immigrant society but it can be used in a variety of ways to serve a variety of purposes. If an organization or community of immigrants adopts a political orientation, for example, certain complications may arise. In the Irish case there were factions which differed as to the methods thought most effective to free Ireland. Factions which existed in Ireland were reflected in the Irish movement in America and John Redmond went to great lengths to establish a viable constitutional movement in the United States which would not be under the control of the revolutionary Irish there. His new organization, the United Irish League of America, was savagely attacked by the Clan na Gael as a result. But Redmond's motive was not simply to ensure that there was a constitutional movement in America, he also wanted to ensure that it remained under his control and that it would be solely devoted to Ireland. When the whole Irish-American movement came under the control of the revolutionary faction after World War I, its leaders were not only concerned with Ireland but also had very fixed ideas about the general principles by which American foreign policy should be guided. Daniel Cohalan and John Devoy, for example, were opposed to any agreement which would leave the power of the British Empire substantially un-impaired. In the tradition of American anglophobia they saw Great Britain as a past, present and future military, naval and economic threat to the United States. They were no respecters of a 'special Anglo-American relationship'. Redmond did not think in their terms and neither did the undoubted revolutionary, Eamon De Valera. Both were concerned with Ireland, not the security and fears of the United States. De Valera, for example, had no fear of the League of Nations but to Devoy and Cohalan the League was an unmitigated evil, a challenge to traditional American isolation and a British plot. They were 'hyphenated Americans', that is, their Irishness had a special American character. When De Valera created the American Association for the Recognition of the Irish Republic in 1920 and split the Irish movement in the United States, he weakened the effectiveness of the Irish movement as a pressure group acting directly on American foreign policy, but he also brought a great number of Irish-Americans back into a movement which was under Irish control and out of a movement, the Friends of Irish Freedom, which was dedicated to a particular philosophy of American foreign policy. This caused some easing of the diplomatic pressure on Britain but it led to even greater problems in Ireland itself because the very influential AARIR, the bond-certificate drive, the American Commission on Conditions in Ireland and the Committee for Relief in Ireland were all organized in America by De Valera or his supporters. They were, unlike the Irish Victory Fund of the Friends of Irish Freedom, devoted solely to the purpose of Irish freedom and numbered among their supporters many Americans who simply wanted to see the Irish problem solved so that Britain and America could be friends and allies. These groups, then, contributed very greatly to Sinn Fein's power and confidence. It certainly appeared that the American Irish were capable of continuing their involvement with Ireland for just as long as it took to satisfy the Irish aspiration for self-government. As long as this was the case, complications in Anglo-American relations could be expected despite divisions and factions amongst the Irish themselves. Nevertheless, what the organization of the Irish movement demonstrated was that decentralization, and any movement separated by a vast ocean must be decentralized, can lead to confusion. Those at home may wage the fight but the propagandists and the fund raisers abroad want to call the tune, although their objectives may not always be identical.

If the Irish were such magnificent organizers, propagandists, conspirators and politicians, and if they so dangerously complicated Anglo-American relations, why could they do so little for so long to settle the problem of Irish self-government? The answer can only be found in the role which the Irish question played in purely British politics. The Irish problem was virtually insoluble and so long as this was true both the United States and Britain had to tolerate the complications it bred for their relations with each other. The Liberal Party, under Gladstone with Irish nationalist support, would have granted home rule to Ireland in 1892 but for the veto of the Conservative House of Lords, and when they finally found a way to by-pass the power of the Lords in 1911 they found that Ulster was prepared to go to war rather than accept home rule. In a memorandum to the Cabinet in July 1914 the military members of the Army Council warned that if a civil war broke out between the 200,000 members of the rival volunteer forces in Ireland it would take the whole British Expeditionary Force to put it down. The army could not then fulfil its obligations in India or Egypt, where civil disturbances might be expected, or fulfil Britain's foreign obligations.[16] Only the war in Europe saved the British government from having to choose between Ulster's military opposition to home rule and whatever political and military weapons the Irish nationalists would have chosen to ensure that home rule was immediately introduced.

Conservatives were opposed to home rule for a number of reasons. They were, of course, the party of tradition, of the integrity of the Empire, of aristocratic authority against the demands of democratic self-determination, and they were Unionists, the party of Union with Ireland and the party of Ulster Protestants. They could not agree that Ulster should be placed under the control of a predominantly Catholic parliament in Dublin against its will. Ulster represented voters and its cause had many supporters elsewhere in Britain. The only Conservative ministry during the period covered by this study was in office in 1899 and was responsible for extensive social and economic reforms in Ireland, but its ideology and membership precluded any concession to the Irish which might have weakened the Empire. Conservatives believed that home rule was simply the first step to Irish national independence which would not only set a disastrous example to the rest of the Empire, but would establish a potentially hostile power astride Britain's Atlantic shipping routes. In fact, after the Irish Party had opposed the Boer War, Lord Salisbury, the Prime Minister, declared at a banquet:

We know now from our South African experiences the danger of

16 Memo by military members of the Army Council, 4 July 1914, *CAB*. 37/120 (81).

letting Ireland have a measure of independence. We know now that if we allowed those who are now leading Irish politics unlimited power of making preparations against us, we should have to begin by conquering Ireland, if ever we had to fight any other power.[17]

The Conservatives were mortgaged to Ulster and the Lloyd George coalition government was in turn mortgaged to the Conservatives. Ulster, Union, and the Empire were articles of Conservative faith and, in the years before the war, Ireland and Ulster were also too useful as electoral issues to be thrown away by the Conservatives. They hoped that a crisis in Ireland and a consequent loss of confidence in the country would be one way of forcing the Liberals to the polls. Whilst not believing that they would necessarily win an election, Conservative leaders anticipated that the Liberal government would be so weakened that its whole radical programme of economic and social reform would be jeopardized.[18]

These were high stakes, then, and to counter charges that Ireland was a threat to friendly Anglo-American relations the Conservatives argued that the Irish question had only been introduced into American politics for party political purposes and need have no influence on the conduct of Anglo-American relations. They were wrong and the Irish question continued to bedevil diplomacy. The longer the problem remained unsolved the harder it was to find terms which were acceptable, even to the Liberals, as moderate Irishmen turned to the extreme Sinn Fein party. The struggle finally ended only when the British capitulated to the nationalists in the south and the nationalists themselves acquiesced in face of a *fait accompli*, the Belfast parliament in the north, which had already been accepted by Ulster and the Conservatives.

The treaty signed in December 1921 granted Ireland, other than the six counties of Northern Ireland, Dominion status with certain British reservations concerning the control of Irish ports. For most Americans who were aware of the Irish problem this marked its solution. Further resistance by Britain to the wishes

[17] *New York Times*, 14 May 1901.

[18] Asquith memos on conversations with Bonar Law, 15 October 1913, *Asquith MSS.*, Box 38, 6 November and 10 December 1913, Box 39; J.A.Spender and Cyril Asquith, *The Life of Herbert Henry Asquith, Lord Oxford and Asquith*, London: Hutchinson, 1932, v. 2, pp. 35–6.

of the great majority of the Irish who lived outside Ulster was no longer feasible without a full-scale war. Ulster's interests were now secured with a separate parliament in Belfast and the rest of Ireland was ungovernable, certainly from Westminster. In America the great bulk of those who supported Ireland had never understood the distinctions between limited autonomy, that is, home rule, Dominion status, or complete republican independence. They were also remarkably ignorant of Ulster and its case for special treatment. This lack of discrimination explains the rapid decline of American interest in Ireland which followed the treaty and the amazement with which so many Americans greeted the civil war which broke out in 1922. So far as they were concerned Ireland now had home rule, or independence, or whatever one chose to call the constitutional manifestation of its freedom. They were largely unaware of the nationalist hostility to partition. The record shows that the American press lost interest in Ireland in 1922, that there was a great diminution in the amount of political material flowing into the State Department from its agents in Ireland, although atrocities in Ireland were well documented, and that in 1922 the American government exchanged agents with the Irish Free State without significant opposition in the United States. When Irish republicans called on Joseph McGarrity to mobilize the full weight of Irish-American opinion to save the republic from the Free State in June 1922, they were referring to a mirage.[19] The campaign for a free Ireland, with all its fervour, its mass meetings, its propaganda and its nation-wide organization, had largely passed away. Some Irish-Americans continued to work for a truly republican settlement but they were no longer in a position seriously to influence either British or American foreign policy. As for the rest, what happened to the hundreds of thousands of Irish-Americans who had packed mass meetings from coast to coast and had contributed such large sums of money, and how their leaders occupied their remaining years, must be the subject of another study. Some quite possibly continued to influence American foreign policy, for example as isolationists and as opponents of American participation in World War II, and their Irish background no doubt influenced their attitudes as Americans towards Great Britain. However, they were no longer able to use

[19] H. Boland to McGarrity, 9 June 1922, *Maloney MSS.*, Box 12.

the Irish question as their major weapon in any public campaign to influence foreign policy, for with the Anglo-Irish treaty of 1921 the British government substantially transferred the burden of the Irish problem to the Irish themselves. They had finally put to the test D.P.Conyngham's statement, made more than fifty years earlier, 'It might be politic to try conciliation, instead of coercion, on such a people.'[20]

20 Conyngham, *op. cit.*, p. 81.

Bibliography

I MANUSCRIPT SOURCES

A *Official Papers*

Public Record Office, London
    Foreign Office and Cabinet Records
    Photographic records in the Public Record Office of original
    letters preserved in the Royal Archives (Cabinet 41) were made
    available by the gracious permission of HM the Queen
National Archives, Washington, DC
    Department of State and Department of Justice Records

B *Private Papers*

Bodleian Library, Oxford
    Herbert Asquith, James Bryce
British Museum, London
    Arthur Balfour
Library of Congress, Washington, DC
    Newton D.Baker, Ray S.Baker, Wharton Barker, Tasker H.
    Bliss, William Jennings Bryan, William Borah, Albert Burleson,
    Joseph H.Choate, Bainbridge Colby, George Creel, Norman
    Davis, Moreton Frewen, Thomas W.Gregory, Leland Harrison,
    John Hay, Gilbert M.Hitchcock, Charles E.Hughes, Philander
    C.Knox, Robert Lansing, William McAdoo, John P.Mitchel,
    George Norris, Whitelaw Reid, Theodore Roosevelt, Elihu
    Root, William H.Taft, Joseph Tumulty, Thomas J.Walsh,
    Henry White, John S.Williams, Woodrow Wilson
Massachuesetts Historical Society, Boston
    Henry Cabot Lodge
National Library of Ireland, Dublin
    John Devoy, John Redmond
New York Public Library
    William Bourke Cockran, Margaret McKim Maloney, John
    Quinn
Plunkett Foundation for Co-operative Studies, London
    Horace Plunkett
Yale University Library, New Haven
    Edward House, Frank Polk, William Wiseman

II SELECTED BOOK LIST

General

NB Journal articles, British Command Papers and US Congressional hearings and reports are not listed here. They will be found in footnotes to the text.

Allen, H.C., *Great Britain and the United States*, London: Odhams, 1954.

Bailey, Thomas A., *A Diplomatic History of the American People*, 6th ed., New York: Appleton, Century, Crofts, 1958.

Blake, Nelson M., *The United States and the Irish Revolution, 1914–1922*, Unpublished Ph.D. dissertation, Clark University, Mass., 1935.

Clarkson, J.D., *Labour and Nationalism in Ireland*, New York: Longmans Green, 1925.

Devoy, John, *Recollections of a Rebel*, New York: Charles Young, 1929.

Fitz-Gerald, William G., ed., *The Voice of Ireland*, London: John Heywood, 1924.

Gerson, Louis L., *The Hyphenate in Recent American Politics and Diplomacy*, Lawrence: University of Kansas Press, 1964.

Greaves, C. Desmond, *The Life and Times of James Connolly*, London: Lawrence and Wishart, 1961.

Gwynn, Denis R., *The History of Partition, 1912–1925*, Dublin: Browne and Nolan, 1950.

Gwynn, Stephen, ed., *The Letters and Friendships of Sir Cecil Spring Rice*, Boston: Houghton Mifflin, 1929, 2 vols.

Jamison, Alden, *Irish–Americans, the Irish Question and American Diplomacy, 1895–1921*, unpublished Ph.D. dissertation, Harvard University, 1942.

Macardle, Dorothy, *The Irish Republic*, London: Gollancz, 1938.

Morison, Elting E., ed., *The Letters of Theodore Roosevelt*, Cambridge, Mass.: Harvard University Press, 1951, 8 vols.

O'Brien, William, *The Irish Revolution and How It Came About*, London: Allen and Unwin, 1923.

O'Brien, William, and Ryan, Desmond, eds., *Devoy's Post-Bag, 1871–1928*, Dublin: Fallon, 1948–53, 2 vols.

O'Dea, John, *The History of the Ancient Order of Hibernians and Ladies' Auxiliary*, Philadelphia: The Ancient Order of Hibernians, 1923, 4 vols.

O'Hegarty, P.S., *A History of Ireland Under the Union, 1801–1922*, London: Methuen, 1952.

—, *The Victory of Sinn Fein*, Dublin: Talbot, 1924.

Phillips, W.Allison, *The Revolution in Ireland, 1906–1923*, London: Longmans Green, 1926.

Porter, Kirk H. and Johnson, Donald B., *National Party Platforms, 1840–1960*, Urbana: University of Illinois Press, 1961.

Roberts, Edward F., *Ireland in America*, New York and London: Putnam, 1931.

Tansill, Charles C., *America and the Fight for Irish Freedom, 1866–1922*, New York: Devin-Adair, 1957.

Wittke, Carl, *The Irish in America*, Baton Rouge: Louisiana State University Press, 1956.

Chapter 1

Brown, Thomas N., *Irish-American Nationalism, 1870–1890*, Philadelphia and New York: Lippincott, 1966.

Handlin, Oscar, *The Uprooted*, Boston: Little, Brown, 1951.

Jones, Maldyn A., *American Immigration*, Chicago: University of Chicago Press, 1960.

Levine, Edward M., *The Irish and Irish Politicians*, Notre Dame and London: University of Notre Dame Press, 1966.

Shannon, William V., *The American Irish*, New York: Macmillan, 1963

Chapter 2

Bagnal, Philip H., *The American-Irish and their Influence on Irish Politics*, London: Kegan Paul, Trench, 1882.

Cambray, Philip G., *Irish Affairs and the Home Rule Question*, London: John Murray, 1911.

D'Arcy, William, *The Fenian Movement in the United States, 1858–1886*, Washington, DC: Catholic University Press, 1947.

Denieffe, Joseph, *A Personal Narrative of the Irish Republican Brotherhood*, New York: Gael, 1906.

Gibson, Florence, *The Attitudes of the New York Irish toward State and National Affairs, 1848–1892*, New York: Columbia University Press, 1951.

Gwynn, Denis R., *The Life of John Redmond*, London: Harrap, 1932.

Healy, T.M., *Letters and Leaders of My Day*, London: Thornton Butterworth, 1928, 2 vols.

Le Caron, Henri, *Twenty-Five Years in the Secret Service*, London: Heinemann, 1892.

Le Roux, Louis N., *Tom Clarke and the Irish Freedom Movement*, Dublin: Talbot, 1936.

Lyons, F.S., *The Irish Parliamentary Party, 1890–1910*, London: Faber and Faber, 1951.

O'Connor, T.P., *Memoirs of an Old Parliamentarian*, London: Benn, 1929, 2 vols.

Chapter 3

Campbell, A.E., *Great Britain and the United States, 1895–1903*, London: Longmans Green, 1960.

Campbell, Charles C., *Anglo-American Understanding, 1898–1903*, Baltimore: Johns Hopkins University Press, 1957.

Dennett, Tyler, *John Hay: From Poetry to Politics*, Pt. Washington, New York: Kennikat Press, 1963.

Ferguson, John H., *American Diplomacy and the Boer War*, Philadelphia: University of Pennsylvania Press, 1939.

Fleming, Denna F., *The Treaty Veto of the American Senate*, New York: Putnam, 1930.

Grenville, J.A.S., *Lord Salisbury and Foreign Policy: The Close of the Nineteenth Century*, London: Athlone Press, 1964.

Heindel, Richard H., *The American Impact on Great Britain, 1898–1914*, Philadelphia: University of Pennsylvania Press, 1940.

Martin, Edward S., *The Life of Joseph Hodges Choate*, New York: Scribner, 1920, 2 vols.

Monger, G.W., *The End of Isolation: British Foreign Policy, 1900–1907*, London: Nelson, 1963.

Chapters 4–7

Bartholdt, Richard, *From Steerage to Congress*, Philadelphia: Dorrance, 1930.

Bernstorff, Count J., *My Three Years in America*, New York: Scribner, 1920.

Casement, Roger, *The Crime Against Europe*, ed. Herbert O. Mackey, Dublin: Fallon, 1958.

Child, Clifton J., *The German-Americans in Politics, 1914–1917*, Madison: University of Wisconsin Press, 1939.

Digby, Margaret, *Horace Plunkett: Anglo-American Irishman*, Oxford: Blackwell, 1949.

Dumba, Konstantin T., *Memoirs of a Diplomat*, trans I.F.D.Morrow, London: Allen and Unwin, 1933.

Edwards, Owen Dudley and Pyle, Fergus, eds., *1916: The Easter Rising*, London: MacGibbon and Kee, 1968.

Gaffney, T.St John, *Breaking the Silence: England, Ireland, Wilson and the War*, New York: Horace Liveright, 1930.

Gwynn, Denis R., *The Life and Death of Roger Casement*, London: Cape, 1930.

Higham, John, *Strangers in the Land: Patterns of American Nativism, 1860–1925*, Brunswick, NJ: Rutgers University Press, 1955.

Hyde, H.Montgomery, *The Trial of Sir Roger Casement*, London: Hodge, 1960.

Jenkins, Roy, *Asquith*, London: Collins, 1964.

Jones, John P., and Hollister, Paul M., *The German Secret Service in America*, Boston: Small, Maynard, 1918.

Link, Arthur S., *Wilson: The Struggle for Neutrality, 1914–1915*, Princeton, NJ: Princeton University Press, 1960.

—, *Wilson: Confusion and Crisis, 1915–1916*, Princeton, NJ: Princeton University Press, 1964.

—, *Wilson: Campaigns for Progressivism and Peace, 1916–1917*, Princeton, NJ: Princeton University Press, 1965.

Lynch, Francis Monteith, *The Mysterious Man of Banna Strand*, New York: Vantage, 1959.

MacColl, René, *Roger Casement: A New Judgment*, London: Hamish Hamilton, 1956.

Marjoribanks, Edward, and Colvin, Ian, *The Life of Lord Carson*, London: Gollancz, 1932, 1934, 1936, 3 vols.

Martin, F.X., *The Howth Gun-Running*, Dublin: Browne and Nolan, 1964.

May, Ernest R., *The World War and American Isolation, 1914–1917*, Cambridge, Mass.: Harvard University Press, 1959.

Mock, James R., and Larson, Cedric, *Words that Won the War*, Princeton, NJ: Princeton University Press, 1939.

Monteith, Robert, *Casement's Last Adventure*, Chicago: Private Printing, 1932 (Revised edition Dublin: Moynihan, 1953).

Park, Robert E., *The Immigrant Press and its Control*, New York: Harper, 1922.

Peterson, Horace C., *Propaganda for War*, Norman: University of Oklahoma Press, 1939.

Seymour, Charles, *The Intimate Papers of Colonel House*, London: Benn, 1926–8, 4 vols.

Spender, J.A., and Asquith, Cyril, *The Life of Herbert Henry Asquith, Lord Oxford and Asquith*, London: Hutchinson, 1932, 2 vols.

Spindler, Karl, *The Mystery of the Casement Ship*, Berlin: Kribe-Verlag, 1931.

Squires, James D., *British Propaganda at Home and in the United States, 1914–1917*, Cambridge, Mass.: Harvard University Press, 1935.

Viereck, George S., *Spreading Germs of Hate*, New York: Horace Liveright, 1930.

Chapter 8

Baker, Ray Stannard, *Woodrow Wilson and the World Settlement*, Garden City, New York: Doubleday, Page, 1922, 3 vols.

George, David Lloyd, *Memoirs of the Peace Conference*, New Haven: Yale University Press, 1939, 2 vols.

Lansing, Robert, *The Peace Negotiations: A Personal Narrative*, Boston and New York: Houghton Mifflin, 1921.

Miller, David Hunter, *The Drafting of the Covenant*, New York: Putnam, 1928, 2 vols.

Tillman, Seth P., *Anglo-American Relations at the Peace Conference of 1919*, Princeton, NJ: Princeton University Press, 1961.

Tumulty, Joseph, *Woodrow Wilson as I Know Him*, New York and Toronto: Doubleday, Page, 1921.

Chapter 9

Bailey, Thomas A., *Woodrow Wilson and the Great Betrayal*, New York: Macmillan, 1945.

Fleming, Denna F., *The United States and the League of Nations, 1918-1920*, London: Putnam, 1932.

Lodge, Henry Cabot, *The Senate and the League of Nations*, New York and London: Scribner, 1925.

Chapter 10

Bromage, Mary, *De Valera and the March of a Nation*, New York: Noonday, 1956.

Gwynn, Denis R., *De Valera*, London: Jarrods, 1933.

McCartan, Patrick, *With De Valera in America*, Dublin: Fitzpatrick, 1932.

MacManus, M.J. *Eamon De Valera*, Chicago and New York: Ziff-Davis, 1946.

O'Doherty, Katherine, *Assignment America: De Valera's Mission to the United States*, New York: De Tanko, 1957.

Chapter 11

Beaslai, Piaras, *Michael Collins and the Making of a New Ireland*, London: Harraps, 1926, 2 vols.

Callwell, C.E., *Field-Marshal Sir Henry Wilson: His Life and Diaries*, London: Cassell, 1927, 2 vols.

Holt, Edgar, *Protest in Arms: The Irish Troubles, 1916–1923*, London: Putnam, 1960.

Macready, Sir Nevil, *Annals of an Active Life*, London: Hutchinson 1924, 2 vols.

Pakenham, Francis A., *Peace by Ordeal*, London: Cape, 1935.

Riddell, George Allardice, Baron, *Lord Riddell's Intimate Diary of the Peace Conference and After, 1918–1923*, London: Gollancz, 1933.

Index

275

www.ingramcontent.com/pod-product-compliance
Lightning Source LLC
Chambersburg PA
CBHW020246030426
42336CB00010B/647